DARKEST AMERICA

Also by YUVAL TAYLOR

Faking It: The Quest for Authenticity in Popular Music (with Hugh Barker)

Growing Up in Slavery: Stories of Young Slaves as Told by Themselves (editor)

The Cartoon Music Book (editor, with Daniel Goldmark)

The Future of Jazz (editor)

I Was Born a Slave: An Anthology of Classic Slave Narratives (editor)

Also by JAKE AUSTEN

Flying Saucers Rock 'n' Roll: Conversations with Unjustly Obscure Rock 'n' Soul Eccentrics (editor)

TV-a-Go-Go: Rock on TV from American Bandstand *to* American Idol

A Friendly Game of Poker: 52 Takes on the Neighborhood Game (editor)

DARKEST AMERICA

BLACK MINSTRELSY FROM SLAVERY TO HIP-HOP

—

YUVAL TAYLOR and JAKE AUSTEN

W. W. NORTON & COMPANY
NEW YORK LONDON

Printed in the United States of America
First Edition

For information about permission to reproduce
selections from this book, write to Permissions,
W. W. Norton & Company, Inc.,
500 Fifth Avenue, New York, NY 10110

For information about special discounts for bulk
purchases, please contact W. W. Norton Special Sales at
specialsales@wwnorton.com or 800-233-4830

Manufacturing by Courier Westford
Book design by Barbara Bachman
Production manager: Louise Mattarelliano

Library of Congress Cataloging-in-Publication Data

Taylor, Yuval.
Darkest America : black minstrelsy from slavery to hip-hop /
Yuval Taylor and Jake Austen. — 1st ed.
p. cm.
Includes bibliographical references and index.
ISBN 978-0-393-07098-9 (hardcover)
1. Minstrel shows—United States—History. 2. Blackface
entertainers—United States—History. 3. Hip-hop—United
States—History. I. Austen, Jake. II. Title.
PN1969.M5T39 2012
791'.120973—dc23
2012007307

W. W. Norton & Company, Inc.
500 Fifth Avenue, New York, N.Y. 10110
www.wwnorton.com

W. W. Norton & Company Ltd.
Castle House, 75/76 Wells Street, London W1T 3QT

1 2 3 4 5 6 7 8 9 0

Dedicated to our families

for all their support

"Here's when blackface is OK . . .

when you have a black face!"

—Larry Wilmore,

The Daily Show, 2009

CONTENTS

FOREWORD BY MEL WATKINS

BOTH LITERALLY AND FIGURATIVELY, minstrelsy cast a grotesque, if strangely conflicted, shadow over the American landscape. From its inception in the 1840s, when it quickly emerged as the nation's most popular entertainment form, until at least the turn of the twentieth century, traditional minstrelsy principally thrived by presenting variety shows featuring burlesqued depictions of African Americans. "Black minstrelsy," authors Yuval Taylor and Jake Austen write, "is based precisely on the adoption of the most slanderous fictions that white people have used to characterize black men."

White and, later, black entertainers corked up, donning absurdly exaggerated, often hideous blackface makeup to create a visual image of the comic Stage Negro; ill-fitting clothing, malaprops, nonsensical chatter, a slavering addiction to watermelons and chicken, a shuffling gait and/or contrasting propensity to break into frenzied dance or flight when in earshot of syncopated music or eyesight of a cemetery were added to complete the picture. By the end of the 1800s this wildly overdrawn, Sambo-like figure was a ubiquitous presence in American culture. Frequently advertised as a true reflection of the character and culture of former black slaves, it was accepted as such by a vast number of Americans.

Formal minstrelsy would gradually disappear, but the stereotypical Negro caricature that it helped etch into the nation's psyche lingered and continued to resurface on- and offstage through the 1960s civil rights movement and even into the twenty-first century. During this time, the authors suggest, black Americans have reacted to the caricatures in three distinct ways: by embracing them, signifying on them, or attacking and refuting them.

The niggling truth about stereotypes and caricatures, of course, is that within their excesses and distortions a shred of reality is nearly always present. And, indeed, close scrutiny reveals that faint *traces* of authentic African American rural folk culture are to be found even in minstrelsy's Sambo characterization. This presence explains why historians and social critics such as Mark Twain, Constance Rourke, and Eric Lott have argued that minstrelsy should be partly credited with bringing aspects of black folkways and folk art to mainstream America's popular culture. It may also partially explain two of the problematic issues engaged by *Darkest America* authors Taylor and Austen: why some African American entertainers willingly incorporate aspects of the stereotype into their acts and why so many members of the black community still embrace the seemingly slanderous stereotypes and find them humorous.

These are among the fundamental questions this work sets out to answer. "The motivation for writing this book is to explore black minstrelsy's artists, art, and audience reactions," the authors write, "the ways the innovative performances of the minstrel stage have affected the subsequent century of African American performance, performances that have consistently defined American popular culture."

Toward that goal, Taylor and Austen have assembled a survey and selective examination of African American culture from the nineteenth century to the present. Beginning with such blackface entertainers as William Henry "Juba" Lane, Billy Kersands, and Bert Williams, the narrative traces the influence of minstrelsy on African American performance for over a century, concluding with an analysis of works by such present-day artists as Dave Chappelle, Flavor Flav, Lil Wayne, Spike Lee, and Tyler Perry.

Examples are drawn from various media, including the stage, radio, music and song, motion pictures, and television. The authors dutifully examine such familiar hot-button phenomena as the *Amos 'n' Andy* show (in both its radio and TV manifestations) and Stepin Fetchit, reaffirming the performers' apparent debts to minstrelsy, and analyze the frequently voiced assertion that much rap music and performance is little more than blackface revisited. But this work is most distinguished and enlivened by its surprising turns (a reinterpretation of Bert Williams's work that takes issue with conclusions drawn by his biographers, for instance) and unexpected subjects such as a firsthand report on the Zulu Krewe, a black group that has marched in New Orleans's Mardi Gras parade wearing blackface for more than a hundred years.

There are also fresh assays and interpretations of artists who have rarely been associated with the minstrel tradition that will likely inspire heated debate and/or dissent. Paul Robeson and Ray Charles, for example, are cited along with the black vaudeville stars Ernest Hogan (who wrote "All Coons Look Alike") and James Bland (who vied with Stephen Foster in penning sentimental odes to plantation life) as having clearly reflected the "minstrelsy revival" in some of their music.

Darkest America is finally a richly detailed examination of the effect that comic minstrel caricatures have had on African

American performers and audiences. The inherent difficulty of the task is evidenced in the last chapter, which is focused on Spike Lee's film *Bamboozled* (described as a bold, angry, "vehement damnation of black minstrelsy") and the rift between Lee and director Tyler Perry (who seemingly enthusiastically embraces many minstrelsy-inspired comic tropes). As the authors conclude, definitive answers to questions concerning the acceptance or rejection of contemporary expressions of minstrelsy-inspired comedy are not easily acquired. Intense scrutiny, they suggest, may muddy the waters rather than clarify them—a consequence that is partially derived from the inherently contradictory nature of humor. As Langston Hughes once observed, comedy is often "what you wish in your secret heart were not funny. But it is, and you must laugh."

Clearly, however, *Darkest America* is a valuable contribution to the growing body of research on minstrelsy and its long-lasting effect on American culture. Yuval Taylor and Jake Austen should be commended for this probing examination of one of the nation's most influential cultural phenomena.

New York City, January 2012

Mel Watkins is the author of *On the Real Side: A History of African American Comedy*.

DARKEST AMERICA

"Never thought I'd say this, but *I'm* embarrassed!" Dave Chappelle's "Racial Pixie" meets the Ying Yang Twins on *Chappelle's Show*.

ILLUSTRATION: K. THOR JENSEN.

1.

RACIAL PIXIES

How Dave Chappelle Got Bamboozled by the Black Minstrel Tradition

THE BLACK MINSTREL TRADITION is a hell of a drug. If taken properly it can relieve tension, produce euphoria, and simulate a sense of freedom for performers and audiences. However, its side effects can include shame, nausea, and short- and long-term cultural memory loss. It has been on the market for over 150 years (despite countless challenges by self-appointed regulators), and over that period there have been very few reported overdoses. That rarity explains why the entertainment world did a double take in 2005 when Dave Chappelle O.D.'d on black minstrelsy.

That was the year that Chappelle, the preeminent comic of the hip-hop generation, stood in a production studio dressed as a "racial pixie," a tiny minstrel performer who appears on the shoulder of African Americans to encourage them to embrace stereotypes. He delivered a manic, absurd performance, in full blackface, wearing a bellhop's uniform and brandishing a cane. Dancing to banjo music, grinning and yelling "Hallelujah," he sent crew members into paroxysms of laughter.

But, as he later told *Time* magazine, when one staffer, a white man, laughed particularly loudly and long, "it made me uncomfortable. As a matter of fact, that was the last thing I shot before

I told myself I gotta take fucking time out after this. Because my head almost exploded." He later told Oprah Winfrey, "It was the first time I'd ever gotten a laugh I was uncomfortable with."

Since its 2003 debut on Comedy Central, *Chappelle's Show* had been a showcase for outrageous sketch comedy that explored and exploited racism and racial stereotypes. Sketches included "Blind Supremacy," a *60 Minutes*–style report on a reclusive, hate-filled white-supremacist author who, because of his blindness, doesn't know that he is African American, and "Racial Draft," a variation of the NBA draft in which executives representing different races negotiate for the rights to claim ownership of multiracial celebrities like Tiger Woods. But Chappelle also parodied more conventional representations of African Americans, from crack addicts to dice players to hip-hop stars, and his parodies often came dangerously close to embracing the stereotypes he was playing with. As the show gained popularity, Chappelle found himself increasingly uncomfortable bringing offensive stereotypes to dramatic life, especially when white fans would quote his characters in black dialect. The "racial pixie" sketch was the tipping point.

Though outrageous, the skit was clearly a multileveled exploration of racism. It was a smart piece that reflected upon minstrelsy's echoes (Chappelle has his blackface pixie pop up in a clip from an episode of *MTV Cribs* that showcased the clownish antics of black hip-hop duo the Ying Yang twins, declaring, "Never thought I'd say this, but *I'm* embarrassed."). But apparently, for a contemporary African American performer, standing in front of a white audience (even a handful of crew and cast members) is not easily reconciled with performing buffoonish comedy in blackface. Immediately after filming the skit, Chappelle, a Muslim, quit producing the show, which had spun off into the all-time bestselling television DVD, and attempted to perform hajj—the pilgrimage to Mecca (he got only as far as Turkey because he couldn't get a visa for Saudi Arabia). A short time later Chappelle walked away from production again, disappeared for days, and eventually was found in South Africa, where he had begun his permanent vacation from *Chappelle's Show*. Forgoing a $55 million contract was, apparently, a fair price to pay to get away from the minstrel imagery that, even when explored from an informed, satirical perch, proved to be too painful a burden to bear. Taking a cue from Spike Lee's *Bamboozled*, the comic decided to destroy his minstrel show before it destroyed him.

The minstrel tradition, as practiced by whites in blackface, was a fundamentally racist undertaking, neutering a race's identity by limiting it to demeaning stereotypes. But what Chappelle and other contemporary performers draw upon is the more complicated history of *black* minstrelsy. Since emancipation, black performers have alternately embraced, exploited, subverted, and turned stereotypes inside out, quite often becoming tremendously successful with both black and white audiences in the process. Black crowds enjoyed early black minstrel shows without shame; black blackface vaudeville stars like Bert Williams were heralded as dignified geniuses; and black performers like Mantan Moreland and the comedian-filmmaker Spencer Williams were able to lead dual performing lives, fulfilling cartoonish minstrel-inspired stereotypes for white Hollywood audiences that drew harsh criticism from the black intelligentsia while presenting almost identical performances that felt unproblematic in productions for black audiences. Critics often posit that these performers were forced to indulge in demeaning caricatures or wear blackface. But in fact, they knew exactly what they were doing: they often had alternatives, and had good reasons for choosing to draw from the minstrel tradition.

Minstrelsy presents a carefree life liberated from oppression, responsibilities, and burdens, where one can be as lazy, crazy, and irresponsible as one wants to be. It held and still holds tremendous attractions for performers and audiences. If you dismiss it as simply "demeaning," you miss half the picture. There are many reasons to be horrified by minstrel material and as many reasons to be attracted to it. The two reactions are equally natural and equally valid.

In the nineteenth century the minstrel show became the most prominent and popular form of American entertainment. Today we instinctively recoil at the sight of performers in the burnt-cork makeup and clownlike greasepaint that turned their skin pitch-black and their lips and eyes into giant cartoon features. But the foundation of American comedy, song, and dance was laid down by white and black minstrel stage legends. For this reason it is absurd to dismiss or bury works because of their minstrel origins. Teen rapper Jibbs had his popular tune "Chain Hang Low" branded as "minstrel-show rap" because it borrowed a melody from the ubiquitous ice-cream-truck theme song "Turkey in the Straw," originally a minstrel tune, and in 2008, Pomona College halted performances of its alma mater, "Hail, Pomona, Hail," when students believed it had been originally composed for a blackface review. But if we were to throw out every song originally composed for the minstrel stage, every joke first uttered by painted minstrel lips, every performer who blackened up, every dance step developed for the olio (variety) portion of a minstrel show, our entertainment coffers might seem bare. We would be denied the tremendous contributions countless black artists made to American popular culture, from dance pioneer William "Master Juba" Lane and composer James Bland (whose "Carry Me Back to Old Virginny" was Virginia's state song until its minstrel heritage doomed it to retirement in 1997) to comedy giant Bert Williams and writer Zora Neale Hurston, whose work was steeped in black minstrel traditions. Imagine your childhood had Charles Hicks's black minstrel troupe not created "Why did the chicken cross the road?" jokes.

But the black minstrel tradition is not relegated to history's pages. It is found on television every day, in the malapropisms on *Tyler Perry's Meet the Browns* sitcom and the giant, bejeweled grins flashed in Lil Wayne's music videos. It went intergalactic with *Star Wars'* Jar Jar Binks character, and viral with Internet sensation Antoine Dodson's histrionic dialect diatribe against an Alabama "bed intruder." And it's referenced online and in print when cultural sentinels like Stanley Crouch or Web sites like Bossip tar popular contemporary black performers with the blackface brush.

And it's not inherently heinous. The black minstrel tradition has provided great entertainment and great art. Black performers have played it shamelessly, signified on it, or attacked it—but they've had to deal with it in one way or another. It's something that every American or fan of American culture should care about. They should care because that culture wouldn't exist without minstrelsy. And because minstrelsy hurts—a lot.

—

Though nineteenth-century white and black minstrel shows (whose history the next chapter describes in detail) are reduced in the collective memory to grinning blackface clowns performing corny comedy or sentimental songs about the South (or "Mammy"), by their very form, with their built-in variety portion, they were showcases for diverse talent. Gifted minstrel-show performers included opera singers like the brilliant Sissieretta Jones, elocutionists, female and male impersonators, magicians, ventriloquists, tightrope walkers, trick skaters, trained French poodles, and oddly attired contortionists billed under names like the Human Corkscrew or the Human Frog.

While black shows also featured performers imitating the dehumanizing stereotypes used by whites in blackface, African Americans were able to distinguish themselves from their pale imitators by bringing humanity to the caricatures and providing coded messages to their brothers and sisters. As an African American theatergoer told a white writer attending a black-written, black-cast play in the early twentieth century, "We *get* things in the show you couldn't possibly react to."

And black audiences have always been there to react. Nineteenth-century traveling black minstrel troupes and popular "legitimate" theater acts like Williams & Walker usually played to mixed audiences, and twentieth-century tent shows often played to predominantly black or all-black crowds. Black troupes at the turn of the century put on shows for crowds of paying black customers numbering in the thousands. A 1908 review in the *Dramatic Mirror* declared it an "undisputed fact that the very sinew of support of a colored show comes more than one-half from the ranks of their own people." A 1926 article in the *New York Herald Tribune* claims that black-cast theater shows typically ran long because of African American audience members' applause and demands for encores.

For decades most of these shows featured African American men and women in burnt-cork blackface performing low, buffoonish comedy, which may make it hard for contemporary sensibilities to believe that they entertained and inspired black audiences. Though many black minstrels throughout history performed without makeup, in his black theater study *Blacks in Blackface*, Henry T. Sampson (an African American nuclear physicist and inventor who in his spare time has become a leading authority on African American entertainment history) demonstrates that blacks in burnt-cork blackface remained popular with black crowds well into the 1930s. The black comedian Pigmeat Markham wore blackface into the 1950s. New Orleans's Zulu Krewe still parades in blackface every Mardi Gras, the majority of their route in front of a mostly black audience.

Black minstrelsy involves not only stereotypes and caricatures, but comic traditions, linguistics, low humor, verbal dexterity, improvisation, and numerous other elements. But stereotypes are a basic building block of the tradition, and identifying these specific figures is crucial to understanding the art form.

Black male minstrels seem to fall rather loosely into three central types, which were seen in white minstrel shows as well. The coon is the shiftless, uneducated, slow-witted buffoon. The dandy is his northern brother, a free man who thinks he's far more eloquent and better dressed than he really is. And the trickster is the fly in the buttermilk, the direct descendent of

Br'er Rabbit, who'll play jokes on anyone, black or white—even himself—and damn the consequences. But it's important to note that actual minstrel personae were rarely so pure—most were a combination of these. For example, most coons had an element of the trickster in them (feigned stupidity and sloth is a trick to lower overseers' expectations); and most dandies were also coons to a large degree (the northern dandy was often called Zip Coon).

There were other nineteenth-century stereotypes that played little part in minstrel shows but have come to be identified with them nevertheless, usually mistakenly so. Two are worth particular mention.

The Tom is the older black man who has seen hard times. Omnipresent in American popular culture after being immortalized by Harriet Beecher Stowe with the publication of *Uncle Tom's Cabin* in 1853, he began to appear in minstrel shows shortly thereafter, but only as an adjunct figure rather than a central character. For Uncle Tom was created to be pitied, and minstrel shows centered around laughter.

The buck—Stagolee, Nat, the dangerous black killer—"was relatively insignificant in antebellum days," as poet Sterling A. Brown wrote in his 1933 study of stereotypes, since "pro-slavery authors were anxious to prove that slavery had been a benefit to the Negro in removing him from savagery to Christianity." He was even more absent on white minstrel stages (and subsequently the black ones that took cues from their forebears) because the harmless, happy, naturally entertaining Negro whites in blackface and their audiences imagined is contradicted by the intimidating stereotypes of virility, savagery, and power that kept miscegenation laws on the books until 1967. He became a stock figure of Ku Klux Klan literature, and was used to justify countless lynchings, but when he appeared as a blackface character (as in the pro-Klan film *The Birth of a Nation*), it was as a distant cousin of the minstrel figures, using the tools of minstrelsy to convey a far different message than that of the traditional comedy-variety shows.

However, the Stagolee figure, with his penchant for violence and his powerful sexuality, became integrated into the figure of the coon in the "coon songs" that became extremely popular in the late nineteenth and early twentieth centuries, and this spilled over to representations of the coon on the popular stage as well. Capable of almost infinite variations, the coon is minstrelsy's primary legacy, with his shucking, grinning, sloth, and mirth—whether he appeared as Sambo, Jim Crow, Zip Coon, or "The Hottest Coon in Dixie."

The trickster, ubiquitous in folklore, cannot be classified as a minstrel creation. The same can be said for the dandy; black figures in flashy, ornate, status quo–challenging attire in fiction and fact existed long before minstrel shows. In England, where slaves were often considered luxury items, it was not unusual to dress them in foppish attire for novelty's sake. In literature the figure of the sharply dressed Negro with attitude emerged in the 1760s, notably in the opera *The Padlock* by Isaac Bickerstaffe, which featured the truth-talking black dandy Mungo Macaroni, whose character soon became a popular costume (for whites) at masquerade balls. Macaroni was later personified by Julius Soubise, black companion to the Duchess of Queensberry. In his powdered wig, silk breeches, and red, diamond-buckled shoes, Soubise became Britain's first black celebrity.

In addition, many of the earliest descriptions of slaves in America note flashy, unusual attire. When slave owners encouraged blacks to embrace Christianity with Sunday services, they were shocked by the creativity and fashion sense their "property" demonstrated. One plantation owner's wife breathlessly described her slaves' church attire as "the most ludicrous combination of incongruities that you can conceive . . . every color in the rainbow, and the deepest possible shades blended in fierce companionship."

Some attribute this fashion sense to West African traditions. Art historian Robert Farris Thompson equates "rhythmized textiles," the bold pattern and color combinations favored by Africans and African Americans, with African music. Certain early African American fashion traditions (including head and body wraps) had obvious motherland ancestry. When given a grander stage, African Americans took these traditions to spectacular extremes in slave festivals like Pinkster, Negro Election Day, and Jonkonnu. There blacks paraded in gold chains, silk stockings, ruffles, silver shoe buckles, and recycled Revolutionary War uniforms ornamented in ways that predicted Michael Jackson's 1980s attire. And though New Orleans's tramplike Zulus are an integral part of local culture, the ornate Mardi Gras Indians became international icons because of their breathtaking, peacocklike costumes.

In *Slaves to Fashion*, scholar Monica L. Miller calls the tradition of black dandyism a "creative, self-defining art form," adding that "black fashion is a form of signifying, not copying white/mainstream style." This signifying—tweaking things to subvert their meaning and employing irony to clarify the performer's distance from them—was demonstrated on the black minstrel stage in ways that often defied the foolish Zip Coon character. The cakewalk was a dance developed as a parody of white balls, and while contemporary eyes may see it as ridiculous and demeaning, it not only functioned as a signifying critique, but became a sensation because of its groundbreaking demonstration of the grace and creativity that are foundations of African American dance. George Walker, the black minstrel era's most acclaimed dandy, dressed sharp to impress, not to clown, and his cakewalk was seen not as comical or absurd, but as breathtaking. An 1897 review in the African American newspaper the *Indianapolis Freeman* credited Walker with possessing "incandescent comportment."

The outrageous attire of minstrel stage dandies seemed to be revived when black stand-up comedians earned mainstream attention in the 1980s on cable TV, and the world marveled at their brightly colored, unusually cut suits. However, similar suits can be seen on contemporary black parishioners, and it would be a cruel leap to equate real-life worshipers to Zip Coon. Thus, despite black minstrelsy's powerful influence on African American theatrical culture, contemporary African American performers draw their dandiness from too many sources to confidently place that aspect of their performance in the black minstrel tradition.

Female stereotypes are harder to enumerate, simply because there were far fewer female characters in the minstrel show. Many minstrel troupes were all-male, with the female parts played by men in drag. (Comic drag and musical female impersonation were common on the American stage, whether minstrel or not. However, many contemporary critics brand any black comic in drag a minstrel.) Two female stereotypes remain associated with minstrelsy. Aunt Jemima, or Mammy, is Uncle Tom's female equivalent—harmless, happy, and sexless. Topsy, the dancing child, is the carefree "pickaninny." Like Uncle Tom, these were familiar characters in literature, the stage, and other media, and the degree to which they figured in black minstrelsy is unclear. Minstrel shows traditionally featured a narrative play as the third act, and these caricatures would often be relegated to these melodramas, which were not unique to minstrel shows. In fact, one parallel to traditional minstrel shows were *Uncle Tom's Cabin* plays (known as U.T.C.'s), performances of Harriet Beecher Stowe's novel that folded a full variety show into loose skeletal interpretations of the story.

These stereotypical caricatures have appeared in pop culture continuously since minstrelsy's heyday, sometimes intact, but more often in bits and pieces: the wide eyes and surprised mouth signified by the blackface makeup; the huge, carefree, tooth-baring grin; shabby rural rags or absurdly ostentatious urban attire; country dialect or would-be-urban malapropisms; superstitious fears of ghosts and boogeymen; comic razor fights; dice games; watermelon and chicken theft; extreme sloth.

Over the years, African Americans have usually approached these stereotypical characters and their traits in one of three ways. Some *embrace* them, playing them straight to make folks laugh (or to ingratiate themselves with a white audience), even to the extent of affirming them as part and parcel of their identities. From the earliest black minstrel shows to today's hip-hop videos and "chitlin circuit" stage plays, this is a charge that keeps black minstrelsy alive as a hot-button issue. Others *signify* on them. This was Dave Chappelle's usual approach, and it can be seen in performers as diverse as Ethel Waters, André 3000, and George Clinton (who funked up the minstrel refrain "Feet don't fail me now"). Still others *make war* on them with such vehemence that they come alive. As seen in Richard Wright's attack on Zora Neale Hurston's *Their Eyes Were Watch-*

ing God, Stanley Crouch calling Tupac Shakur a "thug minstrel," and Spike Lee's unforgettable *Bamboozled*, black minstrelsy rears its ugly head whenever black critics worry that black artists are reinforcing negative stereotypes.

Whichever approach is taken, the black minstrel image remains inescapable, something that every black performer, critic, and thinker has to reckon with.

Performers adopt personae when they go out on stage. They can be exuberant or cool, clumsy or smooth, shiftless or industrious, cowardly or brave, submissive or angry, embarrassed or proud, gluttonous or abstemious, stupid or smart, devious or honest. Throughout American history whites have had the freedom to choose any of these traits without being accused of anything worse than playing to the crowd. But whenever a black performer chooses a persona featuring several of the traits we've named first in this list of opposites, the accusation of minstrelsy tends to follow.

Many of the most popular and revered black performers of the last fifty years—Marian Anderson, Halle Berry, James Brown, Bill Cosby, Miles Davis, Ella Fitzgerald, Aretha Franklin, Mahalia Jackson, Michael Jackson, Tupac Shakur—have mainly embodied the latter positive traits enumerated above. But are these the only ones black entertainers should adopt? Many prominent black cultural commentators—Jesse Jackson, Stanley Crouch, Wynton Marsalis, Spike Lee, Albert Murray, Oprah Winfrey, and several of those on the above list, including Brown, Cosby, and Davis—have publicly denounced black entertainers who choose to embody less positive traits, as have organizations like the NAACP. They all have good reason for doing so, for those negative traits are precisely the ones that whites have used for centuries to create demeaning stereotypes of blacks.

Yet throughout history, some black entertainers have deliberately adopted these negative traits. This is only natural, for those traits, being more subject to ridicule, are more conducive to laughter. It is easier to make your audience happy by acting devious than honest, exuberant than cool, clumsy than smooth.

"The humor of nearly all minorities reveals a tendency toward self-deprecation," writes Mel Watkins in his definitive history of black American humor, *On the Real Side*. And certainly this has been a constant theme in black American writing: the self-contempt induced by minority status, by oppression. W. E. B. Du Bois wrote about the "double-consciousness" of black Americans in *The Souls of Black Folk*: "this sense of always looking at one's self through the eyes of others, of measuring one's soul by the tape of a world that looks on in amused contempt and pity." Ralph Ellison echoed Du Bois when he wrote of the "double vision" of black Americans. And indeed, as Jewish humor also so richly shows, oppressed people have a natural tendency to exaggerate their perceived faults.

Yet the notion of self-deprecation doesn't necessarily include the adoption of the point of view of the oppressor. The Jewish comic, for example, rarely jokes about the money-grubbing miser or the manipulator of the world's finances. Black minstrelsy, by contrast, is based precisely on the adoption of the most slanderous fictions that white people have used to characterize black men.

Is this a remainder of the slave mentality, as some argue? Is this simply an example of black people giving white people what they hope and expect? Or is it something more complex?

These are the fundamental questions this book is trying to answer.

And perhaps this desire for laughter is at the heart of the problem. In Wright's review of *Their Eyes Were Watching God,* he wrote, "Miss Hurston *voluntarily* continues in her novel the tradition which was *forced* upon the Negro in the theatre, that is, the minstrel technique that makes the 'white folks' laugh." Du Bois foresaw comments like Wright's when he wrote, "The more highly trained we become, the less we can laugh at Negro comedy." Dave Chappelle's horror at a white man's laughter echoes Du Bois and Wright. The minstrel tradition was designed to provoke laughter above all, and it has thus tainted that desire in the eyes of many African Americans.

The thriving black minstrel shows of the nineteenth century were designed not only for laughs, but for comfort: their formal structure usually echoed the familiar outline of the traditional minstrel show. But in the twentieth century they took more contemporary forms. Traveling tent shows traversed the rural South; black vaudeville developed the rhythms of minstrel-show end men into a more intimate exchange; proper black revues and narrative plays were developed for small black halls and grand Broadway theaters. And with each development in technology (from cinema to sound recording to television to Internet) black artists continued to practice tried-and-true techniques that were developed under a layer of ebony paint.

One of the best examples of the tradition surviving into the twentieth century and exerting influence on all areas of American popular culture is the lengthy career of the Rabbit's Foot Minstrels, a troupe Sampson declared "the best of the minstrel companies owned and managed entirely by blacks." Pat Chap-

An early twentieth-century Rabbit's Foot Minstrels poster printed by, and still hanging at, Hatch Show Print in Nashville, Tennessee. JAKE AUSTEN.

pelle (no relation, to our knowledge, to Dave) opened a vaudeville theater in Tampa, Florida, in 1899 and began assembling a new ensemble to perform in a revue he commissioned entitled *A Rabbit's Foot*. In 1900 the show began a monthlong tour, making it up to New York City. Despite the *Indianapolis Freeman* declaring that "the Foots" transcended the stigma of tent shows, Rabbit's Foot *was* a tent show, albeit a high-end one, pulling in $1,000 a week (at 35¢ a ticket, a dime above its competitors' prices) primarily in the South. The troupe often entertained mixed or all-white crowds but also frequently performed for thousands of rural blacks. They had over forty performers, five custom railway cars (valued at up to $10,000 each), a tricked-out automobile which they paraded through towns before shows, and bragging rights that they had "not one pale face among us—even our advance agents are colored" (though the company would lose that boast after Chappelle's 1911 death when white carnival man Fred S. Wolcott purchased the troupe).

Though the Rabbit's Foot Company still performed traditional minstrel comedy and lowbrow musical material like "Phrenologist Coon," "Cannibal Love," and "Dis Ain't de Kind a Grub I Been Gittin' Down Home," twentieth-century tent shows combined elements of vaudeville, blues, jazz, the circus (the Rabbit's Foot Company had an "educated goat which does seventeen tricks"), and sports (by 1905 the company had a baseball team that played a local club in each city while the concert band played classical music to accompany the contest). Several of the greatest black comics of the twentieth century passed through the Foots' ranks, including Tim Moore (who a half-century later starred in that milestone of minstrelsy, the *Amos 'n' Andy* TV show), and the raunchy duo Butterbeans and Susie. But it was the troupe's legendary blues musicians, artists rarely associated with minstrelsy, that have kept the Rabbit's Foot name alive despite a century of minstrel-show deniers. Gertrude "Ma" Rainey (along with her husband Will "Pa" Rainey) joined in 1906, years before becoming "Mother of the Blues." Rainey is said to have recruited and mentored a teenage Bessie Smith in 1912. Ida Cox was briefly with the show in 1913. Delta bluesman Big Joe Williams played with the company in the 1920s. And in the 1930s, Brownie McGhee, who became an international star during the blues revival of the 1960s, cut his teeth accompanying the comics and blues shouters in the show.

But the Rabbit's Foot veteran who did the most to keep the black minstrel tradition alive was far from a traditional bluesman. As a teenager in the mid-twenties, Louis Jordan's first important gig was joining his father in the Rabbit's Foot Minstrels, where he played clarinet, sang, and danced. Jordan would take the wide-eyed clowning, raucous humor, and corny jokes ("Ain't nobody here but us chickens . . .") he learned with the Foots to stage, screen, and recording studios, where his R&B/jump blues music made him a superstar, one of the first *Billboard* crossover artists, and a pioneer of rock 'n' roll.

Though the glory days of tent shows and minstrelsy were long behind it, the actual Rabbit's Foot Company persisted in some form until at least the early 1960s. In 1957 the *Chicago Defender* ran a photo of a blackface comic routine that it called the Rabbit Foot Minstrels' most popular act among both white and black southern viewers. The account books of Nashville's famed Hatch Show Print document the Foots ordering posters until December 1959. And in 1960 photographer Henry Clay Anderson shot fourteen young members posing in front of a truck trailer painted with the circus-style declaration "GREATEST COLORED SHOW ON EARTH!" The company's legacy lasted far longer, as Rabbit's Foot alumni continued to perform for decades. Memphis soul legend Rufus Thomas worked as a comic in the show in the 1930s, and took that training into the recording studio, where he made clownish R&B records from the 1940s through the late 1990s, including the 1969 novelty hit "Do the Funky Chicken." Mary Smith McLain, Bessie Smith's half-sister, who joined the troupe in the mid-thirties, had a late-in-life revival on the blues circuit in the 1980s as Diamond Teeth Mary (her diamond-studded dentures blazing the trail for Lil Wayne's hip-hop "grill"). She starred off-Broadway, performed for Reagan, toured internationally, released an album in 1993, and played Tampa clubs until her death in 2000. Outlasting her was Arnold "Gatemouth" Moore, the singer who billed himself as the last surviving Rabbit's Foot minstrel (though he also spuriously claimed to have been Buckwheat in the *Our Gang* comedies). Best known for writing songs recorded by B.B. King and others, Moore cut excellent jump blues records in the 1940s, became a Memphis disc jockey in the 1950s, and was a successful preacher. He continued to sing gospel (and occasional blues) until his death at age ninety in 2004, which perhaps closed the century-plus history of the Rabbit's Foot Minstrels.

During the Rabbit Foot's reign and the decades preceding and following it, instances of African Americans acting like minstrels raised the question of how these performers could enthusiastically participate in demeaning acts of self-representation. There is no definitive answer to this question, and this book does not aim to deproblematize black minstrelsy. The vast majority of viewers and listeners remain uncomfortable with it, with good reason. But reluctance to dig deeper than the usual reaction consigns the entire enterprise of black minstrelsy to the shadows of history.

The motivation for writing this book is to explore black minstrelsy's artists, art, and audience reactions, and the ways the innovations of the minstrel stage have affected the subsequent century of African American performance—performances that have consistently defined American popular culture. There have been countless fascinating books written about white minstrel shows. There have also been a number of excellent books about African American theater and comedy history that include brilliant research on black minstrel performers. These include the work of the tireless Henry T. Sampson; the exhaustive ragtime research of Lynn Abbott and Doug Seroff; the passionate explorations of black humor history and theory by Mel Watkins; Errol Hill and James V. Hatch's definitive history of African American theater; and even an encyclopedia/partial memoir cowritten by stand-up legend Redd Foxx. However, there has never been a study fully devoted to black minstrelsy and its legacy. And there will never be a book long enough to cover the immenseness of the subject. We don't expect *Darkest America* to be the last word on the black minstrel tradition, but rather hope that it will be an eye-opening conversation starter that will fuel discussion and debate among scholars, performers, and fans.

Though there are many challenges to approaching the history and legacy of this thorny subject, one refreshing aspect of this study is that it doesn't ask the student to choose sides, identify villains, or make declarations of good and evil. Any ire that works its way into *Darkest America* is reserved for scholars who knowingly truncate quotes, ignore inconvenient data, and rewrite history to make black minstrels of yore fit into contemporarily acceptable molds. Everyone else's hands are clean. Performers perpetuating stereotypes and pandering to the expectations of white audiences were also helping to keep alive and move forward important African American comic traditions. And these traditions had a purpose. Rather than simply reenacting degrading stereotypes invented by whites, blacks used these stereotypes to momentarily liberate themselves and their audiences from white oppression. While a Stepin Fetchit movie, a Jimmie Walker sitcom, or a Flavor Flav reality show may have earned charges of coonery, they also brought laughter and pride to black viewers who at some level appreciate that these artists demonstrate nuances and rhythms of African American humor that will always be out of the reach of white performers in (literal or proverbial) blackface.

Minstrelsy's critics are similarly justified, even when their criticisms are flawed. Richard Wright may be wrong for dismissing Zora Neale Hurston's writing as vapid, but when he called it a "minstrel show," he was making a valid point. Critics of gangsta rap who may be well aware that their provocative charges of millennial minstrelsy are an ill fit for the noncomical, murder-themed music they abhor have invoked the names of Amos 'n' Andy and Sambo with good reason—they sincerely thought such efforts were necessary to protect young fans of the music from negative influences.

"Blackface is a very difficult image," Dave Chappelle told Oprah Winfrey, adding that he was disturbed by how it "got me in touch with my inner coon." But Chappelle was right to "blacken up" for the racial pixies skit, because it perfectly served his astute, powerful, hilarious examination of the inner conflicts fueled by centuries of hurtful stereotypes. When *Chappelle's Show* added tragic, tangible humanity to a minstrel chestnut like a dice-playing routine, took a watermelon skit to an extreme (murderous gunplay instead of petty theft), or histrionically exploited the worst stereotypes imaginable in their African American version of *The Real World*, Chappelle was appropriately, even admirably, following in the footsteps of black comics who were tweaking, updating, and making minstrel show content their own before the ink was dry on the Emancipation Proclamation.

Yet he was equally right to walk away from the show. It is impossible to find fault when Chappelle explains, "I don't want black people to be disappointed with me for putting that out." The black minstrel tradition is an umbilical cord that feeds contemporary performers both the genius and the frustrations of their ancestors. It allows artists and audiences to feel the shameless liberation of laughter, and it undercuts that with a shame born of bearing the weight of generations of racism and oppression. It's a legacy in which two dissonant instincts attempt to harmonize. Audience members shouldn't apologize for their joy, but critics shouldn't hesitate to challenge content they deem harmful. Entertainers are not required to fret about acting a fool, and offended souls shouldn't stifle their tone when they voice disdain. Regardless of one's reactions to low, incautious, stereotype-flaunting comedy, everyone can benefit from knowing its history. That history is what *Darkest America* humbly attempts to survey.

John W. Vogel's *Darkest America*, circa 1898.

DR. HENRY T. SAMPSON COLLECTION OF AFRICAN AMERICAN CULTURE.

2.

DARKEST AMERICA

How Nineteenth-Century Black Minstrelsy Made Blackface Black

OF THE MANY BLACK AMERICAN entertainments of the 1890s, the most popular—among both blacks and whites—may well have been a theatrical extravaganza entitled *Darkest America.* As the *Colored American,* a black newspaper, described it, *Darkest America*'s "delineation of Negro life, carrying the race through all their historical phases from the plantation, into the reconstruction days and finally painting our people as they are today, cultured and accomplished in social graces, holds the mirror faithfully up to nature."

Yet *Darkest America* was a minstrel show. The performers, even though they were black, wore blackface. A photograph of an 1898 performance shows two of them playing banjos, with xylophones by their sides. One has big white circles painted around his mouth and eyes and grins widely; his collar, tie, and checkered jacket are all several sizes too large; he wears fake bare feet much bigger than his head.

It is difficult for us today to look at this photograph—it induces a cultural nausea comparable to that produced by Nazi cartoons of hook-nosed Jews. Yet none of the published descriptions of *Darkest America* paint the show as racist caricature. In fact, mainstream newspapers went out of their way to emphasize the differences between *Darkest America* and white minstrel shows. "If you . . . have formed your own ideas of Colored folks from the stage Negro and Darktown sketches, you will be instructed and amused," wrote the *St. Louis Dispatch.* The performers "would [at times] lapse into the real Negro eccentricities, which are only burlesqued in the attempted imitations so common to the burnt cork drama," commented the *Miners' Journal* of Pottsville, Pennsylvania. In other words, because they were black, these performers were truer to real life than were white minstrel shows.

Unlike *Darkest America*, many white minstrel shows did not center around plantation life—the minstrel show was a vehicle for parodying almost anything whatsoever, white or black. In fact, a great number of the minstrel skits that survive in acting editions are loosely based on Shakespeare plays, and not only *Othello*. Shakespeare's characters would be exaggerated in obvious ways, the actors wearing burnt cork and speaking a so-called Negro dialect generously peppered with malapropisms and pretentious nonsense; in these skits the blackface performances would be almost entirely unconnected with the customs and habits of blacks.

Darkest America was thus seen as a refreshing change of pace. Although it went through a number of changes through the years, at one point the show opened with a scene of "a crack colored military company" performing "funny scenes in camp life," according to the *New York Clipper,* and included a "watermelon scene [which] was funny enough to make an Indian laugh" (Indians were thought of as stone-faced). It featured, according to the *Miners' Journal*, "corn husking scenes in the barn, [and] massing singing and the wild antics of the dance in perfect time with the music[:] a perfect reproduction of the actions of the people they represented both on festival occasions and in a measure at Sunday wood's meetings."

Were the performers signifying on minstrel traditions? Blacks who performed in or saw black minstrel shows left a number of written accounts, and to the best of our knowledge not one mentions any kind of signifying whatsoever. For black writers, black minstrelsy was either a source of shame or a source of pride as the foundation for American entertainment, never anything more complicated. Was it too early in American history for these stereotypes to be recognized for the slander that they constituted? Hardly—prominent black Americans had registered their disgust for America's most popular form of entertainment since the 1840s.

In fact, we can make no excuses for these performers. These African Americans took pride in deliberately replicating racial stereotypes that are, to contemporary sensibilities, truly nauseating, and their African American audiences ate it up.

Here is the conundrum at the heart of this book—blacks in blackface wholeheartedly took part in the minstrel tradition and were popular among black audiences, despite the occasional vocal objections of black intellectuals. *Darkest America* is not an isolated example. The minstrel tradition had its roots in the folklore of both blacks and whites, and by the end of the nineteenth century a solid black minstrel tradition had developed, one that drew from and remained intimate with the white minstrel tradition.

But, it turns out, there is a rather simple, elegant, and ironic solution to this conundrum. Despite the appearance of black minstrelsy as a servile tradition, there were elements of *liberation* in it from its very beginning, and these were instrumental to its popularity.

A full examination of the black minstrel tradition requires us to take a brief look at its antecedents. One of these was the white minstrel tradition, but another—the black comic fool—predates minstrelsy.

It is in the nature of human society that those in a lower position try—or are forced—to please their masters, who reward them for this behavior. One way that the slaves pleased theirs was by making them laugh. Examples are too numerous to recount—even on slave ships from Africa some of the captives would sing and dance to amuse their captors or, alternatively, were forced by their captors to sing and dance. Because of the lack of freedom of the slave performer, the difference between a voluntary and a compelled performance is small—indeed, the performer would often be compelled to reenact a voluntary performance. In the many contemporary historical portrayals of slave life, this constant and vital part of it is often overlooked—the sight of blacks clowning for whites seems to be harder to watch than that of whites whipping blacks. Clowning can only be demeaning; suffering ennobles. Yet both slaves and slave owners told hundreds of stories about casual performances ranging from offhand remarks to elaborate charades, all cunningly designed to curry favor with and garner affection from the master. In this clowning the slave would usually appear to act stupid rather than clever, as that was more flattering to the master and would result in greater approbation.

Antebellum fiction is full of slaves entertaining their masters by acting foolish, and so offensive are these scenes to modern tastes that the possibility that this really was an important facet of everyday life on the plantation is barely subject to discussion. But we don't have to go to fiction to find corroboration. Many ex-slaves, when interviewed long after emancipation, testified that masters wanted to see them happy and singing. Frances Anne (aka Fanny) Kemble, one of a number of antislavery visitors to the South, visited Georgia plantations in 1838 and wrote that many of the masters and overseers prohibited "melancholy tunes or words, and encourage[d] nothing but cheerful music and senseless words." The sociologist Charles S. Johnson wrote, "A master, unless he was utterly humorless, could not overwork or brutally treat a jolly fellow, one who could make him laugh." And Mel Watkins, the leading authority on African American humor, writes, "Since rebellion was nearly always futile or fatal, 'playin' the fool' or 'puttin' on massa' became staple techniques for surviving and even maintaining some semblance of self-respect."

Small wonder that southern theoreticians such as Thomas R. R. Cobb, who wrote an influential defense of slavery in 1858, concluded that blacks were "mirthful by nature"; and he was hardly alone—this idea has long been one of the cornerstones of American racism. Even visitors from other countries made similar comments: The English traveler J. F. D. Smyth wrote in 1784 that blacks were "blessed with this easy, satisfied disposition of mind [and] seem to be the happiest inhabitants of America, notwithstanding the hardness of their fare, the severity of their labour, and the unkindness, ignominy, and often barbarity of their treatment." The eighteenth-century French immigrant J. Hector St. John de Crèvecoeur wrote that blacks were "as happy and merry as if they were freemen and freeholders," and in the early years of the nineteenth century the Englishman John Bernard similarly called blacks "the great humorists of the Union, and notwithstanding all that has been said of their debasement and wretchedness, one of the happiest races of people I have ever seen."

The psychology of entertainment outlined here—that the slave entertains the master by acting ridiculous, and thus appears happier than his condition warrants—is intrinsic to the master-slave relationship. It can be observed wherever slaves—or even servants—have existed. The literature of performance is therefore rich in clownish servants and slaves, who usually play either the fool or the trickster, and often both. The most ready examples can be found in Molière's plays; but in almost every comedy that deals with servants or slaves, from the ancient Greeks (the slave in Aristophanes's *The Acharnians*) to the twentieth century (Clov in Samuel Beckett's *Endgame* or Florence on *The Jeffersons*), the servants wield a double-edged sword, provoking laughter either through foolishness, guile, or the guile of feigned foolishness.

The more brutish the relationship, the less sophisticated the foolery—brutes have little capacity to appreciate subtlety or nuance. In America, where slavery was particularly brutish, slaves had to act particularly clownish; the wittiness of Molière's servants would have been lost on most American overseers. Similarly, the less educated the master, the less intelligent the slave had to appear, so as to remain the master's inferior while keeping him amused; and since American slave owners were usually less educated than Europeans, the kind of comedy that arose in American life featured a more dim-witted fool than had ever been seen on stage before. Every idiocy had to be exaggerated for effect, from misuse of language to physical ineptitude.

What arose, then, was an African American comedic tradition, some of whose components were motivated by the status of blacks as an enslaved people. This tradition encompassed songs, dances, stories, and performances, and incorporated elements of African, English, and Irish folklore. Perhaps the most fondly remembered element of this comedic tradition was the figure of the trickster.

Servitude induces tricksterism; in every culture in which servitude is a fact of life, tricksters are prominent in folklore. African American folklore is especially rich in these figures, who often play the fool. Yet every trickster requires a fool on whom to play his tricks, and while that fool was often the master, it was just as often another slave. And this black fool would soon metamorphose into that stock figure of white minstrelsy, Sambo.

Even under the strict limits that harsh slavemasters imposed, African Americans maintained an extraordinarily rich performance tradition. And white blackface performers usually claimed that they took their songs, dances, and routines from this tradition.

Only some of these claims, particularly those of early performers, were rooted in fact. Many of the most famous white minstrels and minstrel songwriters were from either the North or abroad, and had very little firsthand knowledge of black tradition and life (Stephen Foster, for example, had never lived in the South and had spent only a few days in Kentucky when he wrote his most famous songs); similarly, about 90 percent, according to one estimate, of minstrel songs are more closely related to other popular songs of their day than to black folk music. Of the many writers on minstrelsy, a few—most prominently Nathan Irvin Huggins and Nick Tosches—even claim that white minstrelsy owed almost nothing to black folklore.

But most writers agree that early blackface performers gleaned some significant elements—songs, skits, melodies, dances—from black traditions. There was, after all, a long tradition of black-white musical miscegenation, stretching back to the colonial period; minstrelsy was just as typical of that interaction as rock 'n' roll would be much later.

Tom Fletcher, who was a member of a nineteenth-century black minstrel troupe, wrote that his grandfather proudly told him, "The plantation is where shows like yours first started, son," referring to parties that slaves would hold when their masters were absent. Fletcher claimed that the cakewalk, which became an essential part of minstrelsy late in its history, originated among slaves, who knew it as the chalk-line walk. He also describes a black family act of the 1840s and '50s whose members performed seated in a semicircle, the father, sitting in the middle, taking the serious role and the sons, on the ends, providing the comedy. According to him, this was the origin of the "minstrel, first part" format. There is nothing implausible about these claims.

It is unnecessary to enumerate here all the correspondences between early blackface and black folk songs, whether tenuous or strong. There are very few if any reliable pre-minstrelsy documentations of the words or melodies to black American songs; one could easily make the case that the black folk songs that resemble minstrel songs in postbellum songbooks evidence a borrowing from the white minstrel tradition rather than the other way around. But a clear resemblance between what little we know of slave songs and certain minstrel numbers seems to lend some credence to the extravagant claims of white blackface performers like Thomas D. "Daddy" Rice, author of "Jump Jim Crow" and considered the "father of American minstrelsy," who said he learned his songs directly from slaves. On the other hand, the distortions he likely introduced may make his claims irrelevant. As Nick Tosches says, "whatever of black culture infused minstrelsy was transmuted into such an exaggerated, expurgated, or comedic form that it was more of a far-fetched funhouse reflection than a real if watered-down representation of the real thing."

But at the time, both blacks and whites consistently claimed black origins for these songs. According to one legend, "Jump Jim Crow" was a black folk song, and the New Orleans black banjo player John "Picayune" Butler, who would later teach banjo to a number of northern white minstrels, sang it to a white blackface circus clown, who later taught it to Rice. Similarly, the authorship of Dan Emmett's "Dixie," which would soon become the national anthem of the Confederacy, was claimed by two black musicians who had been Emmett's neighbors. And many of the most famous later minstrel numbers and coon songs were written by blacks.

Perhaps, as historian Dale Cockrell concludes, "It is impossible to separate out independent white or black strains of musical culture." Both blacks and whites performed minstrel standards like "Jump Jim Crow," "Jim Along Josey," and "Zip Coon," and it's only logical to conclude that both races had a hand in their composition. White blackface performers traveled all over the country looking for—and finding—folk material suitable for their performances. Why would they ignore black songs, dances, and stories? They had every reason to use them. Moreover, lower-class urban society during the era in which these songs originated was remarkably integrated. Cockrell rightly says that "this time and place found the races living together as easily as any before and perhaps more so than any since."

At any rate, it's clear that the rhetoric surrounding minstrelsy promulgated a strong belief among both its white and black audiences that its songs, dances, and comic routines were authentically black. Minstrelsy, whether black or white, was almost without exception viewed as a black art form during its nineteenth-century heyday and for quite some time afterward. It was probably only a little more than fifty years ago that this belief was questioned and found wanting.

Those songs and routines that minstrelsy borrowed were subsequently expunged from the black tradition by those who wanted to keep black culture untouched by blackface. An early example is the 1867 *Slave Songs of the United States*, compiled by three northern abolitionists; among its 136 songs are 124 spirituals (or otherwise religious numbers), seven songs in French (from Louisiana), and only five secular songs: "Shock Along, John," "Round the Corn, Sally," "Charleston Gals," "Run, Nigger, Run," and "I'm Gwine to Alabamy." (At least three of these correspond to white minstrel numbers: the first to "Walk Along John," the third to "Buffalo Gals," and the fourth to the song of the same title.) The reason for this paucity of secular material is given as follows: "All the world knows the banjo, and the 'Jim Crow' songs of thirty years ago. We have succeeded in obtaining only a very few songs of this character. Our intercourse with the colored people has been chiefly through the work of the Freedmen's Commission, which deals with the serious and earnest side of the negro character. It is often, indeed, no easy matter to persuade them to sing their old songs, even as a curiosity, such is the sense of dignity that has come with freedom."

As is made clear here, after emancipation those blacks whom the compilers of *Slave Songs* interviewed—and, presumably, a number of others—did their best to hide their secular folk traditions from the whites on whom their future treatment relied, and tried to emphasize only the more dignified aspects of their culture. This stands in sharp contrast to the situation prior to emancipation, when whites expected blacks to sing and dance in joy and merriment, and blacks, being slaves, complied; it also stands in sharp contrast to the attitude of the many blacks actively engaged in promoting and performing black minstrel numbers at the time. (A far more representative compilation was Newman I. White's 1928 *American Negro Folk-Songs,* which includes 680 items gathered from a number of sources mostly in the 1910s. Of these, 104, in White's reckoning, displayed "traces of the ante-bellum minstrel song," with another 58 "showing traces of coon songs, vaudeville songs and ballets.")

Unlike the compilers of *Slave Songs,* W. E. B. Du Bois, James Weldon Johnson, and J. Rosamond Johnson, all immensely influential black critical thinkers in their fields, viewed the role minstrelsy played in their people's history with favor. In his 1921 essay "The Negro in Literature and Art," Du Bois asserted that Stephen Foster's "Old Black Joe" and "Old Folks at Home" were "built on Negro themes" (this is not true, but was widely believed at the time) and included them in his claim that black music was "the only real American music." In *Black Manhattan* (1930), James Weldon Johnson wrote that minstrelsy "was the first and remains, up to this time, the only completely original contribution America has made to the theatre. Negro minstrelsy, everyone ought to know, had its origin among the slaves of the old South"; and of white minstrelsy, he wrote, "towards the end of the last century it provided the most gorgeous stage spectacle to be seen in the United States." When J. Rosamond Johnson compiled *Rolling Along in Song: A Chronological Survey of American Negro Music* in 1937, he included, after sections on ring shouts, spirituals, jubilees, plantation ballads, and "plantation and levee pastimes," a section on "minstrel songs," followed by sections on jailhouse songs, work songs, street cries, etc. (he concluded with an excerpt from George Gershwin's *Porgy and Bess*). Even if many of these "minstrel songs" were actually written by whites, Johnson assumed that they were at least based on black folklore. He took pains to point out that Stephen Foster's "Old Folks at Home" uses the same scale and intervals as the traditional spiritual "Deep River." For Du Bois and the Johnson brothers, minstrel songs were nothing to be ashamed of, but rather a source of considerable pride.

White minstrelsy has its origins in blackfacing for comic effect. This practice, which has been traced back to ancient Greece, was common during Shakespeare's day, and was continued by callithumpians, mummers, and morris dancers through to the twentieth century. Very little of this form of masking was race-related. But in America we also find blackface actors playing ignorant or comic blacks as early as the first American musical, *The Disappointment* (1767), which featured a black character named Raccoon; foolish and ignorant black characters with names like Sambo, Caesar, and Pompey soon followed in other plays, all in the eighteenth century. Cockrell estimates that between the first American performance of *Othello* in 1751 and the first full-fledged minstrel show in 1843, around 20,000 blackface performances were given in American theaters. At the same time, blackface clowns were extremely popular in circuses, almost all of which featured at least one.

The eighteenth century also saw the rise of so-called "Negro" songs, performed on concert stages or published in collections. These generally portrayed blacks sympathetically, either as tragic or pitiful figures. Their titles included "Poor Black Boy," "I Sold a Guiltless Negro Boy," "The Desponding Negro," and "The Negro's Humanity." But by the nineteenth century, a majority of such songs were of a far more disparaging nature.

In 1827, George Washington Dixon and his troupe hid their white faces behind blackface makeup, put on exaggerated clothes, and sang "Coal Black Rose" and "My Long-Tailed Blue," the former the plaint of the plantation darky and the latter that of the city dandy. These two types would remain constant throughout minstrelsy's long history (though the dandy would often not be in blackface and would instead portray a white parvenu). The popularity of blackface performance exploded the next year with Thomas D. Rice's performance of a tune with words derived in part from black folklore entitled "Jump Jim Crow." And in 1843 came the real breakthrough: the performance in the Bowery Amphitheatre in New York of an entire minstrel show by Dan Emmett and his Virginia Minstrels (none of them were from Virginia, and only one was from a slave state), the first blackface performers to play real instruments (violin, banjo, bones, and tambourine)—and the first to call themselves minstrels.

This was something new—as minstrel historian W. T. Lhamon points out, the Virginia Minstrels insisted that their performances portrayed life on the old plantation, thus defining their art as "straight-up faux anthropology, done as theatre." At the same time, their show featured lively, rhythmic street stories, improvisation, and audience participation. In other words, this was genuinely popular entertainment, a performance mode that in its looseness was able to draw upon and accommodate both the basest and the friendliest impulses of its audience.

The Virginia Minstrels combined all the mischief and fun of the era's comic presentation of frontiersmen with material that audiences thought was genuinely African American. Perhaps never before had the American stage seen such an exuberant and fast-paced performance. According to one review, tambourinist Dick Pelham's "looks and movements [were] comic beyond conception. He seemed animated by a savage energy; and [his tambourine playing] nearly wrung him off his seat. His white eyes rolled in a curious frenzy . . . and his hiccupping chuckles were unsurpassable." There were similar descriptions of the other members, and contemporaneous drawings of the troupe show them full of motion and sprightliness.

At the same time, this wasn't just street theater, but also something more proper. When the Virginia Minstrels advertised their first engagement in the *New York Herald,* they called themselves a "novel, grotesque, original and surpassingly melodious ethiopian band," but also took care to note that they provided "*exclusively musical entertainment*" (emphasis in original) "entirely exempt from the vulgarities and other objectionable features, which have hitherto characterized negro extravaganzas." Even the word "minstrel" signified, at the time, a singing group in a concert hall performing in front of a middle-class white audience.

The genius of the Virginia Minstrels lay in placing plantation comedy and music, however ersatz, in the heart of civilized northern white society, rather than among the lower-class audience it had formerly enjoyed. This was the key to their success—now not only could lower-class whites join in masking and merrymaking, but everyone else could too. This wild and uninhibited portrayal of the most extreme stereotypes of black Americans made them America's central comic figures. And, as Watkins points out, "a grossly distorted public image of black Americans and their humor was being persuasively etched into the American mind."

Suddenly hundreds of performers, all northerners with very little contact with southern culture or slavery, began putting on minstrel shows, making it America's most popular form of entertainment. At its peak in the decades right before and after the Civil War, at least thirty full-time companies were making a living off of minstrelsy, even introducing it to England and France with considerable success. And besides the professionals, amateur groups sprung up around the country, both in cities and small towns.

One of the best descriptions of a minstrel show is by Mark Twain, who later in life remembered one he saw in the 1840s. The description, which lasts many pages, is too long to quote in full, but is well worth reading (it can be found in several early editions of his autobiography, though not in the 2010 volume). Twain describes the exaggerated makeup and clothing well—skin too dark, lips too red, clothes far too large (one of his most vivid passages runs "Their lips were thickened and lengthened with bright red paint to such a degree that their mouths resembled slices cut in a ripe watermelon"). He outlines the function of the end men, "Bones" (named after the castanets he played) and "Banjo" (or, more commonly, "Tambo," short for "tambourine"), who spoke loudly in exaggerated Negro dialect and quarreled with each other while telling "stale and moldy" stories; the middleman, or interlocutor, who spoke proper English, wore elegant clothes that fit well, rarely sported blackface, and was the straight man of the show, trying unsuccessfully to keep order; and the remainder of the minstrels, who performed "rudely comic" songs such as "Buffalo Gals," "Camptown Races," and "Old Dan Tucker."

While white minstrel shows varied tremendously, in general (about half the time) they adhered to a three-part structure, formalized in the 1850s.

At the outset the troupe would march onto the stage, perhaps singing a lively song, and parade around the chairs, arranged in a semicircle, until Mister Interlocutor said, "Gentlemen, be seated." Mister Interlocutor would stand in the middle, Tambo and Bones would sit on the ends, and at least a dozen other performers would be between them. The Interlocutor never laughed or used dialect; Tambo and Bones would play on his straight-faced manner by indulging in all manner of anarchic jokes and routines, punctuated with their rudimentary instruments and loud laughter. This first part was full of humorous songs, dances, jokes, and sentimental ballads; in later years it also included a "walkaround," in which finely dressed couples would parade on the stage, often doing a cakewalk; and a big production number would conclude the act.

The second part was the "olio," a sort of variety show featuring singers and dancers, vocal quartets, acrobats and contortionists, magicians, impersonators and ventriloquists. It usually opened with a monologue or "stump speech," full of malapropisms and delivered in a fake "darky" dialect, burlesquing anyone and anything that wasn't working class, from suffragettes to doctors. It culminated in a dance featuring the entire company.

The third part was a musical afterpiece, or comic play, often with a plantation setting, but more often a parody of a Shakespeare play, an Italian operetta, or something else well-known to the audience. The whole lasted a little less than two hours.

The primary character in the minstrel show, whether he was named Sambo, Tambo, or something else, was a white invention. Perhaps the best description of him is Carl Wittke's, from a 1930 history of minstrelsy:

> The stage Negro loved watermelons and ate them in a peculiar way. He turned out to be an expert wielder of the razor, a weapon which he always had ready for use on such special social occasions as crap games, of which the stage Negro was passionately fond. . . . He always was distinguished by an unusually large mouth and a peculiar kind of broad grin; he dressed in gaudy colors and in a flashy style; he usually consumed more gin than he could properly hold; and he loved chickens so well that he could not pass a chicken-coop without falling into temptation. . . . Moreover, the Negro's alleged love for the grand manner led him to use words so long that he not only did not understand their meaning, but twisted the syllables in the most ludicrous fashion in his futile efforts to pronounce them.

Most people nowadays think of the presentation of blacks in minstrelsy as uniformly like this. But while this character was usually present in some variation, minstrels also sang about and played the part of sorrowful, overworked slaves; old slaves pining for their youth; happy, dancing slaves with hardly a care; lovers grieving for their dead mates; religious slaves afraid of the devil; rough slaves fighting over a woman; female slaves mourning their stolen children; and so on—as even a cursory glance at any antebellum minstrel songbook will make clear. Some of the 1830 lyrics to "Jump Jim Crow" even portray an openly rebellious slave: "Perhaps de blacks will rise, / For deir wish for freedom, / Is shining in deir eyes. / . . . An I caution all white dandies, / Not to come in my way, / For if dey insult me, / Dey'll in de gutter lay." And in addition, of course, hundreds of characters in minstrel shows played white characters, even if they wore blackface for convention's sake.

The aim here was not just to provoke laughs, but also to portray in song and in performance the full panoply of life, so sad, sentimental songs and situations were prominent along with the mass of parodies. The great black songwriter W. C. Handy, who was in a minstrel troupe himself, described a black minstrel show at the turn of the twentieth century, but his words apply to white minstrelsy as well: "Everyone knew that there were those who came to a minstrel show to cry as well as to laugh. Ladies of that mauve decade were likely to follow the plot of a song with much the same sentimental interest that their daughters show in the development of a movie theme nowadays. The tenors were required to tell the stories that jerked the tears."

Because of minstrelsy's widespread popularity, and because it played to many audiences who were little concerned with plantation life or even the very existence of blacks, its thematic material included an astonishingly wide variety of subjects unrelated to slavery. The ridicule was not directed exclusively at blacks, but at other things whites enjoyed laughing about. If its lectures, sermons, and orations massacred the English language with malapropisms and fake Negro dialect, this was often done not only to ridicule blacks but also to poke fun at the vacuous and wordy speeches so common in that era. Much of the repertory of white minstrel shows was, in fact, nonracial in character. The sketches in the afterpiece were not always played in blackface, and included, besides parodies of other plays and series of short skits, plays about the circus, high society, spiritualists, poverty, medical charlatans, and domestic issues. While many of these featured black characters, there were plenty of exceptions.

The essence of minstrelsy was parody. The fact of a blackface show itself was a parody of serious theatrical productions;

and almost every part of it was a parody of something more specific. Not only were speeches and operas parodied, but so were ballet, polka, and other dances; popular songs and singers; foreign bands; ethnic customs and manners ranging from American Indians to Chinese to Irish; a huge range of theatrical productions—in short, if something could be parodied, a minstrel show probably did so.

By the turn of the century, nearly every community, whether urban or rural, enjoyed the performances of amateur minstrel groups, who had ready access to hundreds of low-cost minstrel books. Even as late as the Depression, the Federal Theatre Project of the Works Progress Administration was sponsoring minstrel shows; and *Dixie,* the 1943 movie starring Bing Crosby in occasional blackface as the minstrel Daniel Emmett, is a Hollywood whitewash of white minstrelsy, including an elaborate and unapologetic minstrel show. (In Britain, blackface minstrelsy lasted even longer—the *Black and White Minstrel Show* was on TV every Saturday night through 1978.)

The appeal of the white minstrel show was that it was an excuse to drop all inhibitions, have a good time, and be liberated from the conventions of everyday life. Nathan Irvin Huggins, an important mid-twentieth-century black cultural critic, put it more pejoratively: "What would be more likely and more natural for men who were tied up in the knots of an achievement ethic—depending almost wholly on self-sacrifice and self-restraint—than to create a *persona* which would be completely self-indulgent and irresponsible? White men put on black masks and became another self, one which was loose of limb, innocent of obligation to anything outside itself, indifferent to success (for whom success was impossible by racial definition), and thus a creature totally devoid of tension and deep anxiety."

"Blackface action," W. T. Lhamon writes, "is usually slashing back at the pretentions and politesse of authority more than at blackness," and the truth of this is incontestable, especially of minstrelsy in its nascent form in the 1830s. "To sign oneself black was unmistakably to acknowledge and choose alignment with the low. . . . To blacken one's face, therefore, was at least in part to profess an oppositional stance." Stephen Foster's biographer Ken Emerson adds, "More than simply a revolt against decorum, blackface was also a veil and a vehicle for discussion of sex and violence, money and class—all the dirty stuff of life that many white Americans preferred to sweep under the parlor rug. Behind a mask of burnt cork, they felt freer to speak their minds and express their urges."

This appears to contradict the now-conventional wisdom that minstrelsy was nothing more than comic performance expressly designed to demean black Americans. Indeed, minstrelsy did present black Americans primarily as figures of ridicule—submoronic, slothful, ugly, bestial—and undoubtedly the joys of racism were often essential to minstrelsy's success. Even as early as 1849, Frederick Douglass recognized that minstrelsy "feed[s] the flame of American prejudice against colored people."

One hundred years later, Ralph Ellison's seminal 1958 essay "Change the Joke and Slip the Yoke" took this long-standard objection one step further. Ellison argued that minstrelsy was solely a white phenomenon, even if it "makes use of Negro idiom, songs, dance motifs and word-play," and that blackface was a "ritual mask." Minstrelsy was only comedy, Ellison argued, in the sense of it being a "comedy of the grotesque and the unacceptable"; it was even more "a ritual of exorcism," of purifying the white race. This ritual was cathartic, Ellison maintained, involving "the self-humiliation of the 'sacrificial' figure"; one of its motives was "a psychological dissociation from this symbolic self-maiming."

Yet dissociation and identification, while opposites, can easily coexist. The best comedians engage in both—while savagely ridiculing the character they portray, they nonetheless engage the audience's sympathies. Think of Steve Carrell in *The Office,* to take just one example, or Jerry Lewis in *The Nutty Professor*—or, for that matter, any number of skits in *Chappelle's Show*. Blackface minstrelsy wasn't like *The Birth of a Nation,* which preyed on its viewers' fears to incite hatred. Instead, as Lhamon puts it, "the minstrel mask encouraged identification, it also encouraged racialist differentiation, [and] both could go on simultaneously."

Watkins puts it differently, but essentially agrees: "The minstrel black man served as a kind of alter ego, providing whites with the vicarious experience of breaking free from the rigid restraints of 'civilized' European behavior and expressing their natural or, as they interpreted it, vulgar instincts. Moreover, they did so while allowing white audiences the luxury of remaining aloof from the ludicrous sable figures that pranced before them." Ken Emerson rightly sees this as the foundation for American popular culture: "It was the fakery of blackface, as preposterous as opera, that made this freedom possible; its very disingenuousness paradoxically encouraged honesty. . . . Gleefully flouting the proprieties of sincerity and sentimentality, blackface delighted unabashedly in its irony and even its humbug. That's what made it 'pop.'" Liberation and ridicule—minstrelsy posed these ideas as inextricable allies.

This racialist differentiation—the ridiculousness of the performer serving to affirm the nonridiculousness of the observer—also partook of the nineteenth-century fascination with the exotic, in this case an exoticism that had the advantage of being peculiarly American. And it showcased often exotic melodies, rhythms, dances, plotlines, characters, and jokes that were not just ostensibly but occasionally actually of African American origin. By the time of minstrelsy's founding, the black American was already widely known as a master of fun; therefore an entertainment that emphasized black culture was bound to enjoy the same reputation. But one shouldn't discount the setting of many minstrel shows—the mythical "old plantation"—as an equally essential part of their appeal. The plantation was a site of warmth, community, and happiness, a kind of paradise in its audiences' eyes, and a wonderful setting for parody, mimicry, comedy, dance, and song.

Upstart movements in American culture lose their rebelliousness as they enter the mainstream and engender a mass following—think of rock 'n' roll or the Beat movement. And minstrelsy was no exception. By the 1850s it had become the dominant form of American entertainment, and in the process lessened its focus on racial difference and the "old plantation" in order to appeal to a wider audience. It became the large umbrella under which all forms of music, dance, spectacle, and theater could coexist—the ancestor of vaudeville and the variety show.

Whites were not the exclusive audience for white minstrel shows. Black people attended too. Ticket prices for "colored persons" were advertised for one of Dixon's 1832 shows; in 1833 a curfew imposed on African Americans prompted the objection of at least one theater owner, who protested that "a great proportion of our audience consists of persons of this caste"; in the early 1840s several papers noted instances of black musical troupes performing minstrel numbers; and some of Thomas Rice's obituaries noted that he was popular with black audiences. For many black people minstrelsy held the same appeal as for its white audience.

Perhaps the first black in blackface was William Henry Lane, better known as Master Juba. According to an anonymous letter in the *New York Sunday Flash*, up-and-coming showman P. T. Barnum (who would later found Barnum & Bailey's Circus) first presented Lane in 1840, blacking him up so that nobody would know he was black. As writer Thomas L. Nichols, who was writing for the *New York Herald* at the time, explained,

> there was not an audience in America that would not have resented, in a very energetic fashion, the insult of being asked to look at the dancing of a real negro. . . . [So Barnum] greased the little "nigger's" face and rubbed it over with a new blacking of burnt cork, painted his thick lips with vermillion, put on a woolly wig over his tight curled locks, and brought him out as the "champion nigger-dancer of the world." Had it been suspected that the seeming counterfeit was the genuine article, the New York Vauxhall would have blazed with indignation.

In 1841, Barnum even pretended that Lane was none other than John Diamond, the most celebrated white dancer of the day, who had just left the company that year.

Apparently it wasn't long until Lane's race was no longer something to hide, for by 1844, he was having public dance competitions with Diamond, and winning some of them; even though these contests were clearly perceived as between a black and a white man, white judges gave Lane the prize.

One of the best descriptions of Lane was written by Charles Dickens, who saw him dance in New York in 1842, while Lane was still a teenager (Dickens did not mention the performer's name, but the *New York Herald* identified him as Master Juba less than a month after Dickens's *American Notes* was published; when Lane made his London debut in 1848, playbills called him "Boz's Juba," "Boz" being Dickens's occasional pen name):

> [This] lively young negro . . . is the wit of the assembly, and the greatest dancer known. He never leaves off making queer faces, and is the delight of all the rest, who grin from ear to ear incessantly. . . . Single shuffle, double shuffle, cut and cross-cut; snapping his fingers, rolling his eyes, turning in his knees, presenting the backs of his legs in front, spinning about on his toes and heels like nothing but the man's fingers on the tambourine; dancing with two left legs, two right legs, two wooden legs, two wire legs, two spring legs—what is this to him? And in what walk of life, or dance of life, does man ever get such stimulating applause as thunders about him when, having danced his partner off her feet, and himself too, he finishes by leaping gloriously on the bar-counter, and calling for something to drink, with the chuckle of a million of counterfeit Jim Crows in one inimitable sound!

Lane toured America and England with white minstrel troupes, performing uniquely African American dances, always in blackface. He even earned top billing, his popularity was so high, and was commonly advertised as "The Greatest Dancer in the World" and "King of All Dancers." He died in 1852 at the age of about twenty-seven from unknown causes.

William Henry Lane should be considered not just the most amazing dancer of his time (even John Diamond admitted as much), the first black minstrel, and an originator of African American dance, but also, if you'll forgive the anachronism, the Jackie Robinson of the American stage. Earlier black American actors had played in black theaters and abroad, and Barnum had displayed a black woman named Joyce Heth as George Washington's nurse; but prior to Master Juba's appearance on the New York stage, there were few if any blacks appearing as performers in a white troupe before white American theatergoers.

Plainly, like the blackface black minstrels who would follow him, Lane was a black man performing as a white man performing as a black man. The pretense of being white was at first a necessity—he was "passing" and his blackface functioned as whiteface. But he quickly became perhaps the only black performer in America who could publicly claim superiority over whites, and it was his blackface mask that had enabled him to do so. This established, from the very beginning, the two-edged sword of blackface for black performers (and audiences)—it was simultaneously demeaning, in that it painted them as figures of ridicule, and liberating, in that it enabled them to escape the oppressive strictures of racist America while on stage.

The first truly successful all-black minstrel troupe was organized in 1865, right at the conclusion of the Civil War. But there were some earlier, unsuccessful troupes. Frederick Douglass provided a rich description of one in 1849. Gavitt's Original Ethiopian Serenaders wore blackface and painted their lips in order to exaggerate their size. "Their singing generally was but an imitation of white performers, and not even a tolerable representation of the character of colored people. Their attempts at wit showed them to possess a plentiful lack of it, and gave their audience a very low idea of the shrewdness and sharpness of the race to which they belong." Douglass's contempt, however, did not extend to the very idea of the black minstrel show:

> It is something gained when the colored man in any form can appear before a white audience; and we think that even this company, with industry, application, and a proper cultivation of their taste, may yet be instrumental in removing the prejudice against our race. But they must cease to exaggerate the exaggerations of our enemies; and represent the colored man rather as he is, than as Ethiopian Minstrels usually represent him to be. They will *then* command the respect of both races; whereas *now* they only shock the taste of the one, and provoke the disgust of the other.

We will see echoes of Douglass's argument throughout this book.

Charles Hicks is commonly viewed as the father of black minstrelsy, and the 1865 troupe he managed was called the Original Georgia Minstrels, billed as "The Only Simon Pure Negro Troupe in the World." It was so popular that it reportedly outdrew all other minstrel troupes, black or white, in 1866. Thereafter, with a few important exceptions, black minstrel troupes could be distinguished from white minstrel troupes by one of the three designations "Georgia," "Colored," or "Slave" ("Negro" was used for whites in blackface). Their presentations were very much like those of white minstrels—in fact, it's difficult to find many differences in contemporaneous accounts and advertisements.

Still, one major difference was that a large number of black performers performed without blackface, especially when they were performing straight rather than comic roles. This practice underlined their "authenticity," which was one of the major bases of their appeal to white audiences. As the minstrel historian Robert Toll explains,

> because these performers stressed their authenticity, they were thought of as natural, spontaneous people on exhibit rather than as professional entertainers. "Being genuine Negroes," one reviewer succinctly observed in 1865, "they indulge in reality." Again and again, critics noted that black minstrelsy was not a show; it was a display of natural impulses. . . . Black minstrels demonstrated to a St. Louis writer that "there is nothing like the natural thing, and that a negro can play negro's peculiarities much more satisfactorally than the white 'artist' who with burnt cork is *at best a base imitator.*" White critics throughout the nation, over decades, echoed the same opinions.

Yet these claims of authenticity, like most such claims, were specious. Authenticity in minstrelsy was nothing more than a pretense. Despite admonitions to be true to the experience of their race from Douglass and subsequent black critics, and despite accolades from white audiences for their genuineness, for the most part black minstrels were not imitating the plantation—they were imitating the white minstrel shows' version of the plantation. The black writer Tom Fletcher, who appeared in Howard's Novelty Colored Minstrels, described a typical show, which had exactly the same features as its white forebears: it had three parts, the first in a semicircle with interlocutor, tambos, and bones; it lasted an hour and forty-five minutes; it featured a quartet and dancers; the entire company appeared in the afterpiece; and "the songs were the regular tunes of the period, spirituals, original songs and songs by Sam Lucas, Stephen Foster and Jim Bland." When Haverly's Colored Minstrels performed in Chicago in 1880, the second part included "remarkable imitations," a "banjo song and dance," a stump speech, Jubilee singers, "barnyard frolics," "plantation songs and dances," a "sextet banjo-orchestra," and a sketch entitled "Brudder Bones Baby." When this troupe played in London, a theatrical journal commented, "The entertainment which these colored folks give is . . . not sufficiently different from that given by artificial blacks [whites in blackface] to endow it with an absolutely special mark." Similarly, when Henderson's Colored Minstrels performed in Cincinnati in 1885, the show began with the traditional first part; the second part featured John Armstrong, "the Alabama Slave," who "imitated steam calliopes, planing mills and dogs, and lifted chairs and tables with his powerful jaw"; and the third part consisted of a farce called *Clarinda's Lovers* followed by another play called *Life on the Old Plantation.* One 1889 afterpiece, *Blackville Twins,* featured the following characters, which give a good idea of the content: two twins named Elmia and Jemina; their parents, Parson and Mama Black; two suitors named Juke and Bud; Dr. Cutum, the family doctor; and two rival suitors, named Zuke and Tony. There are plenty of descriptions in the contemporary press of other black troupes performing such songs as

"I'm a Jolly Little Nigger" and "Massa's in de Cold Cold Ground" and plays like *Justice in a Coloured Court; or the Dutchman's Monkey, Holiday on the Old Plantation, I Gits Mine,* and *Southern Home Scenes.*

Just like the white minstrel shows, black shows also included numerous skits, routines, and songs that did not center around the lives of black Americans. An 1889 play, *The Miller and the Sweep,* featured the following plot: On a big holiday in a country village, Ouph, a female fairy (played by a man) and Adonis, a village "flop," arrive and are welcomed. But they quarrel, and soon Adonis and Jupiter, the right-hand man of Diana, Queen of Fairyland (played by a woman), hatch a plan. Jupiter steals Ouph and carries her off to Fairyland. The miller and the sweep, both in love with Ouph, meet with Satan and are transformed into fairies; they go to Fairyland, where a duel ensues. The remainder of the plot is unclear, but concludes with a "night of horrors." An 1890 play, *Somnambulism: Or, He's in the Asylum Now,* included characters named "Oofty Goofty," "Won-a-pe-tie, a Piute Indian," "Shadow," "Good Morning," "Ed. Boots, a dilapidated tragedian," and "Midnight Visitors from the Silent Grave." Also in 1890, Charles B. Hicks' Minstrels concluded their show with a parody of Bellini's opera *La Sonnambula.* Clearly, black minstrelsy wasn't *only* about plantation scenes.

On the other hand, some true black folk elements not featured in white minstrel shows did find their way into black ones, heightening their "authenticity." Spirituals, which were popularized by the Fisk Jubilee Singers in the 1870s, were quickly added to black minstrel shows, heightening the realism of their portrayal of the old plantation. Occasionally the minstrels interpolated comic verses into classic songs like "Let My People Go"; but, as Toll points out, black minstrels' presentation of African-American spirituals were more true to the way slaves had sung these songs than any other presentation of the time, including that of the troupes of jubilee singers.

Black minstrels may also have incorporated some folk-derived innovations into minstrelsy's many dance steps. William Henry Lane's jig had modified the Irish step and added black folk elements to create a breathtaking, exhilarating spectacle. Billy Kersands's "essence of old Virginia" perfected a black variation of the shuffle in which "the performer moves forward without appearing to move his feet at all, by manipulating his toes and heels rapidly, so that his body is propelled without changing the position of his legs," according to ragtime composer Arthur Marshall. The origins of the cakewalk are at least partly African, and in the 1890s it became one of the main attractions of the black minstrel show.

Another factor in the success of black minstrels was their musical skill. In the 1870s, James M. Trotter, who had escaped slavery in 1852 and fought for the Union in the Civil War, set out on a mission to give the fullest possible account of the black American contribution to music. As part of this project, "he had to force himself," despite his strong distaste, "to witness the performances of the Georgia Minstrels" (Trotter wrote of himself in the third person here). "He was not pleased, of course, with that portion of the performance (a part of which he was compelled to witness) devoted to burlesque. Nevertheless, he found in the vocal and instrumental part much that was in the highest degree gratifying."

The troupe at the time was composed of twenty-one performers, many of them exceptionally accomplished musicians. "From the instrumentalists of this company either a fine orchestra or brass band can at any time, as occasion requires, be formed," Trotter concludes; they were also excellent harmony singers. At least four of them had been music teachers, one had played in European orchestras, another played four instruments very well and twelve others fairly, several others had mastered two or three instruments, and three of them arranged and wrote music themselves.

The Georgia Minstrels were indeed world-renowned for their accomplishments. As the *Boston Herald* noted, "Each performer seems to be not only a natural, but a cultured artist." By this time they had given over three thousand performances, and even appeared before the Queen of England. Reviews of the troupe were unanimously laudatory.

But what exactly was their talent in service of? It seems to have been solely to perpetuate the kind of minstrelsy originating with whites. Look at the songwriters, for instance. A northern, college-educated black man, James A. Bland, was billed as "The World's Greatest Minstrel Man" and "The Idol of the Music Halls." This widely successful minstrel comedian wrote some 700 minstrel songs; he was almost as admired as Stephen Foster. His more well-known numbers include "Carry Me Back to Old Virginny" and "Oh! Dem Golden Slippers." The writer of many of the most famous "coon songs" (racist malarkey that largely supplanted minstrel numbers at the turn of the twentieth century) was a black man, Ernest Hogan, who was billed as "The Unbleached American," and who was a huge star in the 1890s for his skill in portraying a malapropism-prone black preacher. Other black minstrel composers include Dan Lewis ("Moses Cart dem Water Melons Down") and Sam Lucas ("Carve dat Possum"). Nothing about their songs separates them from the compositions of white minstrels. For example, "Carry Me Back to Old Virginny," published in 1878, was preceded by white-authored minstrel songs entitled "I Wish I Was in Ole Virginny," "Carry Me Back to Old Virginia's

Shore," "Carry Me Home to Tennessee," and a host of others. Bland's lyrics are written from the point of view of ex-slaves fawningly nostalgic for the old plantation, mourning the death of kind old massa. Sam Lucas's "Dar's a Lock on de Chicken Coop Door" perpetuates the image of the semi-intelligible colored man out to steal his favorite food from whites. It begins, "Dis kintry's gone to de dogs at last / When de farmer gets a watch / And a big bull dog and a big steel trap / In de water million patch." (Unlike Bland, Lucas did sing about the joy of emancipation, but never approached the rebelliousness of Thomas D. Rice's "Jump Jim Crow.")

Today, minstrelsy and "tomming" are almost synonymous, but this was far from the case in the nineteenth century. Harriet Beecher Stowe's *Uncle Tom's Cabin* had condemned minstrelsy in no uncertain terms. Stage adaptations of the novel swept the country almost immediately after its massive success in 1852, since copyright protection did not extend from the printed page to the stage until 1856. These plays soon began to integrate blacks with blackfaced whites, and black stars came to play both Uncle Tom and Topsy, validating and continuing a tradition of successful black actors on the American stage dating back to the 1820s.

Many versions of the play were soon amalgamated with minstrel elements—an unsurprising development, since blackface was an integral part of both minstrelsy and the Tom shows. Thomas Rice even played Uncle Tom in one early version. In 1863 four different productions played New York at the same time, all featuring banjo and minstrel numbers. And meanwhile, white minstrel troupes started incorporating vicious parodies of *Uncle Tom's Cabin* into their programs.

It wasn't long before most major *Uncle Tom* productions featured "authentic" black performers singing and dancing plantation and jubilee songs and performing so-called "Negro specialties." By the end of the century, 400 to 500 Uncle Tom troupes were active, providing a major source of employment for black actors. Both Charles B. Hicks' Georgia Minstrels and Ernest Hogan's Minstrels presented serious all-black *Uncle Tom's Cabins*—in Australia and Hawaii, but not in the United States. And in 1906, the black comedian Tim Moore, who would much later play the Kingfish in the CBS series *The Amos 'n' Andy Show,* staged a one-man *Uncle Tom's Cabin,* playing all the characters, with one side of his face painted black and the other white.

With a few exceptions, however, the Uncle Tom shows were aimed squarely at a white audience and held little appeal for blacks. The Uncle Tom and the minstrel show certainly intersected but were at heart quite different entertainments.

Although at first black minstrels, like all black entertainers, found it difficult to play below the Mason-Dixon Line, by the mid-1880s they were a formidable force there. Black minstrel troupes, unlike the dignified and high-class jubilee singers, who by and large avoided the southern states, were accepted by southern whites as posing no threat to the idea of the Negro as an inferior race; in addition, because they traveled and lived in private railroad cars that shuttled from town to town, they didn't have to face the most common Jim Crow restrictions. And they proved wildly popular with black audiences. When Richards & Pringle's Georgia Minstrels played Memphis in 1896, for example, they drew an audience of 5,000 people (4,000 blacks and 1,000 whites), "the largest indoor paid audience ever known in that city," according to the *Indianapolis Freeman.* (It is important to note, though, that nineteenth-century minstrel troupes rarely, if ever, played to an exclusively black audience: a portion, and often the majority, of the audience was always white.)

One reason for this group's extraordinary popularity was the presence of the first real black minstrel star, Billy Kersands. Born in 1842, he was noticed by Charles Hicks in 1870, and joined Hicks' Georgia Minstrels the following year. Kersands, who typically played a slow and ignorant man (he played Dr. Cutum in *Blackville Twins*, the play alluded to above) and didn't wear blackface, was equally famous for his "essence of Vir-

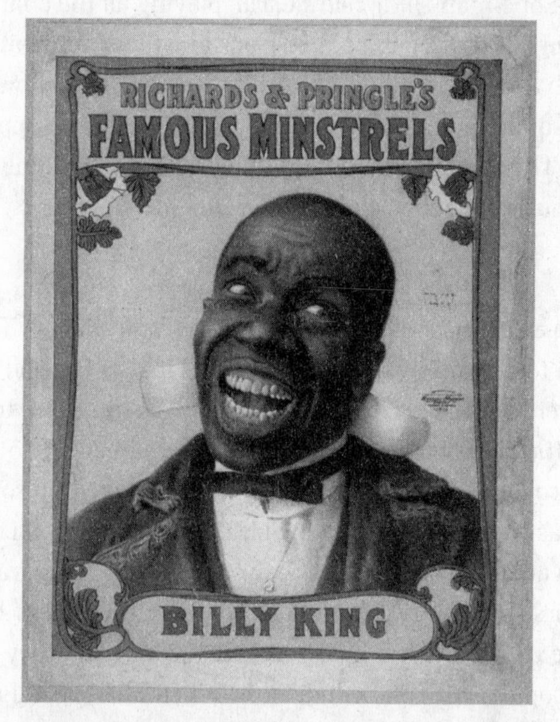

Billy King (1875–1936) was a prominent black comedian; he joined Richards & Pringle's Famous Georgia Minstrels in 1907. He ended up writing dozens of musical shows for his stock vaudeville company in Chicago.
MINSTREL POSTER COLLECTION, LIBRARY OF CONGRESS.

ginia" dance; his theme song, "Old Aunt Jemimah"; and "Mary's Gone Wid a Coon," an 1880 lament that the singer's daughter is about to marry a "a big black coon"—a forerunner of the "coon songs" that would soon dominate the minstrel repertoire and become popular far outside of the minstrel show. (The prominent black critic Sylvester Russell wrote in 1902 that "the Negro race has no objection to the word 'coon.' " Later in the decade, however, a number of black critics were decrying coon songs.) But Kersands's most astonishing feature was his extraordinarily large mouth, which he would contort into wild shapes. He held a cup and saucer inside it; he was known to sing "Swanee River" with two billiard balls in it (the famous photograph of him with the balls in his cheeks forms a part of Robert Frank's photograph that graces the cover of the Rolling Stones' *Exile on Main Street*). The distorted mouth reinforced stereotypes of blacks as having exaggerated features and was a staple of minstrel shows: one review of Hicks's Georgia Minstrels commented on the "enormous mouths" of the performers, which, "every time they open them, they seem as if they were trying to swallow their own heads."

Kersands performed with a large number of minstrel troupes, including Haverly's Genuine Colored Minstrels. Their 1881 performances in London gave rise to perhaps the fullest description we have of a black minstrel show, found in Harry Reynolds's 1928 *Minstrel Memories*. According to it, the curtain went up to disclose sixty-five black men and women of varying complexions and ages, ranging from dark to "octoroon" and from baby to aged (apparently they did not use blackface). "Their costumes were of the plantation, in a picturesque plantation setting," Reynolds wrote. Among the troupe were sixteen corner men—eight bones and eight tambourines—arranged in two rows; a disciplined troupe, they worked together in a "smart manner."

"The programme was a mixture of plantation solos, concerted numbers, Jubilee quartets, and spirituals, interspersed with comic nigger ditties and witticisms by the comedians." The songs included "My Sweetheart When a Boy," an old ballad; "Mary's Gone Wid a Coon," performed by Billy Kersands; and "O Dem Golden Slippers," the James Bland classic. Twenty dancers and a banjo orchestra performed. One actor, Bob Mack, was dressed as a big rooster and "had a combat with a genuine bantam, with most amusing effect. There was a burlesque on the Jubilee singers." Another comedian "made some excellent comedy with a big drum with which he got terribly entangled. First he dived right over it, then underneath it. He was all over it, everywhere in fact but inside it; but he always came up just in time for his beat." The show also included high-pedestal clog dancing; and the Bohee Brothers performed "ballads, banjo song and dance" wearing "velvet coats, knee breeches, and jockey caps."

Black minstrel-show programs confirm that Reynolds's description could, with some small variations, apply to other black minstrel shows of the time. But when Callender's Georgia Minstrels played Virginia City, Nevada, in 1883, they mixed minstrelsy with higher-class black entertainment. The first part of the program, called "Up North," included both minstrel and nonminstrel songs; the second part included not only "Alabama Pickaninnies," a "Grand Military Pagent" [*sic*], Billy Kersands doing his usual gags, and Bob Mack's rooster/bantam performance, but also "The Famous Hyers Sisters," a well-known and decidedly nonminstrel theatrical troupe.

Shows like these represented the black minstrel show at its zenith. However, black audiences had other opportunities to watch black entertainers. In the northern states especially, black minstrels continued to vie with the Uncle Tom shows; the far more dignified jubilee singers; black theater troupes, both amateur and professional; and, by the early 1890s, black vaudeville, burlesque, circus sideshows (which featured both black bands and black minstrel troupes), and baseball.

Given these alternatives, minstrelsy's immense popularity among black audiences can only be explained by supposing that these audiences genuinely enjoyed it. For example, a lukewarm 1891 review of Cleveland's Colored Minstrels in the *New York Clipper* included the following comment: "The large audience included a goodly number of colored people, who seemed to vastly enjoy the ludicrous portion of the program." That "ludicrous portion" consisted of, among other things, "facial distortions and 'mouthings'" and "a short sketch [called] 'stealing Chickens.'"

On occasion, the players asserted their equality with whites. When the black minstrel troupe McCabe & Young's Minstrels played in St. Augustine, Florida, in 1889, they refused to yield to the demand of white citizens to ban blacks from the main floor seats, replying, according to several newspapers, "Any colored lady or gentleman will have the equal right of any white lady or gentleman at our performance in this or any other city."

It is difficult to reconcile this forthright heroism with what the same troupe did the following year in Los Angeles: they put on what was perhaps the most appalling black minstrel show of all time. The Reconstruction period, which lasted from 1865 to 1876, was the high point of black achievement in nineteenth-century America—not for another hundred years would such a large proportion of political offices be held by blacks, who had been given full and unprecedented voting rights. Yet McCabe & Young's Operatic Minstrels made minstrel mincemeat out of that very achievement. The first part of their show was given to "a Senatorial Assembly" in which the comedians ("Ebony Hued Monarchs of Merriment") played senators and representatives, whose assembly is "interrupted by Billy Wisdom telling them of a grand time in Opossum Hollow," and soon devolves into a spat centering around a "Flower Girl who is called the Missing Link of Mo." The olio then featured a sketch called "The Senator's Flirtation," starring minstrels playing Frederick Douglass, P. B. S. Pinchback of Louisiana (the only black man to serve as a state governor prior to the 1990s), and Senator Blanche Bruce of Mississippi (the second black man to serve as a U.S. senator). Clearly any lingering pride which McCabe and Young might have taken in the political achievements of their fellow African Americans had been overwhelmed either by southern propaganda, which painted these politicians as buffoons and which the show reprehensibly echoed, or by their own desire to make fun at any expense. A contemporary equivalent might be a black theater putting on a play ridiculing Martin Luther King Jr. and Malcolm X.

It is not surprising, then, that middle-class and intellectual blacks either ignored or criticized minstrel shows—the black population of Toronto even tried to get the city government to ban "caricatures of their race." But, as Watkins recognizes, these blacks also denounced or labeled vulgar other more "legitimate" aspects of black folk culture, including work songs, spirituals, and black dances. They went for more "high class" entertainment, as exemplified by the enormously successful Hyers Sisters, a black theater company that specialized in uplifting musical dramas such as *Out of Bondage, The Underground Railway,* and *Princess Orelia of Madagascar*. As the *Chicago Inter-Ocean* put it in 1889, "There is an indescribable charm, an originality and feeling of reality about the songs of these dark-skinned artists which is positive relief from the hackneyed rubbish of the bogus, cork-grimed variety man." (Despite the nonminstrel character of the Hyers Sisters, they shared many musicians, actors, and occasionally a stage with the Georgia Minstrels.)

By the early 1890s the minstrel show was commonly perceived as being in decline. It had become more and more circuslike over the previous decade, increasing in size and variety, while decreasing in quality. For example, Haverly's Mastodons, a white troupe, boasted 100 members in 1880, rather than the 40 members it had boasted of a few years earlier; Haverly's Colored Minstrels, meanwhile, employed over 100 black performers. By the late 1880s, the Billy Sweatman, Billy Rice & Barney Fagan Minstrels, another white troupe, boasted a company of 110 members, two bands of 14 musicians each, a sextet of saxophone players, two drum corps of 8 each, 2 drum majors and a quartet of mounted buglers. And in 1887, Gorman's Spectacular Minstrels advertised "The Siamese Twins! The Hindoo Ballet Dancers! The Trick Elephants! The Chinese Giants! The Headless Man!" billing this as the introduction of a "new era in minstrelsy" and "the climax of minstrel greatness."

At the same time, mixed minstrel shows arose, offering black performers in one part and white performers in another. Primrose and West's Big Minstrels, for example, included 40 whites and 30 blacks. Characteristically, the blacks "dressed in the old-time style," according to the *New York Clipper,* and sang classic minstrel numbers like "Nellie Was a Lady," "Suwanee River," "Kentucky Home," and "The Virginia Rosebud." We have no evidence that the black entertainers had any say in what they performed, unlike in all-black troupes, nor that they performed for black audiences. Another mixed troupe, W. S.

Cleveland's Massive Minstrels, boasted "35 white minstrel stars, 15 male and female Japanese, 35 genuine colored minstrels, [and] 15 Moorish-Beduoin Arabs." Clearly, mixed minstrel troupes did not signify an increase in racial tolerance but rather a willingness upon the part of some black performers to perform white characterizations of black life for white audiences, just as they had done in the days of slavery.

These two developments created room for a far more genuine presentation of black life. *Darkest America,* which premiered in 1894, represented a purification of the black minstrel show. Together with the 1895 *Black America,* it was the most "authentic" minstrel show in history and marked a fundamental change in direction. It was also, in a sense, the nineteenth-century black minstrel show's last hurrah.

Other black minstrel acts had also been billed as more authentic than white ones. But, as the *New York Clipper* wrote of *Darkest America,* "The show will not be of the old style of negro minstrelsy. To introduce scenes peculiar to the South will be the aim of the management." By 1897, its scenes included a cotton field with a fully operating cotton gin, a Louisiana sugar plantation like the one made infamous by *Uncle Tom's Cabin,* the levee at New Orleans, a panorama of the Mississippi showing the famous 1870 race between the *Natchez* and the *Robert E. Lee,* the interior of the South Carolina State House during the 1876 Hayes-Tilden election dispute, a gambling scene, a camp meeting, Jacksonville on the night of the 1894 Corbett-Mitchell prize fight, and a black ballroom scene in Washington. It required two seventy-foot railroad cars simply to carry the scenery from town to town.

The show was wildly successful. In 1896, for example, it played for twenty-eight weeks in fourteen different states, traveling over 12,000 miles. And it featured a large number of the major black entertainers of the time, including Sam Lucas (and his wife), Billy Miller, and Florence Hines, the premier black male impersonator.

Undoubtedly the most elaborate and authentic black minstrel show was *Black America*, an 1895 theatrical extravaganza that took place in Ambrose Park in Brooklyn. "An outdoor environmental theme-park extravaganza," as Abbott and Seroff put it, it was advertised as a "Panorama of the Negro, from the Jungles of Africa to the Civilization of America."

The show was the brainchild of an immensely talented freeborn black minstrel comedian and entrepreneur named Billy McClain, who had helmed a successful show in 1892 called *South Before the War* with a mixed cast of 50, including a brass band, and would go on to helm *Darkest America* in its later years. Despite the disbelief of his friends, McClain managed to secure financing from Nate Saulsbury, who had promoted Buffalo Bill's Wild West Show. He collected a cast of over 500 people, including "all of the top show people of the period," many of whom needed summer employment. He also roped in 63 vocal quartets from all over the country along with a group of men who had served in the Ninth U.S. Cavalry, commonly known as the Buffalo Soldiers, to perform their regular army maneuvers. At some point the park, according to Tom Fletcher, "was transformed into the likeness of a southern plantation. Cotton bushes, with buds blossoming, were transplanted. Bales of cotton were brought in and a cotton gin in working order set up." McClain also brought in chickens, mules, and other livestock, and built real log cabins both for performances and for living quarters for the entertainers. People could come before the show and pretend they were strolling through an old-time plantation.

It should be noted that full-scale re-creations of the old

plantation were hardly unique at the time. The Centennial Exhibition in Philadelphia in 1876 had featured a concession called "The South" featuring "a band of old-time plantation 'darkies' who will sing their quaint melodies and strum the banjo," according to a guidebook. In 1879 and 1880, Haverly's Colored Minstrels had featured "the darky as he is at home, darky life in the cornfield, canebrake, barnyard, and on the levee and flatboat"; their replica of a southern plantation even featured "overseers, bloodhounds, and darkies at work." The 1895 Trans-Mississippi Exposition in Atlanta, the 1897 Tennessee Centennial Exposition in Nashville, and the 1898 Cotton States Exposition in Omaha all featured a concession called the Old Plantation, managed by a former white minstrel, where "young bucks and thickliped [*sic*] African maidens 'happy as a big sunflower' dance the old-time breakdowns, joined in by 'all de niggahs' with wierd [*sic*] and gutteral [*sic*] sounds to the accompaniment of 'de scrapin' of de fiddle an' de old bangjo [*sic*].'" When the Old Plantation reappeared at the Pan-American Exposition in Buffalo in 1901, it included fifty "genuine negros" from the South who had secretly attended a performance school in Charleston in order to satisfactorily portray "jocular, careless serfs, who in the South before the war gave slavery the deceptive hue of contented and oft-times happy dependence." The Old Plantation reappeared in the St. Louis World's Fair in 1904, the Alaska-Yukon-Pacific Exposition in Seattle in 1909, and the Panama-Pacific International Exposition in San Francisco in 1915.

None of these plantation re-creations, however, were nearly as big or elaborate as *Black America.* Fifteen minutes before showtime the crowds would take their seats in the huge outdoor amphitheater, which was covered by canvas. Soon they were presented with a variety of music: singing field hands, featuring a number of the 63 quartets; operatic selections sung by black opera singers; and the (black) Baltimore Brass Band. The program continued with a company of the Ninth U.S. Calvary, black boxers, vaulters, jugglers, acrobats, jockeys, foot races, fancy skaters, quadrilles on horseback, buck-and-wing dancing, historical pictures, and more. An advertisement in the paper used more colorful language: "500 Southern Colored People, presenting Home Life, Folk Lore, Pastimes of Dixie, More Music, Mirth, Merriment for the Masses; More Fun, Jollity, Humor and Character presented in Marvellously Massive Lyric Magnitude for the Millions than since the days of Cleopatra." Two weeks after opening, "real living scenes in the life of the Southern negro, amid cotton fields and in cabins" were added, according to the *Clipper*, along with racers, hurdle riders, gladiators, athletes, banjoists, "specialists, . . . and a perfect presentation of the Old Plantation Darkey." Reviews echoed this rhetoric—according to one, "all the features of Southern plantation life . . . are faithfully and picturesquely re-produced"; according to another, "one of the chief charms of the exhibition is its naturalness"; according to a third, the performers "were brought direct from the fields and plantations of the South and put before the Northern people, presenting animated scenes of rural simplicity in Dixie"; and according to a fourth, "the true Southern darkey is seen just as one might see him in a journey to the land of cotton."

Clearly this was much more than a minstrel show, since the emphasis was on authenticity rather than buffoonery. Yet the old-fashioned minstrel elements were undeniable: minstrel songs like "The Old Folks at Home" and "Carry Me Back to Old Virginny"; a band of tambourine and banjo players; and "the quaint and fantastic cake walk." And when a watermelon cart appeared, "the entire cast," according to Toll, "broke ranks and descended on the melons, 'uninhibitedly' breaking them open and gorging on the sweet contents." Photographs of the show, however, show the actors without blackface, and dressed in clothes that actually fit them well.

Unfortunately, the black press did not see fit to write about the show, and there's no record of how many blacks were in the audience.

These presentations of the 1890s attempted to display *real* blackness—the players in *Black America* were not advertised as "entertainers" but as "participants." This was the culmination of the black minstrel show—an idealized vision of plantation life on display for white northerners. Still, it really was a sign of progress that so many of these shows balanced their nostalgic portrayal of slavery days with positive portrayals of genuine black achievement.

In the South, however, black minstrelsy did not develop into this kind of extravaganza. Black minstrel troupes, along more traditional lines, continued to tour there (as did numerous white minstrel troupes), playing, often in blackface, for both white and black audiences, until well into the 1950s, giving rise to such popular performers as Lincoln Perry (aka Stepin Fetchit, Hollywood's first black superstar) and Dewey "Pigmeat" Markham, the comedian responsible for "Here Come da Judge."

It is difficult to discern any difference between the minstrel show and black comic performance in general in the nineteenth century. But by the turn of the twentieth century, black comedy would move away from minstrelsy—the wildly successful Smart Set was billed as a comedy company, not a minstrel show, despite the fact that Ernest Hogan and Billy McClain, two of the greatest minstrel performers, were their leaders and biggest stars. Sylvester Russell, the foremost black theatrical critic of his day (and a former Georgia Minstrel himself), wrote a review of their 1902 show in the *Indianapolis Freeman* that is instructive in pointing out the differences. The scenes were all set in Honolulu rather than on a southern plantation. The roles generally steered clear of the standard minstrel caricatures; instead, flower girls, sailors, racetrack gamblers, lovers, missionaries, Royal Rooster Lodge members, drunks, and a hunchback were featured. The clothing was formal, elaborate, and fit the actors well: McClain "has suits of all shades and changes clothes every minute. Any other actor on the boards who aspires to be a 'swell' will have to bring three new suits of clothes and have a new green English tailor-made suit made to order, at once, to even approach him." Moreover, the actors did not wear blackface.

The *Freeman*'s review goes out of its way to distinguish this show from the minstrel shows that had preceded it. There was one exception, however: Ben Hunn, who remained in a minstrel rather than comedy mode, singing "Turkey in the Straw" and dancing minstrel dances. "Of course," the *Freeman* commented, "the common people accept that. It makes the hit of the evening with the people in the gallery."

The Freeman's castigation of Hunn and its praise of the rest of the show is telling. Russell continues:

> The question is: Where are we at? Mr. Hunn must remember that he is now in a modern production, which caters only to the requirements of a legitimate standard. The lines of comedy are not across the footlights. When a man is on the stage alone he is supposed to talk to himself and not the people. The common element of white

> people (about two-thirds of the Empire Theatre audience) care nothing about the boundary lines of coon comedy or anything else that colored actors may do as long as they get lots of fun. But we have got to establish these precedents ourselves, and those in comedy who do not will be creatures of criticism.

Russell here echoed Frederick Douglass's comment on Gavitt's Original Ethiopian Serenaders over fifty years earlier. In that short column Douglass had admonished the Serenaders to "seek to improve, relying more upon the refinement of the public, than its vulgarity; let them strive to conform to it, rather than to cater to the lower elements of the baser sort, and they may do much to elevate themselves and their race in popular estimation." Following Douglass, Russell drew clear lines in the sand: Comedy is elevated, minstrelsy is low. Comedy is modern, minstrelsy is old-fashioned. Comedy is "legitimate," minstrelsy is "common."

After this, black minstrelsy would persist for many decades, but it would always be associated with the nineteenth century, only a dark shadow of a bygone art form.

One hundred years after its first successful productions, black minstrelsy, in its true nineteenth-century essence, enjoyed its last gasp. In the mid-1960s, dancer Dewey Weinglass and composers Noble Sissle and Eubie Blake staged a minstrel revival show starring a group of men whose average age was around sixty-five. Marshall and Jean Stearns, authors of *Jazz Dance,* saw them at Fordham University on September 25, 1964. The performance was titled "The Grass Roots of American Folklore," and opened with Sissle's lecture on the history of black theater. He then announced that the remainder of the program was going to be a faithful re-creation of the Georgia Minstrels.

> A cast of eighteen strutted noisily on stage playing tambourines and singing. They were dressed in garish red-striped jackets and wore boaters. As they sat down in a half circle facing the audience, Sissle stood in the center as interlocutor, and Sidney Easton and Willie Glenn, clad in suits with blindingly large blue and white checks, took their positions as end men.
>
> Two dozen or so numbers followed—songs, dances, skits, instrumental solos—alternating with jokes so ancient that, delivered with reckless assurance, they seemed new-minted from another world. . . .
>
> After intermission, an olio follows, with a brief concert by the [Don] Redman band, a tear-jerking song, a comedy violinist, and a medley of favorites by Noble Sissle and Eubie Blake. The show ends with a lively Walk Around—struts, twists, prances, taps, rubberlegs, and even splits—and exit.

Unfortunately, the Stearns neglected to mention whether or not these 1960s minstrels wore blackface.

It is not easy to quickly characterize the nineteenth-century black minstrel tradition. It could be broadly defined to encompass the entertainments that slaves put on for their masters, the proper black minstrel shows that did little more than imitate white minstrel shows, and the theatrical extravaganzas like *Darkest America* and *Black America.*

At first, these entertainments seem to have little in common besides being performances put on by black people. As we have seen, they played a huge variety of roles, ranging from plantation slaves to fairies, Indians, and opera singers; they mixed pure comedy with noncomic song, dance, and drama; they often appeared without blackface, or didn't call themselves minstrels.

But there are seven features that broadly characterize these disparate presentations.

First, these performances either were mostly comic in nature or included a substantial amount of comedy. And this comedy was more often buffoonery than wit.

Second, black minstrelsy usually treasured, re-presented, or reinforced established negative stereotypes of blacks. The blacks wore blackface, either literally or metaphorically. Minstrel stereotypes of blacks emphasized qualities—laziness, thievery, dishonesty, mispronunciation, putting on airs, exaggerated physical features—that enabled whites to feel inherently superior to them. Admittedly, the stereotypes of stupidity, sloth, and unwarranted pomposity, while effective tools for dehumanizing blacks, were also comic tropes that comedians throughout history have indulged in without shame. Some minstrel performers may have even turned these negative stereotypes on their heads and signified on them, emphasizing the trickery involved in playing the fool. Moreover, as blues historian Paul Oliver suggests, "by adopting the image of the minstrel figure of ridicule, black entertainers defused the charge. When the butt of the joke participated in the joke much of its effect was discharged." Yet no matter how black entertainers approached them, these stereotypes remained "negative" since whites had used them for dehumanizing purposes.

Third, black minstrelsy rarely aspired to high art; it was

down-to-earth. It was often contrasted with the theatrical performances of such artists as the Hyers Sisters, who performed dramas for the cream of society; and we've seen how Sylvester Russell contrasted it with proper comedy. Minstrelsy had wide appeal, from the working classes to the queen of England, and it often showcased the most impressive talents; but it always mixed in low, crude elements that those in high society might look down upon.

Fourth, black minstrelsy delighted in variety. It combined song and dance, comedy and tragedy, clowning and acting; the action was rarely unified; seldom did one narrative unite the whole of a black minstrel show.

Fifth, nineteenth-century black minstrel shows were designed for an audience that was at least partially white. A plantation frolic performed solely for the enjoyment of the slaves may have been comic, full of variety, and firmly low-brow; but it was not a minstrel show—it had no white audience. Black minstrel shows played in mainstream theaters that also featured white troupes and were advertised to the general public. (In the twentieth century, this would change: black minstrel troupes in the Deep South sometimes played in tent shows to exclusively black audiences, even if many of their routines and customs—including the wearing of blackface—had been developed by whites for whites.)

Sixth, black minstrel shows were often presented, either by the management or by white viewers, as authentic representations of black life. No matter how wild or ridiculous the appearance and behavior of those onstage, and no matter how ludicrous they might appear to a sophisticated viewer, for many white audiences, these black performers were tethering a wild theatrical event to "reality."

Seventh, black minstrelsy refrained from any explicit delineation of interactions between whites and blacks. While white "massa" might be discussed or even be implicitly offstage, he almost never actually appears; the stage remains a space free of white presence. Even mixed minstrel troupes most likely refrained from this type of interaction, the white performers wearing blackface and not appearing white, with the probable exception of the interlocutor in the first part of the show.

If one insists that any definition of the black minstrel tradition be based purely on the art's nineteenth-century heyday, one can define the black minstrel performance as *a comic, low-brow variety show in which all-black troupes re-present negative stereotypes as authentically black for a white or mixed audience.* One can easily see how this definition can encompass a wide variety of twentieth- and twenty-first-century black performances as well, ranging from hip-hop concerts to *Chappelle's Show.*

However, black minstrelsy no longer reflects only nineteenth-century traditions. In the twentieth and twenty-first centuries, it took on a host of new aspects. Performers drew on the minstrel tradition for purely black audiences, shutting out whites; the pretense of authenticity all but vanished; irony and signifying infiltrated all of black comedy; the set of negative stereotypes it drew from changed; elements of minstrelsy were adopted in new forms while others were discarded. It would be counterproductive to limit our concept of a living tradition to a definition suited to its long-ago heyday. But at the same time, we should not lose sight of that definition, especially when called upon to decide whether a particular performance deserves the appellation in its most pejorative sense.

What made the black minstrel show so popular, and why did it become more popular than white minstrel shows?

First, there was the undoubted skill of the performers. Between the end of the Civil War and the 1890s, black minstrel shows, Uncle Tom shows, black theatrical productions, and jubilee singers were the best professional opportunities for black entertainers, the sole institutions to welcome and develop their skills. Of these, minstrelsy employed far more black performers than the others. Even after the rise of black vaudeville, black minstrel shows continued to serve as a good source of employment.

One of the primary appeals of the white minstrel show at its inception was its pretense of authenticity; obviously, the black minstrel show, because the performers were actually black, trumped the white minstrel show in that regard. American entertainment has always had a desire to "keep it real," and the black minstrel show was necessarily more real than the white minstrel show could be.

The white minstrel show began earlier than black minstrelsy. It had become codified over the years as its producers and performers stuck to the tried and true. Its staleness caused its popularity to wane. Audiences eager for novel entertainment gravitated to the innovations of black minstrels.

Whites could feel good after seeing black minstrelsy. It confirmed and reinforced white ideas about the inferior nature of blacks and the merits of continuing their degradation by staging elaborate plantation fantasies in which blacks were happy and foolish, while the whites, by implication at least, were benevolent and protective.

While white attendance at black performances therefore makes sense, what made these shows popular among black audiences? Undoubtedly the chance to see others of their own color as successful performers was hard to pass up, and these entertainers likely included material designed specifically for black audiences. But there must have been more than that.

This question, which is seldom asked, brings up another one, which is more often discussed: What made black performers so interested in presenting such a questionable representation of their race? Was it simply to please whites? Or was there another, more fundamental reason?

The conventional conclusion is, as Nathan Irvin Huggins wrote, that "The mask was a means of survival—only by wearing it in some form could black entertainers find work." This assumption is shared by the large majority of minstrel historians. For instance, cultural critic Eric Lott refers to "minstrelsy's century-long commercial regulation of black cultural practices" which "stalled the development of African-American public arts." Lott's celebrated book, *Love and Theft: Blackface Minstrelsy and the American Working Class,* steadfastly denies, throughout its pages, that African Americans had any agency in their theatrical fate: they are simply "powerless." In one fell swoop, he relegates all the triumphs of black minstrelsy and its vaudeville successors to nothing more than a parroting of "racist ideology, a historical process by which an entire people has been made the bearer of another people's 'folk' culture." Black minstrelsy's imitation of white minstrelsy, according to Lott, "indicates minstrelsy's fundamental consequence for black culture[:] the dispossession and control by whites of black forms."

Very few if any contemporary historians view nineteenth-century black minstrel performers as triumphant entertainers.

Most agree with Robert Toll, who concluded, "black minstrels had to work within narrow limits because they performed for audiences that expected them to act out well-established minstrel stereotypes of Negroes." Cultural historian Ann Charters went even further out on a limb, stating that American "audiences expected any man with dark skin, no matter what his background or inclinations, to be a 'real coon.'"

Did whites really force black minstrelsy upon blacks? No support for this assumption can be gleaned from the many firsthand accounts that black minstrels left us. Moreover, nonminstrel black performers—including black theatrical troupes like the Hyers Sisters; black performers in the Uncle Tom plays; and musicians like the Fisk Jubilee Singers, Elizabeth Greenfield (the "Black Swan"), M. Sissieretta Jones ("Black Patti"), and Blind Tom, all of whom many minstrel historians ignore—enjoyed wide success among both black and white audiences. This success is evidence that, if black minstrelsy had been only "a means of survival," a whole host of other serious acts would have predominated in its stead. On the contrary, the majority of nineteenth-century black performers, no matter how accomplished, made a conscious choice *not* to perform in the lofty manner of the Hyers Sisters and the Jubilee Singers, and instead decided to entertain audiences of both races via a medium they considered rightfully theirs.

The opinions of minstrel historians are based on erroneous assumptions. In the nineteenth century, black audiences, like white ones, viewed black minstrelsy not as a borrowing from white culture but as an authentically *black* art form, and the most popular black minstrels were triumphant examples of black entertainment at its best. A host of immensely talented performers threw themselves into the contradictions of black minstrelsy with gusto, verve, and ingenuity—not with reluctance. They must have had a good reason to do so, for alternatives were available.

Ellison, Huggins, Lott, and their peers have always discounted the *liberating* potential of wearing the blackface mask—not just for whites, but for blacks as well. As Lhamon points out, an actor in *Pitch a Boogie Woogie,* a 1947 movie made by blacks in Greenville, North Carolina, for a black audience, was later asked why only some of the actors wore blackface. He divulged, "We put on blackface when we had something really *crazy* to say."

This helps answer the question posed at the outset of this chapter—how could black performers adopt the most demeaning caricatures of themselves, and how could black audiences lap it up? If whites found a sense of comic triumph and underlying rebellion in the minstrel caricature, this appeal would logically be even greater for an oppressed people. Sambo, Zip Coon, and Jim Crow are not slaves in any conventional sense: they don't work hard, they don't get whipped. Instead, they eat a lot, sing and dance, and poke fun at each other. They never worry about what white people think, or interact with them at all. Ostensibly they may be plantation slaves, but they are far freer than any slave ever was, and far freer than the black members of their audience, who had to constantly bow to the authority of whites, and be on their best behavior no matter their station. They are free to be as *crazy* as they want to be.

Black minstrels led a hard life, especially during the twenty years following the Civil War, for they had to put up with not only the denial of food and lodging by segregationist whites, but occasional violence as well. Admittedly some of them earned substantial sums—the leading black minstrels were among the richest black Americans of their era. Yet could the prospect of monetary gain alone explain why, in 1894, some

2,000 blacks responded to a New York advertisement for forty black minstrels?

There is an obvious yet widely overlooked reason why black minstrelsy appealed to black performers and audiences more than any other form of entertainment. Offstage, blacks had to work hard, be submissive and reserved, and endure a host of daily humiliations. It must have been a great joy to act silly, lazy, foolish, and free while contributing to a tradition widely viewed as their greatest gift to American entertainment—and an equally great joy to watch other blacks do so. And this joy defines the legacy of black minstrelsy as, paradoxically enough, a liberating force.

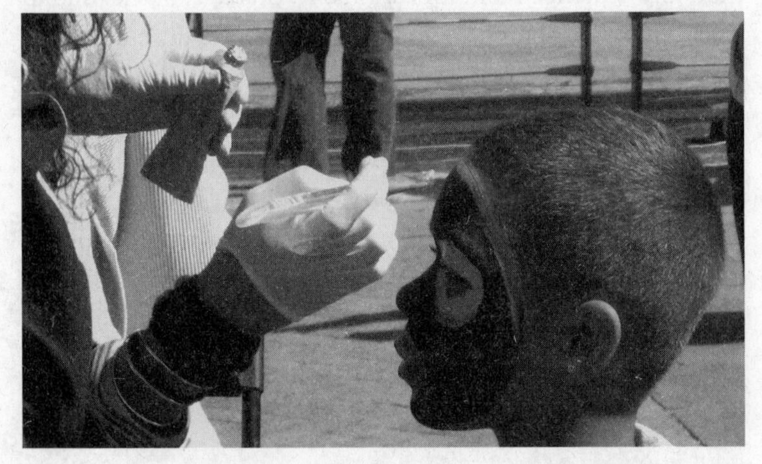

If you want to get your face painted at the Lundi Gras festival in New Orleans, one option is blackface. YUVAL TAYLOR.

3.

OF CANNIBALS AND KINGS

How New Orleans's Zulu Krewe Survived One Hundred Years of Blackface

ONE MIGHT THINK THAT BLACK PEOPLE painting their faces black would be a bygone practice. Yet in one American city, at least, it's more popular than ever. New Orleans, the site of black America's worst tragedy of recent years, celebrated 2009 as the hundredth anniversary of the only black performers still practicing blackface on a large scale: the Zulu Krewe.

Mardi Gras carnivals had been celebrated in New Orleans almost since the city's birth, but it was only in the 1850s that they became what we now see: processions of floats organized by quasi-mystical societies, each with strict rules guiding their membership and specific traditions to uphold. One of these traditions was that of the wild man. From their beginning, the all-white carnival parades featured whites dressed as Indians—in headdresses and war paint—and as blacks—in blackface, playing banjoes. An 1873 illustration in *Scribner's Monthly* shows both, along with assorted other clowns and masked musicians, cavorting around a central square. As the eminent historian of carnival Samuel Kinser puts it, these are "exotically marginal figures who on this topsy-turvy day of excess can and should be exhibited at or near the center of things." This wild-man imagery would soon be adopted by New Orleans's blacks and made their own.

In November 1909 a group of black vaudevillians called the Smart Set (described in the previous chapter) enjoyed a monthlong residence at New Orleans's Pythian Temple, a black-owned-and-run theater that was the largest of its kind. One of their skits, according to a review in the *New Orleans Item,* was all about cannibals. In it, Ezy Amos, Sam Slick, and their friends are about to be eaten when the cannibals mistake Amos for a king whom they had been told would come from across the water.

In the audience were members of a group of poor black Mardi Gras revelers known as the Tramps, who used to parade in hobo costumes through the black part of town. At some point they had decided to put on the black equivalent of Rex, the grand white parade designed to show off all the pageantry of the old South. To do this, they needed floats, costumes, and, of course, masks. And they also needed a theme.

After seeing the cannibal skit, the Tramps changed their name and became Zulus. They could have just as easily called themselves Cannibals, but took the name from a "Zulu King song and drill" that the Smart Set performed. This was only thirty years after the Zulu War, in which the South African tribe had displayed an astonishing tenacity in fighting the British, and only three years after the final Zulu uprising. But for the Tramps, the Zulus did not represent heroic blacks fighting oppressive whites. "Zulu" was just as pejorative a term in the United States at that time as "cannibal," as music scholar Thomas Brothers points out: "'Zulu' was a common racial slur, used right alongside 'nigger,' 'darky,' 'coon,' and 'monkey.' . . . Taking the name ['Zulu'] was an indication of distance from

Africa, not an embrace of it." Certainly, Zulu did not represent ancestry—as far as we know, no Zulus were ever taken to the Americas as slaves. Zulus simply represented brutal savages far removed from civilization and were stock figures on the vaudeville and minstrel stage. As New Orleans historian Ned Sublette writes, "in dime museums and circuses, a caged 'Zulu,' eating raw meat, might be displayed next to the Wild Man of Borneo and the Snake Charmer."

The New Orleans Zulus adopted the crude blackface costumes that the performers wore, except, since they couldn't afford burnt cork, they used chimney soot to paint their faces black and lard to make white circles around their mouths and eyes. For the rest of their costume, the Zulus wore grass skirts, black-dyed turtlenecks and tights, and frizzy longhair wigs; the first king, William Story, also carried a banana stalk for a scepter.

What remains unmentioned in the standard histories of the New Orleans Zulus is the basis for this costume. The caricaturing of Africans as cannibals was a standard typology that long predated the skit and featured exactly the same look that the Zulus adopted. One sees this image in countless cartoons of cannibals, ranging from the mid-nineteenth century to today. The Zulus were vivifying a racist caricature without changing it one iota.

The New Orleans Mardi Gras we know today was imported from Mobile, Alabama, in the 1850s. Earlier parades were open to all revelers and were disorderly and disreputable. The exclusive "mystick krewes" were introduced to impose order upon chaos. They originated in Mobile in the 1830s, drawing from the callithumpians of Pennsylvania and other quasi-mystical societies, who enjoyed a great vogue at the time. They soon spread to several other cities.

Two of Mobile's mystic societies came to New Orleans in 1850, by which time the white Protestant Mobile tradition had solidified. It featured mule-drawn floats, elaborate and colorful costumes, themed parades, and thrown gifts. In 1857 three members of Mobile's Cowbellion de Rakin Society (the name is gibberish), along with a number of white New Orleanians, founded the Mystick Krewe (the spelling is without precedent in English—its anachronism is fake) of Comus in New Orleans, named after the Greek god of mirth, a figure known primarily from John Milton's masque *Comus*.

Throughout its history, Comus has been a social club of New Orleans's white American elite, excluding both the French Catholic and the black elements of New Orleans society. Its parades reflected the southern white Protestant values of the Civil War era, featuring blackfaced participants as slaves, apes, and wild men. They drew on masking, secrecy, anachronistic terminology, racist ideology, and an ethos of disruption that celebrated the thrills of sacrilege—exactly the same traditions as did the Ku Klux Klan, founded nine years later. The word for it at the time was "mummery," and mummers parades swept across the South (and persist in Philadelphia today). As Ned Sublette writes, "The Mardi Gras krewes and the Ku Klux Klan were quite different organizations that took very different paths. . . . But in the early days of the Klan, it was part of a single movement with the krewes—masked, mysticalized, anonymous resistance to Reconstruction, [and this resistance] was in turn identified with race hatred, terror, and repression of the rights of African Americans."

The era of Reconstruction (1867–1876) was one of the

most extraordinary in the history of the South. Blacks voted, owned land, and held political positions in a measure almost commensurate with their population. Even the public schools were integrated. For a short time in 1872 and 1873, Louisiana's governor, P. B. S. Pinchback, was a black man (portrayed in Comus's carnival as an ape). Meanwhile, southern Klan members, especially in Louisiana, led a campaign of terror in which over a thousand Republicans and blacks were murdered.

It was during Reconstruction, when southern society was turned on its head, that Mardi Gras traditions solidified in New Orleans. "The carnival themes of this era display an obsession with proper social order," writes Sublette. "These were public declarations of wealth, power, and order. . . . The plebes were allowed to witness the edifying spectacle of royalty being revered in the street but not to enter the sacred precincts of the masked ball." A new krewe, Rex, was founded in 1872, and it organized all the various small societies and unaffiliated maskers into one big event. An annually crowned king, usually one of New Orleans's richest men, who wore no mask, led the parade on horseback, followed by a group of whites in blackface.

In 1874, a new organization, made up primarily of members of Rex and Comus, sprang up—the Crescent City White League, a paramilitary organization dedicated to the subjugation of blacks, some of whose members had murdered Republican officeholders and "troublesome" black people. They threw blacks out of the schools and won a pitched battle against thousands of government troops. President Grant sent additional troops to occupy the city, and the carnival parades were suspended. But Reconstruction ended with the Hayes-Tilden compromise of 1876, and an era of white supremacy, complete with segregation, widespread lynching, and the effective reenslavement of thousands of black Americans under the practices of peonage and sharecropping, began. Comus's theme for the 1877 parade was "The Aryan Race." And not much really changed in New Orleans's Mardi Gras for the next twenty-five years. The city was mired in corruption, filth, poverty, illiteracy, prostitution, and a hatred of its black citizens.

The early years of the twentieth century were marked by an increase in violence between blacks and whites in New Orleans—"we are on the threshold of a race war," declared the white New Orleans paper the *Times-Democrat* in 1900, three years after the effective disenfranchisement of blacks by Louisiana's notorious "grandfather clause"; a similar paper, the *Daily States*, upped the ante with an editorial headlined "The Negro Problem and the Final Solution," which threatened that "a race war means extermination." Mardi Gras, like everything else in Louisiana, was supposed to be segregated, but in the crowds, that proved to be next to impossible. According to the whites, the crowds of blacks attending had become increasingly unruly. In the parades themselves, however, no blacks were allowed. The absurdity was greatest, perhaps, in one 1939 parade, when a krewe of schoolchildren marching as the "Peoples of New Orleans" included Greenlanders, Persians, and Siamese—but no blacks. Even Filipinos joined the official parade in the 1930s and were allowed to parade as "Caucasian"; blacks were the only ethnic group excluded. (Fake blacks, of course, were allowed—an entire krewe of whites in blackface, the Boll Weevil Social Club, had sprung up in 1910.)

When the Zulus arose, they marched separately, though along many of the same streets as the white parades. They adopted various outlandish costumes at first: In 1914, King Henry

Harris, riding in a buggy, wore a suit made of the tinfoil insides of cigarette packs. In 1917, the Zulu king arrived in a skiff rowed through the New Basin Canal, imitating the arrival of Rex in a yacht, and carried a huge hambone for a scepter. (This waterfront arrival, which drew huge crowds, fell by the wayside in the 1950s when the city filled in the canal, but was reprised in 1993 on the riverfront.) Throughout the teens, many Zulus masqueraded as various local figures, from the terrifying municipal policemen to New Orleans's elite society members. In 1923 a Zulu queen was inaugurated; she was portrayed by a man in drag until a Ladies Auxiliary (which, oddly enough, also included some men) was formed in 1933 (the regular Zulus remained all-male for decades). And the constant throughout this varied history was, of course, the blackface makeup with white paint around eyes and lips.

Perhaps the most vivid description of the early Zulus is found in Lyle Saxon's 1928 *Fabulous New Orleans*, a thick volume that's part travelogue, part history, and part fantasy. The first part of the book is given over to describing a Mardi Gras that Saxon claims to have witnessed around 1903, when he was a boy; but the fact that the Zulus play such a big part in his tale gives the lie to that. From the details Saxon gives, the parade he witnessed seems to have taken place between 1918 and 1922.

The Zulu king and his "henchmen" arrived on a sparsely decorated barge tugged by a tiny motorboat. "He represented a savage chieftain," wearing "a suit of black knitted underwear, . . . bunches of dried grass at throat, ankles and wrists, and a sort of grass skirt such as hula-hula dancers wear, and he wore a fuzzy black wig surmounted by a tin crown. In his hand he carried a scepter—a broomstick—upon which was mounted a stuffed white rooster." His four companions were dressed just like the king except without the crown. All of them wore blackface with stripes of red and green paint on their cheeks.

The king and his company climbed aboard a mule-driven wagon decorated with some potted palms, flags, and flowers; this led a procession featuring a guard of honor consisting of Zulus on mules. A woman on a second wagon fried catfish over a wood-burning stove and handed it out to spectators. Next came decorated horse-drawn carriages with the elite of black society aboard. Men marched alongside, some costumed, others wearing their best suits. The parade proceeded slowly through the crowded streets, with frequent stops for Zulus to exchange greetings with people they knew, banter with women, and dole out catfish. The whole was accompanied by "a band boom[ing] out a ragtime march."

Considering that American blacks were constantly being insulted as coons, darkies, Zulus, pickaninnies, Africans, monkeys, and gorillas, why would the Zulus want to reproduce these racial clichés?

From the evidence available it seems that the Zulus simply saw something they thought was funny and easy to imitate, something that would perfectly fit with their aim to entertain. These costumes, this act, could display far more pageantry than the Tramps ever had.

The controversial use of blackface, an obvious minstrel traditon, however, seems to demand a deeper answer than this one. And the one that most historians rely on is that the Zulus were parodying racist caricatures. As the 2009 Mardi Gras exhibit in the Louisiana State Museum put it, "Zulu[s] ridiculed white pomposity by using white notions of black savagery; in short they reclaimed black stereotypes."

But while a contemporary blackface performer might be calling attention to racist stereotypes by vivifying them, these early Zulus, on the other hand, were mainly trying to satirize Rex. Some Zulu historians deny this, but in 1914 and for some years afterward, the Zulu Krewe made the satire of white carnival explicit by directly following the Rex parade along the same route. In 1928 the black newspaper *Louisiana Weekly*'s headline straightforwardly announced, "Zulu Burlesque on Rex to Be Most Elaborate Ever."

Thomas Brothers gives perhaps the most accurate, succinct, and direct elucidation of the meaning of Zulu: "King Zulu is not an African but rather a minstrel parody of an African. His true object of satire is Rex, the white Mardi Gras king. He does everything that Rex does, only upside down. Rex arrives by yacht . . . so Zulu arrives by a rowboat named the 'royal barge.' Rex is protected by the city police, King Zulu by his comical Zulu police. It is a classic example of carnivalesque release of class tensions with the special twist of African-American signifying." Similarly, black theorist Albert Murray writes, "the specific traditional ritual function of the outrageous costume and conduct of the King of the Zulus is to ridicule the whole idea of Mardi Gras and the Lenten season." Rather than parodying racist caricatures of blacks, Zulus were parodying the white Mardi Gras institution that best embodied the racism of the era.

The fact that this parody currently precedes what it parodies also gives rise to a less charitable interpretation. As Daniel Thompson, a black sociologist from Dillard University, told *New Yorker* writer Calvin Trillin in 1964, "Zulu has the same psychological function as a clown at the circus. A man going up on a high wire is more effective if two clowns fall off first, and Rex is more beautiful because Zulu is ridiculous. The clown doesn't have to be a Negro . . . but in this area . . . it's logical that it should be a Negro. This ludicrous individual, to make himself really ludicrous, has to be black."

Dressing up as a cartoon cannibal is indeed ludicrous, but is that all it is? Mardi Gras carnivals have always been staged as battles between order and disorder, logic and nonsense, rule and misrule. Parody is a weak word to describe the desire to outrage that has always characterized carnival, from medieval times to today. For example, in Trinidad a "molasses devil" (*jab molassie*) would lead the carnival dance. Think of the signification of molasses in the nineteenth-century Caribbean, where life expectancy on the sugar plantations was well under ten years. To combine blackface with molasses is not an innocent gesture, but one fraught with danger and potency.

Not only was blackface theatrical and over the top, comical and bold, parodic and gleeful, it was *threatening*—after all, cannibals *killed* white people. And it was in that comical threat that the Zulus found longevity.

At the same time, the practices of the Mardi Gras Indians, who are commonly referred to as "gangs," have always revolved around the language and signs of warfare. Though their tradition of violent brawls with competing "tribes" has largely been replaced with ritualized confrontations decided by the quality of costuming, choreography, and taunting chants, the Indians still enjoy a reputation as dangerous, mysterious figures. The ornately attired African American carnival revelers, who have been active since the mid-nineteenth century, have steadfastly refused to assimilate into the structures and strictures of the parade. Their Mardi Gras appearances are unofficial and unpredictable; their organizations are shrouded in ritual and secrecy. If the Zulus posed a threat, so did the Indians.

In both scholarly and popular treatments of black culture, wild rebellion is valued more highly than comic rebellion, and thus the Indians have generally been regarded with far more favor than the Zulus. And indeed, compared to the Indians, the Zulus have been much less militant: they simply made those who hew to conventional standards uncomfortable. But the Indians exist independently of the white order, and have thus been outside it altogether; the nature of their threat is therefore quite different. While the Zulus were not as easy to assimilate into the conventional social order as the Tramps had been, when they finally became part and parcel of Mardi Gras they placed themselves at the very heart of that order—as the black answer to Comus and Rex, the center of the New Orleans tradition.

Further echoing their minstrel roots, the Zulus, early in their history, developed a cast of characters to complement the Zulu King, many of whom are still around today, including the Witch Doctor, the Ambassador, the Big Shot, the Governor, the Mayor, and the Province Prince. The Soulful Warriors are pan-African pride characters established in the 1970s, and Mr. Big Stuff was named after Jean Knight's hit single of 1971. More short-lived characters included Chief Ubangi, Zambango the Snake Man, the Head Hunter, the (*Amos 'n' Andy*–inspired) Kingfish, and Jungle Jim.

But parody was not the whole of the Zulu endeavor. In 1916, the Zulu Social Aid and Pleasure Club was founded to provide insurance to aid sick members and the families of the dead. In this, they followed tradition: there were many such benevolent societies among black Americans in the nineteenth century. This club quickly established itself as a social organization whose cohesion embraced the entire New Orleans black community and formed an essential part of that community's identity.

Yet that cohesion was, on occasion, broken. For example, in 1933, a second black krewe was founded—the Jolly Boys. As the *New Orleans Item-Tribune* wrote in 1941, "Unlike the Zulus, this Negro group patterns its floats and costumes after those of the white groups and instead of including the downtown commercial district in its parade route traverses only those sections of the city with large Negro populations." The Zulus, while the most prominent black parade organization, never held a monopoly on black participation in Mardi Gras.

Meanwhile, in Mobile, the black population founded a Zulu Club in 1938, clearly in imitation of their New Orleans brethren. If anything, the jungle references in the Mobile parade outdid those in New Orleans: floats included "Flying Alligator of the Jungle," "Monster of the Jungle," and "The Wild Man and the Dragon." In 1947 the black association of carnival societies in Mobile called the Zulu parade "a burlesque of which we colored people in Mobile are truly ashamed," so there was no Zulu parade that year; the Mobile Zulus disbanded altogether five years later, prefiguring what would happen to the New Orleans Zulus in the 1960s.

At their height in the 1930s and '40s, the New Orleans Zulus boasted close to 400 members, including 30 or 40 dukes riding mules and 30 or 40 warriors with spears. A lot of them were drunk, as the parade would make frequent stops at taverns. And then there were the Baby Dolls, originally bands of prostitutes dressed as little girls, who used to follow the parade and fight with each other. It was during this period that the signification of Zulu began to be reversed—now the Zulus' own literature proudly described them as masquerading as the real African tribe: "There was a time the Zulus were . . . great warriors; their battle cry was 'wash your sword in the blood of your enemies.'"

In 1949, King Zulu was portrayed by none other than Louis Armstrong, who wore the traditional blackface for the occasion. Armstrong had left New Orleans as a young man, but had fondly remembered the Zulu parade, recording "The King of the Zulus" in 1926. And what he remembered most fondly was that the Zulus offered blacks a chance to satirize white society. "Every member of the club masquerades in a costume burlesquing some famous person," he wrote. "It had been my life-long dream to be the king of the Zulus." During the parade, overenthusiastic Second Liners (dancing parade followers) destroyed the royal float. (As Armstrong so richly put it, "Just then, my float commenced to crumbling down to pieces.") Afterward, Armstrong went to City Hall and met with Mayor Morrison, who gave him the keys to the city.

He was then forced to spend the night at a Jim Crow hotel.

By 1954 criticism of the Zulus as minstrels had grown. Manuel Wilson, Zulu king that year, announced: "Zulu is going to be modern from the word go. Some of our folks have been kicking about how the parade . . . is a disgrace to the Negroes. So . . . we're going to be a comic strip right on." The next year a new king appeared wearing silk clothes and no blackface; as soon as more traditional members saw this, they hurriedly painted his face, and did so again when he wiped it off.

The 1960s saw a marked drop in popularity for the Zulus due to harsh criticism. In 1960 a group of black social clubs promoted a black boycott of carnival as a response to the Louisiana legislature's attempt to block the desegregation of New

Orleans public schools. A petition was signed by 27,000 people, reading, in part, "we resent and repudiate the Zulu parade, in which Negroes are paid by white merchants to wander through the city drinking to excess, dressed as uncivilized savages and throwing coconuts like monkeys. This caricature does not represent us. Rather, it represents a warped picture against us." Faced with this and other pressure, the Zulus voted to cancel their 1961 parade, but were persuaded by the mayor and superintendent of police to march under full protection from hostile elements. The king and queen had, meanwhile, abdicated under pressure, and the identity of the new king was kept secret. Thus began the identification of the Zulus as minstrellike blacks who conformed to the wishes of whites. The Zulus had been transformed from fierce African cannibals to happy plantation slaves.

The Zulus had always been problematic for some members of the black community. One major Zulu historian and former parade chairman, Alex T. Rapheal Jr., remembered, "For many years we were regarded as heathens by other Negroes." The black *Louisiana Weekly* tended to ignore the krewe when it wasn't carnival time and complained about its "grotesque mimicry of the whites' observance," calling for a parade that would "portray Negro achievement" instead. But now, in some sense, the tables had turned—the Zulus, who had been seen as riffraff, were being portrayed as part of the (white) establishment.

But in another sense, the complaints were the same. Leonard Burns, the boycott's leader, called the Zulu parade "a symbol of everything contrary to the hopes, aspirations, and desires of responsible Negro citizens." Zulu leaders responded, rightly, that the Zulu Krewe was a black working-class tradition.

In the parades held from 1961 to 1964, the Zulus received the same kind of police protection that was turned on civil rights activists—dogs—and these prevented the Second Liners, those who follow the parade to hear the music, from doing so. In 1962 the boycotters met with the Zulus to try to work out a compromise, but, as Burns told Trillin, "negotiations broke down. We were willing to keep the name but *not* the blackface King. We thought we'd have a dignified parade, showing the progress the Negro has made in America." The calls for boycotting Mardi Gras increased, and by 1963, the NAACP was involved. Together with the Congress of Racial Equality (CORE) and some Christian churches, they called on the Zulus to tone down their undignified act, but the Zulu parades had already been stripped of their vibrancy. That year the Zulus mostly stayed above Canal Street so as to avoid their opponents. In 1964, the year the Zulus celebrated their inaccurate fiftieth anniversary, membership dropped to twenty-five men. In June, Trillin's outstanding and very long profile of the Zulus' decline appeared in the *New Yorker.* It may be the saddest article ever written about Mardi Gras; after reading it, it's hard to conceive of the Zulus ever holding another parade.

However, the leaders of the other black clubs had decided to infiltrate the Zulus, and by 1965, the reformers outnumbered the traditionalists. The Zulu Krewe gave up blackface and grass skirts; their "dignity parade" depicted the Watusis ("children of the Lion") instead of caricatured cannibals. Despite the new direction, the decline continued: membership at one point dropped to sixteen; the factions deepened, and the club split in two, each electing its own king, and taking each other to court.

The Zulus weren't the only ones suffering. Mardi Gras in general reached a nadir in its popularity at this time. The hotels were only a little more than half full. But by the late 1960s, new krewes like Endymion and Bacchus had injected fresh ideas into the old traditions, and the Zulus were slowly recovering, reclaiming their heritage, and becoming a decent middle-class institution. What had been founded in a spirit of rebellion and comic outrage was now a source of community pride, as upstanding an organization as the Elks Club. In 1969 the city granted the krewe permission to parade on Canal Street, the historic route of Rex and other white parades, thus making Zulu the first black carnival organization to be a part of the city's official Mardi Gras festivities. In the 1970s, whites started joining the Zulus, though none of the characters were white until 1988. Under the leadership of Roy Glapion Jr., president of the Zulus from 1973 to 1988, Zulu became much more of a community organization, with an active Community Involvement Program; membership swelled to 375. By the time of his retirement, the coronation ball was held at the Convention Center, just like those of the white societies; Zulu members included some of the richest black families in New Orleans. One Zulu president, in his introduction to a coronation ball program, spoke of introducing "sound fiscal policies while cautiously implementing cost effectiveness in an effort to safeguard new investments and liabilities." The Zulus still wore blackface, but few of them sported the other elements of the traditional costume—there were no more nose rings or gold earrings, no more references to caricatured Africans. In 1987 they even discontinued giving coconuts to the crowd, a practice dating back to 1920.

But lately there has been an increase in the respect paid to tradition. In 1993 a Zulu Lundi Gras festival was born. On the day before Mardi Gras, the Zulus hold a public fair, including live music and crawfish eating at a riverfront park. In the evening, King and Queen Zulu arrive, disembarking from a Coast

Guard boat along with their costumed entourage. The next morning the Zulus parade in full makeup with their grass skirts and Afro wigs, and once again give coconuts to the crowd. And it certainly seems that their presentation, like those of the original black minstrels, is unironic. After all, President Obama even named a two-time Zulu queen, Desirée Rogers, as his social secretary.

The signification of Zulu had clearly shifted over the years. At first, the Zulu was a buffoonish cannibal, a savage Hottentot. Soon he was a parody of Rex, the black king opposing the white one. By the 1940s he had become a brave warrior on a drunken rampage. By the 1960s he was a happy plantation slave, playing to a white audience. And by the end of the century he was a successful black businessman simply letting off steam. Yet almost the whole time, he kept wearing blackface and a grass skirt.

How could such an apparently demeaning performance last for a hundred years and be more popular now than ever before? Has an unironic tradition accrued layers of irony with time? Has it ossified into ritual or degenerated into camp? Or has its initial appeal—an implicit comparison of black Americans with "savage" Africans—been stood on its head and transformed from degradation into pride?

That's what we went down to New Orleans for the hundredth anniversary of Zulu on Mardi Gras 2009 to find out.

Dozens of krewes parade through the streets of New Orleans during Mardi Gras season (roughly from early January to Mardi Gras day in February or March), ranging from krewes of cats (Endymeow) and dogs (Barkus) to the Krewe du Vieux, which includes a float of a giant, dripping penis. Comparatively few of these krewes actually parade on Mardi Gras Day itself; among

This group of Zulus is known as the Tramps, in tribute to the original Tramps, who morphed into the Zulus back in 1909. YUVAL TAYLOR.

those that do, Zulu is the first and one of the biggest. It is also by far the largest African American krewe. Comus stopped parading in 1991 because of a law outlawing segregation in parading krewes; it remains an all-white society with an annual private coronation ball on Mardi Gras evening that is shown live on local television. Zulu, on the other hand, is integrated, with a significant white minority. Rex too allowed a few blacks to join; its parade is, for whites, the crowning glory of Mardi Gras.

Each krewe's parade, whether on Mardi Gras Day or earlier, goes through a number of different neighborhoods and generally takes between three and five hours. Usually it consists of masked riders on floats throwing beads and other prizes to the crowd, interspersed with high-school and Marine marching bands and various other organizations on foot or horseback. Unlike most American parades, Mardi Gras features no commercial advertising or corporate sponsorship (there's actually a law forbidding advertising on Mardi Gras floats); instead, the krewes spend a great deal of money simply to entertain onlookers, a phenomenon unexplainable by traditional economic theory.

The day before Mardi Gras we attended the Lundi Gras Festival. In many respects it's a typical African American fair. It features two or three stages, on which soul, blues, funk, and gospel groups perform (the Zulu Ensemble, founded in 1980, is one of the latter). Vendors sell soul food staples like turkey legs, greens, cornbread, and, because this is New Orleans, spicy crawfish. Other vendors sell African American crafts and Zulu memorabilia; and there is at least one activity for the kids—face-painting. To watch, in 2009, a black child getting his face painted black with white circles around his eyes and mouth is not something one can easily forget.

The most traditional Zulus at the fair call themselves "tramps"; they wear costumes almost exactly like their forebears of the 1910s and '20s, and one of them even carried around a bone. But while these comprise the majority of Zulus on Mardi Gras, Lundi Gras Zulus emphasize variety. The makeup of many is far more artistic, with zigzags that reference African ornamentation around the eyes or on the cheek

Straight off the boat, Zulus parade on New Orleans's waterfront on Lundi Gras evening, 2009. YUVAL TAYLOR.

and forehead, and a variety of colors and shapes. Costumes range from the traditional grass skirts to elaborate beads and feathers reminiscent of the Mardi Gras Indians, most of them tied to African animals (zebras, lions, leopards, snakes); sequined and embroidered jackets, sashes, crowns, headdresses, beaded necklaces, plastic shark's teeth, helmets, boots, wigs, stovepipe hats, nose rings, whistles, and spears are all common. The costumes of the main Zulu characters are quite huge, towering over their heads with beads, feathers, lettering, and so on. These characters wandered back and forth along the waterfront with a small brass band.

At the end of the festival, the Rebirth Brass Band got the crowd excited playing their usual amazingly funky set. Meanwhile, a Coast Guard boat moved up and down the Mississippi River with a crowd of Zulus on it plainly visible to all, preceded by a Coast Guard officer in a dinghy equipped with a machine gun, while a Coast Guard helicopter hovered overhead. After the king and queen, who wore no masks or blackface and dressed formally, disembarked with their elaborately costumed retinue, they paraded up and down the waterfront for a few minutes before going to the stage. Mayor Ray Nagin spoke about the Zulu legacy (without, of course, mentioning minstrelsy), read a proclamation, and gave the king and queen an award. It was all quite well organized, neither over-the-top nor unduly modest, and the crowd had an excellent time.

The next morning we awoke early to catch the launch of the Zulu parade at 8 A.M. in Central City, an exclusively black and somewhat impoverished neighborhood. Though the near-dawn launch time might be earlier than many Lundi Gras revelers care to think about, it was still shocking that in a city bursting with parade enthusiasts and curious tourists, a pair of European women who stayed less than an hour were the only white faces in the crowd other than our own. Though cautious tour guides likely steer visitors away from "the hood," it would seem that the welcoming spirit of Mardi Gras would blur traditional neighborhood lines, and the crowd was certainly friendly to us. This may have had something to do with our attire. We had been told in no uncertain terms to wear costumes—"Everybody wears costumes on Mardi Gras. You'll feel weird if you don't." But we were alone in our finery. The black audience in Mardi Gras wears no costumes, unlike the white audience downtown. Our embarrassment was modest, however, as the neighborhood residents were welcoming to a superhero and a zebra, and our ridiculous garb likely earned us a few coconuts that morning.

The parade kicked off relatively on schedule, with Mayor Nagin leading the way on horseback, wearing a full Roman centurion outfit. He was followed by a succession of marching bands and floats. The names of these floats played on African themes—Mandela, Griot, Imani, Shaka Zulu; some floats were clearly recycled from other krewes that no longer needed them—a Beatles float, a Casey-at-the-Bat float. The vibe in the crowd felt warm and open, the kind of comfort that comes with a long tradition, a familial energy. The parade was hands-on, with plenty of audience interaction with the Zulus. It felt intimate, like a big neighborhood party. There were no barriers separating the crowd from the horses and floats. We heard anecdotes of kids who had gotten hurt in previous years from running too close to the horses, but we saw no trouble. The police presence was minimal; the lack of safety precautions seemed to bother no one.

The Zulus on the floats toss out soft spears, beaded necklaces, Zulu dolls, and shaved, drained, and elaborately hand-painted coconuts—the most intensely valued and coveted of all the tosses of the Mardi Gras season. The gifted seamstress we were staying with half-jokingly asked us to catch one for her, with modest expectations. She had lived in the city for ages, and even the paraders whose costumes she had crafted had only deigned to pantomime a toss her way. "The Zulus are just mischievous," she explained, shaking her head. The float riders were picky about whom they chose to give each present, favoring people they knew over tourists, children over adults, and in more integrated areas of the route, blacks over whites. One woman covertly signaled her membership in the AKA black sorority, earning a knowing nod, and a coconut from a sister. Our absurd outfits paid off as we left with a few coconuts, one adorned with the hand-painted, glitter-accented logo of the New Orleans Hornets, the NBA team that had returned to the city for the 2008 season after a two-year Katrina-forced exodus. We gave a spare coconut to our hostess, who was shocked and thrilled to receive it.

All the Zulus (except the president and his entourage) wore blackface, thickly applied, with white around the mouth and either one or both eyes. It was quite a sight to see hundreds of African Americans in blackface. Talking to many spectators during the parade—soldiers, blue-collar workers, unemployed single parents, college students—not one of them mentioned minstrelsy; none of them commented on the blackface.

It was clear that the most important thing about Zulu today is tradition. This is the value that gets lip service; it seems to trump entertainment, partying, showing off, rebelling, or any other reason to hold a parade. There's no shame in blackface here: Zulus are proud of their tradition, and blackface has ceased to be demeaning. At the same time, the campiness is contained, not over the top.

Overall, our 2009 Mardi Gras experiences were overwhelming. The night before the Zulu parade had been exhausting and bizarre, beginning with a failed attempt to have a recovering crack-addict one-man band we had met get us into a sold-out show by New Orleans eccentrics Quintron and Miss Pussycat, and ending with us following an ersatz parade of teenage hipsters to a private party where transgendered rapper Katey Red delivered some of the most dynamic dance music we'd ever heard. With that long night behind us, we had planned to wind down after the Zulu parade's launch with some relaxed socializing at the Mother-In-Law Lounge, the Tremé bar founded by late R&B legend Ernie K-Doe.

However, when none of our friends were reachable, we decided to make the long trek to the end of the Zulu route to catch the parade's conclusion. Here we saw white firemen, seemingly on duty, in blackface. Whites in blackface are not uncommon at the Zulu parade—not only are there white members of Zulu, but sponsors who help pay for a float and its tosses can ride along, in full Zulu tramp regalia (including blackface), regardless of race. We saw white staff members of the Louisiana State Museum (which was hosting an exhibit commemorating the Zulu centennial) riding in blackface, including Charles Chamberlain, one of the two historians behind the exhibit. Oddly, Chamberlain, a man who had negotiated the politically correct world of academia to earn his position, unselfconsciously posted blackface photos of himself on Facebook.

We soon learned that the reason we had not been able to reach any of our friends was that they were reeling from the news that Ernie K-Doe's widow Antoinette (proprietor of the Mother-In-Law, and a longtime member of the Baby Dolls marching organization) had died of a heart attack that morning. Her lounge, severely damaged in Katrina, and reopened relatively swiftly, had always been a hub of funky activity. It hosted a party that night, where Antoinette's memory was toasted. As Mardi Gras Indians marched past, actors from the upcoming *Treme* television show visited for research, and musicians jammed, friends shared stories about the woman who for the last eight years had been accompanied by a fully costumed mannequin of her late husband. She had just ridden in Thursday's Muses parade with "Ernie."

We mention all these extraneous anecdotes mainly to convey the excitement, weirdness, and specialness of Mardi Gras season. In this context it was easy to forget how bizarre it is to see blackface, and how shocking and negative it usually feels to encounter that signifier of racism. Eating our last meal in New Orleans Wednesday night in a restaurant popular with tourists, we noticed a rack of souvenir books about parades and Indians and floods and wondered aloud why there were no tourist books about the rich, visually compelling history of the Zulus. On no other week would we have wondered why shops couldn't sell photo books of blackface revelers with fake bones through their noses. Getting swept up in the tradition of Zulu made us understand how a historian could think it was okay to post a blackface photo online, how a fireman could sit casually on his truck as if he weren't wearing ebony greasepaint, and how thousands of black residents in a city with as deep a history of racial strife as any in America could shamelessly cheer for hours at cannibals in ratty Afro wigs waving bones and throwing coconuts.

The day after Mardi Gras we went to the Louisiana State Museum's impressive exhibit called *From Tramps to Kings: 100 Years of Zulu* at New Orleans's Presbytere. It included costumes, photographs, memorabilia, movie footage, coconut-decorating instructions, a long letter from Louis Armstrong describing being king of the Zulus, and much more. We spoke at length with Chamberlain and spent hours poring over the artifacts.

But even with the impetus of this exhibit, New Orleans's Zulu historians (both the organization's official ones and the ones at the museum) seemed confused about a huge number of questions—whether or not the Zulus wore blackface with white circles around the mouth and eyes in the teens and twenties (they did—one can tell from photographs); whether or not one is required to mask on a float (one isn't, but almost everyone does it); whether or not Zulu was intended to parody Rex (there's no question that it was, but it was often a friendly parody: at one point, one of Zulu's main sponsors was a prominent member of Rex); what the significance of the white circles around the mouth and eyes might be (they were standard in American minstrel shows and appear in caricatures of cannibals).

More damning, perhaps, is the fact that among the thousands of words of text devoted to the tradition, both illustrating exhibits and providing overview, there was not one mention of minstrelsy or cannibals.

Back in "Zululand"—South Africa—there's a parade that turns Zulu on its head. It's called the Coon Carnival, and dates back to the nineteenth century. It takes place in Cape Town on the first few days of the new year. For the parade, thousands of "coloureds"—mixed-race working-class people—put on *white-face* and dress up like stereotypical American plantation slaves—or blackface minstrels. They pick banjos, eat water-melon, and drink a soft drink called "Jive." Like the Zulus, they were also inspired by a troupe of black comedians—in this case, McAdoo's Original Colored American Minstrel & Vaude-ville Company. One couldn't ask for a neater reversal. Yet there seems to be no connection—nobody in New Orleans seems to have heard of the Coon Carnival, and the Africans behind the Coon Carnival seem unaware of Zulu.

Like Zulu, the Coon Carnival has become a long-standing tradition without much reference to what inspired it. But it's clear that oppressed South Africans admired American blacks because they had become emancipated, and when McAdoo's minstrel troupe spent a few years in South Africa in the 1890s, the Capetownian coloreds started celebrating the triumphs of black Americans by adopting costumes similar to those of the only black Americans they had seen. As with Zulu, there's very little if any signifying going on here.

This gets to the heart of what we concluded after our trip to New Orleans. For their mostly African American audience, the painted faces of the Zulus no longer evoke minstrelsy or can-nibal caricatures at all. The primary association for New Orlea-nians when faced with blacks in blackface is simply Zulu.

In other words, blacks wear blackface in New Orleans today not due to its symbolic value or African connotations, not to comment ironically on racial stereotypes or to parody the white parades, not even as an act of liberation. These were all reasons for wearing it in the past, but Zulu history has been largely whitewashed, scrubbed clean of its origins in caricature, parody, and stereotype. Instead, blacks paint their faces out of respect for a tradition that, like the rest of the black minstrel tradition, has always focused on entertaining its audience. For the Zulus, as for many black and white minstrels in the nineteenth century and earlier, blackface simply stands for a very good time.

Bert Williams in New York, 1921, wearing blackface;
his shadow is also enjoying a smoke.

4.

NOBODY

How Bert Williams Dignified Blackface

WHEN THE GREAT COMEDIAN BERT WILLIAMS died in 1922 from a heart condition at forty-seven, the African American newspaper the *New York Age* wrote, "From last Sunday morning until Wednesday afternoon, [tens of thousands of] people in every walk of life, irrespective of race, creed or color, paid homage to one who, during his life, helped to drive away dull care and worry with his original, quaint humor, always clean and at no time suggestive of ridicule."

Yet Williams had, for almost thirty years, performed only in blackface,* the burnt cork hiding his light complexion, the white outline around his mouth emphasizing the absurdity of his mask. How, one wonders, can a blackface performer be "at no time suggestive of ridicule"?

Paradoxically, Bert Williams had succeeded in bringing dignity to blackface, and single-handedly, if temporarily, freed blackface from ridiculing his race. And he did so through sorrow.

Bert Williams set out to portray the most comically miserable and unfortunate of creatures, and did so with such cunning and

* Several historians have suggested that in his first film, *Darktown Jubilee* (1914), Williams uncharacteristically appeared without blackface, wearing a top hat and a zoot suit. Other historians disagree. The film is now lost, and no contemporaneous descriptions of it seem to exist.

grace that he transformed the blackface minstrel character into a figure not only of comedy but also of equal pathos and warmth. As the great theatrical producer David Belasco put it, "His audiences laughed at him and at his strange, grotesquely serious proceedings; but also, from the first moment when they saw him, they *liked* him."

Bert Williams was born in 1874 in the Bahamas; according to some sources, his father was one-eighth black and his mother one-quarter. Although he might have been able to pass for white, he always thought of himself as black; yet he also thought of himself as West Indian, even though he lived in the United States from the age of ten.

After some failed theatrical experiences in his late teens with Martin and Selig's Mastodon Minstrels, a small ("Mastodon" was ironic) group of five blacks and five whites based in California, Williams became partners with George Walker, another young black entertainer. According to Williams, his eureka moment came when, "just for a lark," he applied blackface one evening in a Detroit theater in 1895 or '96. He recalled: "Nobody was more surprised than I was when it went like a house on fire. Then I began to find myself. It was not until I was able to see myself as another person that my sense of humor developed." Like so many minstrels before and after him, wearing blackface liberated Williams to develop an entirely new persona. Walker, meanwhile, avoided blackface.

Williams and Walker first tasted success in a New York vaudeville theater in late 1896, but this was followed by several failures. It wasn't until 1901 that they became major stars, due to the success of their musical comedy *Sons of Ham*.

Soon they were collaborating with many of the most successful black performers of the era, including Bob Cole, Ernest Hogan, and J. Rosamond Johnson, and became wildly popular among both black and white audiences.

While Williams dressed in ill-fitting and worn-out clothing, Walker wore flashy yet impeccably tailored suits. Together they developed a kind of manic-depressive act, with Walker as the manic one and Williams the depressive. "In all of their sketches," observed the playwright Rennold Wolf, who would later write material for Williams, "Williams was the slovenly hard-luck coon and Walker the elegant bunco steerer. . . . Always did Walker, by some sort of confidence game, gain control of Williams' funds." This was also reflected in their offstage personalities: Walker was an ambitious, clever, yet scrupulously honest businessman, who would never yield when he thought he could get a more advantageous deal; Williams was a quiet, accommodating partner who would do anything to avoid even a hint of conflict. They billed themselves, presumably with a modicum of irony, as "The Two Real Coons," in contrast to whites in blackface.

In 1903, Williams and Walker produced and starred in Broadway's first all-black musical, *In Dahomey*, which was a tremendous hit; *Theatre Magazine* called Williams "a vastly funnier man than any white comedian now on the American stage." The show's success was due far more to the music and comedy than to the nonsensical plot, which revolved around two detectives trying to locate a missing treasure and ending up in Africa. *In Dahomey* soon traveled to London, where, after singing "Evah Darkey Is a King," Williams and Walker personally taught Edward VII not only how to do the cakewalk, but how to play craps, including "the humorous expressions identified with the playing of the game." Success followed success, and the pair were firmly established. Their shows were clean—no double entendres were allowed—dignified, and uproarious.

In 1909, Walker became too ill to continue the partnership (he had contracted syphilis), but Williams's fame only increased. Newspapers often called him America's greatest comedian black or white. He became the first black man to appear in the Ziegfeld Follies, sharing a bill with many of the major white stars of the time but receiving the most prominent billing. Producer Florenz Ziegfeld called him "a consummate artist in a sea of banality; technically perfect, timing immaculate, his portrayal of his people his only flaw in his otherwise perfect diamond."

Williams took an intellectual approach to the art of impersonation. "I try to portray the shiftless darky to the fullest extent," he told an interviewer in 1916, "his fun, his philosophy. . . . There is nothing about this fellow I don't know. I have studied him; his joys and sorrows. Contrast is vital. If I take up a lazy stevedore, I must study his movements. I have to. He is not in me. The way he walks; the way he crosses his legs; the way he leans up against a wall, one foot forward." Rather than exaggeration, the typical approach of minstrels, Williams favored subtlety.

Likewise, Williams, who spoke perfectly correct English with a slight West Indian accent, made a special study of African American dialect. As Mabel Rowland, Williams's longtime secretary, noted, "He studied the negro. He caught him in his laziest linguistic moments; he waited patiently for new dialectic twists and turns and when he discovered, for instance, that in a certain section the negro says 'cuccus' instead of 'circus,' he has rejoiced."

His impersonations became controversial when Williams appeared in the Follies, since he now played in an all-white show to all-white audiences (blacks were routinely excluded from the major New York theaters). The black critic Sylvester Russell scolded Williams for lacking racial pride, for not being as assertive as Walker had been, and for having "no backbone"; other black critics were equally disparaging (though black audiences, when he made appearances outside the Follies, responded enthusiastically). Williams replied to such criticism that while he was proud to be black, he was treated with more respect by the members of Ziegfeld's Follies than he was by his "own people." That may have been a veiled hint at the contempt in which many blacks—including George Walker—held blackface performance in general.

At the same time, some blacks recognized Williams's enormous contributions to the advancement of their people. One was Charles W. Anderson, a respected New York politician known as the "colored Demosthenes," and a close friend of Williams's. He later wrote: "His services to the race were great and multiple. He blazed a pathway from the minstrel house to the legitimate theatre: he unlocked the door, which had, for centuries, shut out colored performers from white shows. He lessened discrimination by conquering the prejudice of managers and producers. He overcame much of the hostility of the press against mixed casts and he reformed and refined the art, so called, of the (white) blackface comedians, by teaching them how to substitute drollery and repose for roughness and vulgarity." Yet the Follies never showcased another black artist alongside Williams—he remained the sole black man on stage for years.

In the meantime, Williams developed an elaborate theory of comedy. In his long 1918 essay "The Comic Side of Trouble," he observed:

> Nearly all of my successful songs have been based on the idea that I am getting the worst of it. I am the "Jonah

> Man," the man who, even if it rained soup, would be found with a fork in his hand and no spoon in sight, the man whose fighting relatives come to visit him and whose head is always dented by the furniture they throw at each other. . . .
>
> Troubles are only funny when you pin them to one particular individual. And that individual, the fellow who is the goat, must be the man who is singing the song or telling the story. Then the audience can picture him in their mind's eye and see him in the thick of his misfortunes, fielding flatirons with his head, carrying large bulldogs by the seat of his pants, and picking the bare bones of the chicken while his wife's relations eat the breast, and so on.

In fact, Williams's most successful songs had been precisely those of utter and complete misfortune—"I'm a Jonah Man" and "Nobody." "I'm a Jonah Man" was written, under Williams's direction, by his close friend Alex Rogers for Williams to sing in *In Dahomey* in 1903, but he never recorded it, despite its popular success. The verses relate the narrator's hard luck—he gets named after his father, who promptly dies; he gets a six-month meal ticket, and the restaurant burns down; he tries to follow the example of a friend who had fallen in a coal hole and successfully sued for $10,000, but instead he breaks both his legs and gets a year in jail. It's almost as if Williams had invented the blues—had any black-authored song expressed the sentiment of being shunned by God and man alike so clearly before?

Williams recorded "Nobody" at least three times, first in 1906—it was his signature song, the song his audiences wouldn't go home without hearing. The 1906 recording is completely unlike any of his previous records. It's essentially a duet between Williams and a moaning slide trombone, with an orchestra behind them. (As Rowland put it so well, "Many a laugh in 'Nobody,' came from the plaintive sound of the trombone and from Williams' apparently desperate efforts to catch up with it.") In the lyrics, Williams delivers a litany of questions, beginning with generalized anguish ("When life seems full of clouds and rain, and I'm full of nothin' and pain, who soothes my thumpin', bumpin' brain?") and proceeding to absurd situations ("I started to whittle on a stick one night—

From the cover of the sheet music to "I'm a Jonah Man," here are Williams and Walker in 1903, at the height of their success. Compare not just their makeup, but their hats.

who cried out, 'stop, that's dynamite'?"), all of them answered with "Nobody." The chorus, however, offers relief to Williams's apparent desolation: "Until I get somethin' from somebody sometime, I'll never do nothin' for nobody, no time." In song after song, despite all the slings and arrows of misfortune, Williams always stubbornly holds his own. In his skits he frequently played the trickster, slyly and quietly getting his revenge after appearing dense and subservient. As historian Ann Douglas writes, "His was the act of patience protracted despite abuse and misfortune, but his act also reminded viewers that all patience wears out sometime."

Williams followed the success of "Nobody" with dozens of other records, making him by far the most recorded black man and, along with Al Jolson and Nora Bayes, one of the three highest-paid recording artists of the time. He was not an especially skilled singer—it was his comedic talents that made him so popular. At least half of his records similarly bemoan the narrator's misfortunes in a comical manner. And Williams's onstage demeanor perfectly matched his songs. He always wore a top hat and tails, but they were ill-fitting and shabby; below them he brandished high-water trousers and scuffed-up shoes. No matter what character he portrayed, he was generally luckless. He never stood up straight; the corners of his mouth were usually turned down.

In the last four or five years of his life, the roles Williams was playing became unsatisfactory, since the writers for the shows were not providing him with very good parts; he was at sea in the Follies and no longer received top billing. He suffered from a heart condition that caused swelling and pain. This, along with the myriad small injustices he was subject to because of his race, turned him melancholy and even misanthropic. According to his wife Lettie and some of his friends, he made up his mind to break free from comedy and fulfill a long-harbored ambition: to play serious black theater. Yet, in his last show, *Under the Bamboo Tree,* he still wore blackface, still did comedy, and was still the only black man on stage. Unfortunately he died before the play had a chance to be a success. The play he had been hoping to perform next was, according to Lettie, "very somber"—he would play a jealous husband who uses voodoo to torture his wife's child, and the wife "dies of horror." (Williams's best biographer, Eric Ledell Smith, suggests that Lettie was confused and that Williams was planning to star in Mary Hoyt Wiborg's *Taboo*, which ended up opening in 1922, shortly after his death, starring Alex Rogers and Paul Robeson. *Taboo*, which centers around curing a white child by means of voodoo, is hardly as horrific as the play Lettie Williams described; it is, however, a far more serious play than any Bert Williams had been in.) After his death, some black critics bewailed that Williams was never given a chance to shine as a serious actor; but, as Rowland points out, this wasn't the fault of the theater world, which would have been ready to give Williams such a part, but of Williams's characteristic hesitancy.

George Walker once traced the evolution of black minstrelsy. White performers, he wrote, "used to make themselves look as ridiculous as they could when portraying a 'darky' character. In their 'make up' they always had tremendously big red lips and their costumes were frightfully exaggerated. The one fatal result of this to the colored performers was that they imitated the white performers in their make-up as 'darkies.' Nothing seemed more absurd than to see a colored man making himself ridiculous in order to portray himself."

Bert Williams wore the makeup his partner Walker so

detested. Still Walker never criticized him for this, since Williams successfully avoided appearing ridiculous by emphasizing human suffering, and by shying away from the extreme exaggeration of previous comics. While minstrel performers had long acted carefree and happy, finding a sense of liberation in impish behavior, Williams took the opposite approach, so overburdened with cares and worries that he was practically paralyzed. As one reviewer of *In Dahomey* wrote, Williams "had his audience shouting with laughter one instant, and the next, with a few peering glances, an intent attitude, and a wonderful manipulation of his lips, he almost made you want to cry. The laughter ceased abruptly, something caught you at the throat, the eyes pulsating, hotly for a second—and then you were laughing again." Douglas comments on his "omnipresent sense of reluctance: he'd really just as soon, as the drooping shoulders, slow shuffle, and mournfully reserved face attest, not perform at all. In every line he spoke, in every step he danced, one felt a dash of death wish." Perhaps Williams himself put it best: "I often think of the old court jesters; how they used to make the guests weep before they would make them laugh."

This combination of comedy and tragedy can be traced back to the character of Pierrot, who first appeared in late-seventeenth-century France and quickly became a stock figure; by the 1880s and 1890s, the apogee of the age of pantomime, he had become ubiquitous. Always in whiteface—Williams's insistence on blackface can be seen as a brilliant reversal of this tradition—Pierrot was the lovelorn, sad, yet funny servant. Alone, estranged, evoking pathos and laughter simultaneously, he was a fool yet nobody's fool, a servant but independent; he used small gestures, in contrast to the exaggerations common in pantomime. Williams, who excelled in the art of pantomime, and (falsely) claimed to have studied it in Europe with "the great Pietro" (probably Pietro Bologna), adopted this character completely. For example, his 1916 film *A Natural Born Gambler* features a brilliant solo pantomime of a poker player, stuck in jail and without any cards or coins, playing a pretend game of draw poker with four imaginary players. Even in this fantasy, he loses all his money.

Williams recognized his style as a departure from the minstrel tradition. "When we picture the negro on the stage," he said, "we think of him singing, laughing and cutting up. That seems to be his nature. But has it ever occurred to you that under his mask of smiles and this cloak of capers there is hidden dire tragedy?" Williams himself experienced a great many of the myriad humiliations, large and small, that blacks in public life were subjected to in those days. When he took this "hidden dire tragedy" and made it evident, there was a sense of having lived it, even within the minstrel context he insisted on.

While he often spoke of the realness of the characters he portrayed, Williams took infinite care to separate them, in the public mind, from the man he was offstage. The tragedy and the comedy of the misfortunes of Williams's singular characters were inextricable. But equally inextricable was the dignity of Williams's nonblackface life (in advertisements he appeared without makeup and dressed in fine, well-fitting clothes, and in interviews he was unfailingly erudite) from the shiftlessness of the "darky" he portrayed. For the success he achieved in his profession, and his reputation as a man of broad knowledge and considerable wealth, only made his blackface performances more riotous. And when Williams would entertain offstage at white society parties, he would appear in full formal attire, according to his biographer Ann Charters, and ask as his opening sally, "Is we all good niggers here?" The irony was delicious, a complete departure from, yet also a perfect continuation of, the long tradition of "good niggers" onstage.

In 1896, Paul Laurence Dunbar, the great black author who was a close associate of Williams and who would write the script of several Williams and Walker vehicles, penned a poem that resonates with Williams's performance and black—and human—life in general: "We Wear the Mask."

We wear the mask that grins and lies,
It hides our cheeks and shades our eyes—
This debt we pay to human guile;
With torn and bleeding hearts we smile
And mouth with myriad subtleties,

Why should the world be over-wise,
In counting all our tears and sighs?
Nay, let them only see us while
        We wear the mask.

We smile, but oh great Christ, our cries
To Thee from tortured souls arise.
We sing, but oh the clay is vile
Beneath our feet, and long the mile;
But let the world dream otherwise,
        We wear the mask!

Williams doubtless knew the poem well, and more than any other black actor of his time, he took Dunbar's words to heart. For him, the mask was blackface, and he wore it with a singular consciousness of what it hid, what it revealed, and what it enabled him to accomplish. He wore the mask—and he simultaneously tore it apart. He allowed the world to "count all our tears and sighs," to hear "our cries" and see our "tortured souls." He wore the mask, but he never "let the world dream otherwise."

W. C. Fields, who knew Williams only near the end of the latter's life, famously remarked, "Bert Williams was the funniest man I ever saw and the saddest man I ever knew." What he didn't remark on was how perfectly those two facets of Williams's character went hand in hand, and how revolutionary was their strange and unique companionship.

Bert Williams's historical importance is often exaggerated. He has been called "the first black performer who could be described as an international pop star," but Billy Kersands has a far more valid claim to that description. He has been called "the first black artist to star with white performers in a major musical production," but William "Juba" Lane did so over fifty years earlier. Williams was certainly the most successful black comedian—both onstage and on recordings—of the first two decades of the twentieth century. He deserves to be placed in the company of Charlie Chaplin, Buster Keaton, Stan Laurel, Jacques Tati, Roberto Benigni, and Bill Murray, all of whom, like Williams, used small gestures to simultaneously invite pity and provoke laughter. Perhaps he even deserves W. E. B. Du Bois's praise of him as "a great comedian, a great Negro, a great man." But he is most notable for being the last of the great black blackface minstrels.

What is never exaggerated is Williams's expressed fondness for blackface. This is almost always either downplayed or outright denied. To be categorical and plain, *Bert Williams trea-*

sured the minstrel tradition. But this fact is too horrifying for contemporary writers to face.

In February 1908, George Walker was at war with racism. During that month, he wrote three letters to the *New York Age*, responding to a white booking agent who had called black entertainers "unreliable," chastising his white managers for the way they handled a black reporter, and accusing a New York private club of racism. Williams, characteristically, approached the *Age* rather differently. In an interview with the newspaper near the end of the month, he seemed to go out of his way to echo the timeworn nineteenth-century condescension of whites toward blacks, stating categorically, "The American Negro is a natural minstrel. He is the one in whom humor is native, often unconscious, but nevertheless keen and laugh-compelling. He dances from the cradle stage almost, for his feet have been educated prenatally, it would seem. He usually has a voice, and there is not much necessity for schools of voice culture to temper [*sic*] with a natural voice. There is soul in the Negro music: There is simplicity and an entire lack of artificiality."

What is one to make of these words coming from a well-read, sophisticated, wealthy, and famous black entertainer? Was Williams adopting the racist, primitivist attitudes of his white audience? Was he justifying his use of blackface by calling the artifice "natural"? Did he, a citizen of the Bahamas, not consider himself an "American Negro" (he only became an American citizen in 1918)? Or was he, perhaps, being completely sincere? The answer to all of those questions is, simply, yes. But it's important to view Williams's words in the context of their time.

Compare Williams's statement to this one, written in 1917:

"We find that there is constant striving on the part of the Negro for beautiful or striking effect, that those things which are most picturesque make the readiest appeal to his nature. . . . There is something very elemental about the heart of the race, something that finds its origin in the African forest, in the sighing of the nightwind, and in the falling of the stars." This may sound like the typical romanticization of the savage Negro by a nineteenth-century white, but it was actually written by the noted black educator and author Benjamin Brawley, who at the time was dean of Morehouse College. Or take this similar statement, written in 1913: "The Negro is primarily an artist. . . . [There is] a sense of beauty, particularly for sound and color, which characterizes the race." This came from the pen of W. E. B. Du Bois. Zora Neale Hurston essentialized the African American character as late as 1934: "The Negro's universal mimicry is not so much a thing in itself as an evidence of something that permeates his entire self. And that thing is drama."

Admittedly, none of these black writers brought up minstrelsy. But it's clear that Williams, like many others of his day, saw blacks as especially skilled in the arts of dance, music, and comedy. Perhaps in that sense to him they were "natural minstrels."

At the same time, Williams was closely allied with the accommodationist perspective of Booker T. Washington, and professed admiration for the man and his philosophy. Washington himself was an ardent admirer of Williams, and in a 1910 tribute to him wrote, "During all the years I have known Bert Williams, I have never heard him whine or cry about his color, or about any racial discrimination." Indeed, time and again Williams had separated himself from the anger over racial injustices that George Walker and other blacks displayed. Only near the end of his life did Williams publicly complain about the numerous discriminatory practices to which he was subject.

In reply to Washington, Williams wrote an article entitled "The Negro on the Stage," which was published that same year both in the *Green Book Album*, a journal about the theater, and in the *New York Age*. Here he once again spoke positively of minstrelsy, calling it "the one new stage form which has been developed in this country." But then he went further than any other black man has ever gone: he went out of his way to apologize for *white* minstrelsy. "My observation has led me to the theory that when a strange unassimilated element exists in a nation, it almost immediately finds its way to the stage in comic types, usually caricatures. . . . I may add that the white men who have interpreted our race in this manner have done us no discredit."

Williams's pontifications, here and elsewhere, may seem disingenuous. How could any African American maintain with a straight face that white minstrelsy had "done us no discredit"? Sylvester Russell's criticism of Williams as having "no backbone" seems apt; time and again, when faced with the choice of standing up for his race or kowtowing to the white man's opinions of it, Williams chose the latter. For years after Walker left, he frequently seemed to turn his back to his black audience both onstage and off, playing for whites in not just his theatrical appearances but also his public pronouncements.

Yet Williams seemed aware of this perception, and took care to address it later in his life. In "The Comic Side of Trouble," Williams wrote, "People sometimes ask me if I would give anything to be white. I answer, in the words of the song, most emphatically, 'No.' . . . I have never been able to discover that there was anything disgraceful in being a colored man. But I have often found it inconvenient—in America."

—

The first biography of Williams was a warm and loving account compiled (and largely written) by his secretary Mabel Rowland and published in 1923, shortly after Williams's death. Here Williams comes across as a personable, lively man, whose talent for impersonating characters and making people laugh is unequaled. It is clear from this book that prior to his last few years there was little hint of sadness in his life, which was characterized by generosity, modesty, and amiability. It would be hard to find an African American who suffered the indignities of his era about whom the word *bitter* would be less apt.

But in 1970, Ann Charters published *Nobody: The Story of Bert Williams,* and in it she set a very different tone for future accounts. In her first paragraph, she stated unequivocally, "When Bert Williams began his career in 1892, he found he had to conform to a theatrical convention that in many ways crippled his talent and limited his achievement. As a pioneer he was forced into a blackface role he detested."

There is no truth to this. Williams was not forced to wear blackface, and there's absolutely no indication that he felt bad about wearing it. George Walker never wore blackface, and had a wildly successful career. When Williams appeared in England in 1903 some Tin Pan Alley publishers tried to persuade him to take the stage without it, and he refused (he even proudly called his performance there of *In Dahomey* "a minstrel show"). In *A Natural Born Gambler,* which features over a dozen black actors, he's the only one in blackface. Rather than limiting his achievement, blackface made it possible for him to adopt his inimitable persona, and he publicly proclaimed that fact.

Only one thing that Williams said might give some credence

to Charters's position: "When a man has no pigment in his skin, it's hard. Just think what I have to do to 'get by.'" But Williams, in this 1916 interview, was *not* complaining about wearing blackface, but about the inability of whites to recognize him for who he was—a black man who, by virtue of his light skin, was different from other blacks. He explained, "The Caucasian believes that every colored man is a 'coon,' that they are all alike, that they should not live in a modern way. This is a mistake. We have as many differences as the white man and no one characteristic covers us all." This is a far cry from the myth that Charters promotes.

This myth actually began immediately after Williams's death. In 1923, a twenty-five-year-old black writer named Eric Walrond, who, like Williams, hailed from the Bahamas and lived in New York City, but who had probably never actually met the man, reviewed Rowland's biography for the *Negro World.* Walrond, who would go on to find acclaim as a writer of fiction, invented a scene in which Williams argues with himself: "'Is it worth it?' One side of him would ask. 'Is it worth it, the applause, the financial rewards, the fame? Is it really worth it—lynching one's soul in blackface twaddle?' 'But it is the only way you can break in,' protests the other side of the man. 'It is the only way. That is what the white man expects of you—comedy—blackface comedy.'" Needless to say, it is difficult to believe that Williams ever thought of what he did as "lynching one's soul in blackface twaddle."

After Charters, Eric Ledell Smith was the next biographer to tackle Williams, and he did so fairly, portraying him through his own words and contemporaneous writings, without resorting to fictionalization. But his well-researched 1992 book, entitled simply *Bert Williams,* was all but ignored: it was published by a small press, McFarland & Company, and saw little circulation outside libraries.

Caryl Phillips, another successful black novelist with roots in the West Indies, published a novel about Williams in 2005 entitled *Dancing in the Dark*, and he seems to have taken Walrond's and Charters's fiction as the basis for his protagonist's psychological makeup. Williams cuts a pitiable figure here, full of shame and doubt, even at the height of his career with Walker. Onstage, Williams plays "a shuffling, dull-witted, clumsy, watermelon-eating Negro of questionable intelligence," but offstage, Williams suffers dreadfully from the guilt of it all. There is no hint in this book of Williams's hobbies and interests—playing piano and baseball; boxing; visiting the zoo; taking photographs—nor of his considerable generosity in helping, financially and otherwise, to educate young men of his acquaintance. Mention of any of those activities would disturb Phillips's portrayal of Williams as a depressed alcoholic with no offstage vitality.

Louis Chude-Sokei, in *The Last "Darky,"* a relatively astute academic analysis of Williams's racial politics published in 2006, unfortunately continues the pattern. Williams's melancholy, he writes, was "the sadness of the black performer held by racialized performance conventions; the tragic sadness of black skin trapped underneath a black mask held firmly in place by racism."

Similarly, Camille F. Forbes, in her widely praised 2008 biography *Introducing Bert Williams,* essentially "blackwashes" her subject. She subtitles her book *Burnt Cork, Broadway, and the Story of America's First Black Star,* but glosses over the subject of burnt cork entirely, saying almost nothing about its history, development, or use; and to call Williams "America's first black star" ignores all the black stars of the nineteenth century, ranging from minstrels to classical musicians. Forbes's biography is full of omissions—when quoting him she omits key words, she omits the most minstrel-like songs and acts he performed, and, worst of all, she omits all mention of his well-known 1910 essay "The Negro on the Stage" (it's not even in her otherwise complete bibliography).

A good example of her technique is how she backs up her claim that Williams tried "to distance himself from minstrelsy's legacy." Here she quotes the 1916 interview previously cited. In it, Williams answered the simple question "Minstrels?" with the following: "Minstrels are a thing of the past—because there are no more minstrels. To cork your face and talk politics is not minstrelsy. There are no more men like 'Daddy' Rice, the originator of Minstrelsy, but I think the art will be revived." But when Forbes reproduces this statement, she omits those last eight words, which can easily be interpreted as one of Williams's ambitions (his innate modesty would have prevented him from saying "but I hope to revive the art").

In fact, Williams deliberately championed almost every aspect of the minstrel tradition. In marked contrast to George Walker, who refrained from using dialect and boldly stated in 1906 that the "old-time nigger act . . . ought to die out and we are trying hard to kill it," Williams took great pains to learn "stage Negro" dialect, which was, he confessed, "to me, just as much a foreign dialect as that of the Italian." He freely dipped into the panoply of minstrel caricatures—chicken-stealing slaves, preachers giving stump speeches, razor-toting poker players—at a time when many black performers avoided such types. He recorded songs of minstrel and coon ilk like "The Mississippi Stoker," "Oh Lawdy! (Something's Done Got Between

Ebecaneezer and Me)," "I'm Gonna Quit Saturday," "'Tain't No Disgrace to Run When You're Skeered," and "I Ain't Afraid of Nothin' Dat's Alive." And in the *Ziegfeld Follies of 1919*, he even played Mr. Bones in a version of a minstrel show and sang a song (written by none other than Irving Berlin) called "I'd Rather See a Minstrel Show."

Bert Williams tried to cultivate the same attitude toward minstrelsy as his contemporary James Weldon Johnson, who, as previously noted, wrote that minstrelsy had its origins among black slaves and "was the first and remains, up to this time, the only completely original contribution America has made to the theatre." Even if the minstrel tradition was a source of shame for performers like George Walker, it was a source of pride for Williams, as for others in the early twentieth-century theater world. And Williams unquestionably suffered for that pride, for it subjected him to the scorn of those blacks who hated minstrelsy and everything it stood for. Even immediately after his death, while most writers were lauding his achievements, one black newspaper wrote that Williams was "a facile instrument" of the "insidious cult" of white supremacy, and that his life was proof that "the oppressed have always acquiesced in and defended their own oppression."

To what extent is this the case? Indeed, Williams's attitude toward minstrelsy had much in common with that of his white contemporaries. This light-skinned Bahamian thought of himself as black, but held himself apart from the common African Americans of his day. His milieu consisted of whites of a theatrical bent and the cream of Harlem society. His defense of white minstrels, taken together with his statement that "the shiftless darky . . . is not in me" and his complaint that his light skin wasn't sufficient to separate himself from the "coon" in white eyes, seems to place him squarely in the camp of his contemporaries Al Jolson and Eddie Cantor, white men in blackface. Indeed, the latter was his partner in the Follies, the two of them playing Tambo and Bones in the 1919 minstrel skit, and they were good friends offstage too. Williams spent his later years trying to ignore the complaints of his more race-proud black contemporaries, and he turned his back on them time and again, most notably when, after leaving the Follies, he put on a show in which he was the only black actor. He evidently felt more comfortable working with white performers and in front of white audiences than with blacks, and this was reflected in his act. As Douglas wisely points out, Williams's performances were built "on his ability to look at the darky as the white man did, purposely to elicit white laughter at black sorrow."

But instead of attacking Williams for his minstrel act, Charters, Phillips, and Forbes all pity him for it. For contemporary writers can't seem to conceive of a black person, no matter how removed from black society, being comfortable with—and even proud of—the minstrel tradition. When Forbes reprints Williams's statement that "the American Negro is a natural minstrel," she calls it "forced and unnatural" and omits the remainder of Williams's interview.

Yet offstage, Williams was not a sad man—at least not before the last few years of his life. Belasco called him one of the most amiable men he had met; Anderson wrote, "Bert's was one of the most buoyant and boyish spirits I have ever known"; and many others attested to his love of humor in his private life. Williams himself once said, "I have no grievance whatsoever against the world or the people in it. I'm having a grand time." He clearly enjoyed himself and the minstrel tradition he partook in, and surely does not need our pity. For by pitying Bert Williams, we rob him of agency, deny the fact that he had options, and fail to respect his choices.

Bert Williams has had a long and complicated afterlife, being resurrected time and again in television documentaries, theatrical tributes, and even Hollywood movies. But his most notable—and saddest—postmortem appearance was the Broadway actor Ben Vereen's portrayal of him at Ronald Reagan's inaugural gala in 1981. Vereen had earlier paid tribute to Williams in a 1970 episode of *Evening at Pops,* portrayed him in blackface for years in his nightclub act, and created an elaborate sketch about Williams in the first episode of his 1975 variety television series *Comin' at Ya*. This sketch, according to one account, was preceded by an introduction describing Williams's travails, the humiliations he had endured, and the sacrifices he made in order to be onstage (including a reiteration of the common misconception that Williams was forced to wear blackface). Vereen then appeared as Williams (in blackface), did some comedy and dance material, sang "Nobody," and invited the white audience out for drinks, only to break off and add mournfully, "For a moment there, I forgot my place."

But at the inaugural gala Vereen sang the demeaning and joyous Al Jolson number "Waiting for the Robert E. Lee" (with its chorus of "Watch them shufflin' along")—a song Williams never sang—and all the audience saw was a man in blackface doing minstrel material. The reaction from black Americans was, according to contemporaneous accounts, unanimously negative. One letter to *Ebony* read, "He eased his way on center stage, shuffling his feet, as if he didn't belong. Bulging eyes darted over the audience. White-painted lips emphasized his Black face. Ashamed, I slid into my seat. My insides shook. My racial pride was crushed. The predominate [*sic*] White audience laughed at the . . . 'stereotyped image' Black people have fought to overcome. I watched President Reagan break into laughter. Why would a gifted man abuse his talent by performing the White man's myth?" Another read, "Never would I have believed that in January 1981 I would behold with my own eyes, at the Inaugural festivity, such regression to the days of minstrel shows, pickaninnys, plantations, and cotton pickin'." A third read, "I consider this outrageous performance as demeaning and an insult to all Black people of the world." And a fourth went even further: "Ben Vereen, you ought to be tarred and feathered for the egotistical, insensitive, stereotypical niggeration of yourself and all Black people in offering that 'tribute' to Bert Williams." Ossie Davis and Ruby Dee expressed their dismay to *Jet*. "Poor Bert is turning over in his grave," Dee offered, "because this was a man of great dignity who would never do a thing like that." And Dee was right: Williams never did perform a song like "Waiting for the Robert E. Lee," with its happy darkies shuffling along. In even his most minstrel- and coonlike songs, his protagonists had real character ("Character" was Williams's reply to the question of what interested him most in his work) and suffered real sorrows.

But Vereen refused to apologize. He explained at length to *Jet* that only half of his performance had been shown on television. In the second half Vereen as Williams offered to buy the audience a drink and was refused by a waiter in the back because he was black and "your money's no good here." (This is a variation on an actual incident in which Bert Williams, because he was black, was charged $50 for a glass of gin in a bar, so he peeled off $500 and said, "Give me ten of them.") Vereen then sang "Nobody," wiped off his blackface with a rag, looked at the makeup there, and handed the rag to the audience. "For how long, how long?" he asked them. "It's up to you to do something about this." According to Vereen, who heard it from Reagan's daughter Maureen, when Reagan saw this, he asked her, "Why is he doing this to me?" Maureen responded, "Because you need to see it." "The message," Vereen told *Jet*, "is 'How long? We are not going to put up with this. . . . I ain't goin' to do nothing for nobody no time until I get somethin' from somebody.'" Vereen clearly wanted to place the blame for the affront to black Americans squarely on the decision not to show the second half of his act.

Like Caryl Phillips, Ben Vereen seems not to have realized that Bert Williams was dignified *not* just when he wiped off his blackface, but *during* his blackface act itself. Williams's posthumous misrepresentation in periodicals and books and on stage and screen has resulted in a widespread myth that he was a gifted, dignified comic forced to do a demeaning minstrel act. Nothing could be further from the truth. Williams deliberately revived the art of minstrelsy in order to expunge some of its demeaning aspects and transform it into an art of humanity and pathos. But since his death, ironically enough, the man who introduced sorrow to minstrelsy to make people laugh has provoked only sorrow. The pity Williams took from Pierrot has completely infected the image of Williams—and minstrelsy—itself. And the laughter—the joy with which he drew on the minstrel tradition—has died.

Publicity still of the cast of the *Amos 'n' Andy* television show. Left to right: Alvin Childress, Tim Moore, Spencer Williams, Jr.

5.

I'SE REGUSTED

How Stepin Fetchit, Amos, Andy, and Company Brought Black Minstrelsy to the Twentieth-Century Screen

IN 1968, NBC PRODUCED *Flip Out with Flip*, a TV special offering Flip Wilson's black variation on the popular sketch comedy show *Laugh-In*, on which the comedian frequently appeared. Though *Flip Out* mostly consisted of brief, wacky skits, the highlight was a poignant twenty-minute piece about a headstrong black youth (Wilson) being put in his place by his wise, cantankerous father as they watch over the family antique shop. The casting of Lincoln Perry as the paternal figure was a notable and bold move.

Perry had come to personify black minstrelsy in the twentieth century when his stage persona, Stepin Fetchit, enabled him to become Hollywood's first black superstar. He did not invent the stereotype of a slow-witted, lazy buffoon that he brought to the silver screen in over fifty movies (mostly in the 1930s). However, his interpretation was so stylized, specific, and memorable that it instantly became the new prototype of this nineteenth-century standard, defining it for modern audiences. Black actors like Willie Best and Nick "Nicodemus" Stewart had lengthy careers doing xerographic impersonations of Perry's heavy-lidded, molasses-witted rube in hundreds of film and television appearances from the 1930s through the 1960s. In a 1965 TV special, *Danny Thomas Presents the Wonderful World of Burlesque,* Thomas (not in blackface) salutes Bert Williams by re-creating several minutes of his act . . . in a Stepin Fetchit voice. Though Williams's cylinder recordings make it clear that he did not employ that vocal style, to audiences in the 1960s it was inconceivable that an early African American comic would use anything other than Perry's "coon show" cadence. In *Hollywood Shuffle*, a 1987 satire about black movie stereotypes, actor-director Robert Townsend used the Fetchit mannerisms as shorthand for all the racist ills of the previous century of cinema.

But on the NBC special Perry did not use his signature voice, or demonstrate slothful passivity. His character is ill-tempered, slick, and quick with words. The sketch even addresses Perry's legacy, when Wilson's character lashes out at his father, who is urging his son to help the community rather than follow his dream of being a downtown lawyer:

LP: You better listen to your old man and stay here where you belong . . .

FW: Here we go again, Ole Uncle Tom telling it like it ain't . . . kiss my NAACP card!

LP: You better hush up, boy. If you want respect make something of yourself right here . . . right here is where we need a criminal lawyer because the worst crime around here is being black.

Perry hoped this new, more dignified persona would spark a much-needed comeback (he fell out of favor in Hollywood by the late 1930s, in part because of excessive off-camera antics, and in part because his comic characteristics were so easily mimicked that audiences were satisfied with copycats). When he visited Earl Calloway's office at the *Chicago Defender* waving the *Flip Out* script, he was "filled with joy and enthusiasm." And the *Los Angeles Times'* TV editor speculated that the sketch "could later be developed into a weekly series, which would restore Fetchit's career in a big way."

However, it was a different 1968 network TV appearance that would be the last word on Fetchit's professional life. In "Black History: Lost, Stolen, or Strayed," part one of a series of CBS specials called *Of Black America*, narrator Bill Cosby essentially blamed Perry for the long-standing resonance of the negative stereotypes he so expertly brought to cinematic life. Although a stone-faced Cosby at one point sympathizes with the "fine actors who had to play baboons to make a buck," he was not particularly charitable with Perry. "The tradition of the lazy, stupid, crapshooting, chicken-stealing idiot was popularized by Lincoln Theodore Andrew Monroe Perry," Cosby lamented. "The character he played was planted in a lot of people's heads and they remember it as clearly as an auto accident."

There were no sitcom offers forthcoming for Perry. NBC never aired *Flip Out*, developing a different special for Wilson, one without Perry's involvement. Though cultural historian Donald Bogle claims the show was shelved because it was "poorly done," Lincoln Perry knew better. For the rest of his life he bitterly blamed CBS for blacklisting him with their harsh attacks. Never ashamed of his signature character ("Because Dean Martin drinks, that doesn't make drunks out of all Italians"), he was devastated by this development. His frustration was magnified when *The Flip Wilson Show* became TV's first smash hit black show two years later, and *Sanford and Son*, a show very similar to his father-son-junkshop skit, later became the second.

Perry might have done better on television if he had not tried to supplant his "chicken-stealing idiot" character. The populist medium has always appealed to the same demographic that had frequented minstrel shows and vaudeville. Thus, black performers doing low, stereotype-laden comedy have become TV perennials, consistently reemerging every few seasons, despite tireless efforts by black activists and actors (and their white liberal allies) to "overcome" the persistence of minstrelsy. Perry's inclusion in two very different 1968 TV productions plots the two major positions in the ongoing cycle of responses to minstrelsy's survival in American mass culture: correction and rejection. Perry's attempt to embody a three-dimensional black character on *Flip Out* represents one strain of antiminstrel activism, in which black performers attempt to counter stereotypes with positive programming, using dignity to upend the legacy of crude clowning. The castigation of Perry/Fetchit on "Lost, Stolen or Strayed" represents the other strain: recurring efforts by activists to protest loudly against mass-media buffoons that threaten to set back the race. That show's host was a fitting choice, because, as we'll see in the following chapter, the most familiar face of both rejection and correction on television would soon belong to Bill Cosby. But Cosby, while effective, was not an antiminstrel pioneer. His efforts to clean up the small screen were built on a solid precedent—the attacks on *Amos 'n' Andy*.

There would not be a black-cast narrative television series until 1951. However, that program, *Amos 'n' Andy*, perfectly reflected the refinements and reactions to the black minstrel tradition developed over a half-century on film and a quarter-century on radio. Lincoln Perry was far from the first black face on motion-picture stock. As would later be the case with American radio and TV, some of the earliest films featured black characters (represented by blacks, by whites in blackface, and occasionally by both commingling). When the Edison Manufacturing Company began producing America's first commercially exhibited films, scores of these shorts mirrored the content and themes of black minstrelsy, and their competitors followed suit. Titles that showcased black dancing included Edison's *The Pickaninny Dance* (1894) and *Buck and Wing Dance*, featuring black vaudevillian James Grundy (1898), and American Mutoscope's *A Coon Cake Walk* (1897). Stock stereotypical comic situations were seen in Edison's *The Tramp and the Crap Game* (1900), American Mutoscope's *The Chicken Thief* (1904), and in so many watermelon movies that when Lubin released their 1903 short *Who Said Watermelon?* they advertised that "the usual watermelon picture shows darkey men eating the luscious fruit . . . but the demand for a new watermelon picture has induced us to pose two colored women."

Black actors, or simulations thereof, have been at the center of many of cinema's milestones, from *The Jazz Singer* to *Avatar*, and no milestone was heavier than 1915's *The Birth of a Nation*. D. W. Griffith's paranoid racist fantasy (in which Reconstruction is cast as a deviant black revolution that can only be quelled by the heroic Ku Klux Klan) perfected many important technical and narrative cinematic techniques, and established the notion of the Hollywood blockbuster that still defines the industry. It also helped develop a model for concerted African American cultural dissent, with the NAACP and the black press rallying together to protest the film, black intellectuals like W. E. B. Du Bois voicing their disapproval, and black artists answering with their own works, including director Oscar Micheaux's 1919 antilynching melodrama *Within Our Gates*.

The Birth of a Nation features some ostensibly comic scenes (notably a session of an all-black Congress, reviving themes from black minstrel performers McCabe and Young's sketch "The Senator's Flirtation"). But with its themes of rape and brutality it predominantly drew from threatening black stereotypes mostly ignored on minstrel stages. Unlike Griffith's masterful techniques, this evocation of black violence did not become a cinematic trope. Most blacks appearing on screen in the next half-century were cast as either broad comic relief or as comforting (sometimes sassy) domestics, a development that likely had less to do with vehement black protest and more to do with the long-proven appeal of minstrel shows (and their faux–country cousins, *Uncle Tom's Cabin* plays). African American musicians and dancers also appeared on-screen, often in "specialty numbers," to provide entertaining diversions, independent of the narrative, that could be spliced out if a local southern censor objected.

In tandem, a fascinating alternative cinema emerged in which low-budget, black-cast films were created for black audiences. Some were produced and directed by blacks, some were helmed by black directors but backed by white independent producers, some had white directors leading black casts, and, in the case of some musical shorts, some were made by major studios. These "race films" played to black audiences at theaters in black neighborhoods, at special screenings at segregated white theaters, and in alternate venues, like the churches and tents black artists also used for live performances.

In many of these films the stereotypes are discarded, as when Micheaux cast blacks in roles reserved for white Hollywood heroes (he promoted actor Lorenzo Tucker as "the Black Valentino"). At other times minstrel-show stereotypes were embraced. Yet without the intrusion of white expectations, they were transformed. In "Lost, Stolen, or Strayed," Cosby's verbal destruction of Stepin Fetchit is mostly illustrated by clips of comedian Mantan Moreland from the 1942 race film *Lucky Ghost* (perhaps Moreland's low-budget film had fallen into public domain, and Perry's high-profile Hollywood films had not). The featured excerpts of Moreland bulging his eyes and nervously vibrating as he rolls dice are damning. The same scenes are shown as part of a much longer excerpt in the 2002 documentary *That's Black Entertainment*, a history of race films. There the offensive segments are contextualized. We see Moreland as the main protagonist, not a comic sidekick to whites (as he was in many of his Hollywood films). We realize that it is a completely black film. And we feel the gravity of the situations making Moreland's character act bizarrely. That the same footage could be used to make opposite points demonstrates the alchemy of audience. Without whites watching, sometimes a funny eye bulge is just a funny eye bulge.

The best race films demonstrated genuine humanity that avoided minstrelsy's shorthand treatment of black characters. With an all-black cast and all-black audiences, vices like sloth, ignorance, and foolishness could be traits of characters without fear of stereotyping. In *Blood of Jesus* (1941), Spencer Williams (who also wrote and directed the film) plays a lazy, hog-stealing loser, but in the context of his loving marriage to a religious wife, he never evokes minstrelsy. Despite being stagey and somewhat surreal, the film is too sincere for the characters to be caricatures. Films like *Blood of Jesus* had Z-grade budgets and used amateur actors, but this often contributed to a documentarylike vibe. "You actually have the feeling the actors aren't performing," film scholar Pearl Bowser notes. "You are seeing a slice of life on screen."

But in mainstream movies blacks rarely got to keep it real.

As a 1972 article from the *Black Panther* newspaper put it, "we can sum up the development of Black people's involvement in the motion-picture industry, at least until the middle 1960's, in just two words, 'Stepin' Fetchit.'" Perry's fool, bumbling on the sidelines, was as high as black actors could hope to rise in Hollywood. It is possible to read that type of comic character as subversive—a trickster who feigns ignorance and sloth to undermine the slavemaster-boss (Ossie Davis said this figure "invented the coffee break in the cotton patch"). But because Hollywood only made a handful of predominantly black-cast films in its first six decades, in their brief appearances as incidental characters in majority white-cast films, black actors and actresses never had enough context to develop characters beyond two dimensions. Thus, Perry and his impersonators played rubes that seemed genuinely dumb and lazy.

Which isn't to dismiss their performances. Comedians like Perry, Moreland, and Butterfly McQueen could take a dismissive, racist script and inject black vernacular between the lines. In the extremely narrow window of expression Hollywood films provided African Americans, the black minstrel traditions of broad humor and extreme stereotypes were useful tools for clever actors. One of Stepin Fetchit's signatures was a mumbling postscript to every sentence. This "audible pantomime" (Perry's term) allowed him to continue making comments and asides beyond his scripted lines, and it's often amazing to see classic Hollywood films in which white actors slavishly follow the script while Perry obviously improvises much of his dialogue. This under-the-breath comic technique (also used in Fleischer Studios' *Popeye* cartoons and, more manically, by Robin Williams) never rises to the level of full subversion—his mumbles don't overtly denigrate white costars—but compared to the characters who played it straight, like Bill "Bojangles" Robinson, Perry's Fetchit could be considered borderline dangerous. This scene from the 1934 film *Judge Priest*, starring Will Rogers, demonstrates the dynamic of subtly talking back to his boss.

SF: Look like that liver done walked off by itself . . .

WR: Lord, how am I gonna catch any catfish and ain't got no bait. Take this dime now and hurry on back to town and get me that beef liver. Hurry up now.

SF: All right. *[slowly walking, carrying his boots]* . . . actually runnin' now . . . *[continues to mumble under his breath]*

WR: You gonna put your shoes on?

SF: I'm savin' 'em in case my feet wear out . . . *[under his breath]* and then I'll have 'em . . . *[continues mumbling as he leaves scene]*

As Perry was establishing his fame, radio was developing as entertainment's new electronic frontier, with black characters quickly staking their claims. On October 11, 1924, only a few years after the medium's birth, WGBH in Massachusetts broadcast a performance of *Shuffle Along*. Written by Flournoy Miller and Aubrey Lyles, with music by Noble Sissle and Eubie Blake, the African American Broadway play had been a big hit when it premiered in 1921. Though the play's biggest song was fairly whitebread (the fox-trot "I'm Just Wild About Harry"), *Shuffle Along* unashamedly let its black minstrel roots show: the African American actors all wore blackface, two characters are named Uncle Tom and Old Black Joe, and there is even some

Lincoln Perry and Will Rogers in a publicity still from *Judge Priest* (1934).

"inside" humor (the song "If You Haven't Been Vamped by a Brownskin, You Haven't Been Vamped at All" is about skin-color politics in the black community).

Miller and Lyles had met at Fisk University in Nashville around 1906 and quickly found work with the revered Pekin Stock Company, at Chicago's Pekin Theater ("The Temple of Music"), considered the first legitimate African-American theater. They soon established themselves in New York and during the next decade created their own shows in Harlem and appeared on Broadway as performers. They also found success in Europe. Onstage the duo prospered by mastering a routine that was far from original. The foundation of most minstrel shows had been the comic interaction between Mr. Interlocutor, a polite straight man, and the two clownish endmen (often called Tambo and Bones) who delivered raucous punchlines. This trio was boiled down to the two-man comedy teams that became vaudeville fixtures (the most enduring being Abbott and Costello, who performed these routines intact through the 1950s). Miller and Lyles's version emphasized character and dexterous wordplay. *Shuffle Along* made it a sensation, with Miller's straight-man character Steve setting the table for Lyle's blustery, arrogant fool, Sam. In 1931 the duo would get their own radio show, but as far as they were concerned, by that point their influence on the medium had long been established. They were convinced that Sam and Steve had inspired two of radio's most prominent performers, Freeman Gosden and Charles Correll.

On January 26, 1926, WGN radio in Chicago broadcast the premiere fifteen-minute episode of *Sam 'n' Henry*, starring Gosden and Correll. The two white performers had worked low-level blackface minstrel circuits before the Joe Bren Company in Chicago teamed them as minstrel-show facilitators. Like hiring a karaoke deejay today, this company rented out professionals to help organizations stage amateur minstrel shows. Developing their own act, Gosden and Correll eventually were hired by WGN, where they developed a radio show about two rural blacks negotiating the big city. The show was a quick success. When they moved the program to rival Chicago station WMAQ a year later, they were legally required to rename their characters. They chose Amos and Andy.

Amos 'n' Andy was a staple of American radio until 1960, and a TV version appeared from 1951 to 1953. If Lincoln Perry personified minstrelsy for the twentieth century, *Amos 'n' Andy* literally became synonymous with it. When Amiri Baraka or Truman Capote or a critic at *Spin* reviewing a Dr. Dre album invokes the characters' names, they do so as a universally accepted substitute for "minstrelsy," "blackface," or "black minstrel tradition." If you type "Amos n Andy shit" into your computer's search engine, you will find dozens of bloggers using it as shorthand for any archaic negative black stereotype rearing its head in contemporary popular culture.

This can be credited in part to the show's ubiquity: it was so popular it virtually erased all prior blackface performers from public consciousness. *Amos 'n' Andy* was a national sensation (it moved to the nationwide NBC network in 1929) that shaped the future of American entertainment. It is credited as the first sitcom, the first original serial for radio, the first soap opera, and a pioneer in the medium for its use of recurring characters, storytelling techniques, and syndication (prior to joining NBC, Freeman and Gosden's "chainless chain" system had them recording episodes and distributing records of the shows to stations around the country). The radio encyclopedia *On the Air* calls it "perhaps the most popular radio show of all time." At its apex in the early 1930s, movie theaters would stop their programs from 7 to 7:15 P.M. and pipe in the show. An estimated audience of 40 million, one-third of the U.S. population, listened to it. The Sky Ride, the 600-foot tall central attraction at the 1933 Century of Progress Exposition, named its rocket cars after Amos 'n' Andy characters. There were Amos 'n' Andy candy bars, comic strips, records, cartoons, and toys. Their catch phrases "holy mackerel" and "I'se regusted" entered the American lexicon.

Miller and Lyles had concerns that *Amos 'n' Andy* ripped off their Sam character, drew on their comic innovations, or stole some of their catchphrases (over the decades Miller decreased his protests and he eventually worked for the show). But there were three distinct reasons the show resonated with the public, and they had little to do with the black minstrel tradition that had been faithfully revived in *Shuffle Along*.

The first was the way the show's narrative fit in with the national mood. Two black southerners, as part of the Great

Migration, end up in Chicago (later shows moved them to Harlem) where they start a lowly business by turning a scrap-heap convertible into the Fresh Air Taxicab Company. Hardworking, simple Amos (Gosden) is the driver, and arrogant, foolish Andrew (Correll) is the CEO. Through vivid descriptions and publicity photos, listeners knew that their clothes were ragged, their car was held together by ropes, and their pockets were empty. During the Great Depression, when every American suddenly believed they knew what it felt like to be a broke Negro, the appeal was universal.

Another aspect of *Amos 'n' Andy* that made it a sensation was its serial nature. The daily fifteen-minute format allowed it to drag out story lines and punctuate drama with cliffhangers. With the perils their business and livelihood faced from smarter and more ruthless rivals, the duplicitous nature of the popular character the Kingfish (a trickster lodge brother, voiced by Gosden), and tender-hearted Amos's lengthy and complicated courtship of Ruby, his middle-class girlfriend, there was plenty of drama to explore.

More important, despite Correll and Gosden drawing from their minstrel-show experience (with strained dialect and ridiculous malapropisms), the show's greatest strength defied the broad, loud, comic nature of classic burnt-cork theater. The program was surprisingly quiet, recorded without an audience and with few sound effects. Gosden and Correll did the show alone, occasionally playing supplemental characters, but more often referring to outside conversations, taking one-sided phone calls, or reading letters rather than introducing new voices. Instead of doing female impersonation, women were rarely featured on early shows. For the first seven years Amos' girlfriend-fiancée-wife Ruby Taylor was discussed but never appeared in an episode. And rather than relying on comic routines or punch lines, the show featured mostly gentle conversational humor. As NBC president Merlin H. Aylesworth put it, "these boys are different from any other comedians . . . they don't have any jokes." Summing up their comic style in an interview with *Psychology* magazine, Gosden concluded, "We don't wisecrack." These elements combined to make *Amos 'n' Andy* feel incredibly intimate, less like a flashy stage show and more like a conversation between two close friends. That intimacy may have been an important factor in helping many Americans become comfortable with inviting electronic media into their private living rooms for the first time. That they were not actually doing minstrel-show routines may explain why no other blackface duo radio show—not *Rufus and Rastus*, *Slo 'n' Ezy*, *Molasses 'n' January*, nor *Sugarfoot and Sassafras*—was a success.

However, the duo sometimes engaged in minstrel show/vaudeville banter during stand-alone episodes that existed outside of the narrative arc, and these were often quite racist. Arrogant Andy and simple Amos would take fifteen minutes to ineptly attempt simple arithmetic or read business correspondence. They fully played upon stereotypes of racial inferiority. But these routines were atypical. They are disproportionately represented in the few recordings that exist today because most of the surviving shows are "chainless chain" copies of the earliest episodes when the program had yet to establish its identity, or episodes after a 1943 format change, when *Amos 'n' Andy* took on a standard half-hour sitcom format, hiring outside writers (including Joe Connelly and Bob Mosher, who later created *Leave It to Beaver* and *The Munsters*) and a full supporting cast of black actors. It seems fair to say that rather than being an example of America's thirst for minstrelsy, the classic *Amos 'n' Andy* was a humorous serial that did not rely upon the minstrel tradition, but occasionally used it as a crutch (the show literally took this route during the 1936 season when one episode a week became Amos and Andy hosting an actual minstrel show, the pretense being that these were fundraisers for their lodge, the Mystic Knights of the Sea).

Despite the blackface roots of its creators and its use of comic dialect, the radio show seems to have been very popular with black listeners, the black press, and some black social critics and activists. At the 1931 Bud Billiken Day (the annual African American parade sponsored by the *Chicago Defender*), 35,000 Bronzeville residents cheered guests of honor Gosden and Correll. *Radio Digest* quoted a Harlem cop saying every radio on his beat was tuned to the show. When the black newspaper the *Pittsburgh Courier* launched a campaign against the program, its letters pages were filled with readers dismissing the protest, and other black papers, including the *Chicago Defender* and Seattle's *Northwest Enterprise*, jumped to the show's defense. A Chicago Urban League survey of prominent black professionals found widespread approval of it too. And civil rights activist Roy Wilkins, in a 1930 editorial defending the program, called it "clean fun from beginning to end." By presenting the complexity of Amos's love life, his noble aspirations, his vulnerabilities, and his heroic pursuit of the American dream, Gosden and Correll subverted decades of dehumanizing blackface practice: African Americans responded to these fake black folk because Amos Jones felt real. Like Bert Williams before him, Gosden subverted classic minstrelsy by making his rube a real character, not a regressive stereotype.

Not that the two actors deserve to be lionized as race men. It's certainly true that their press material had the actors posing with black fans, that they made public donations to black charities, and that Gosden's backstory of growing up with a black best friend panned out (the hard-to-believe tale of his family taking in a black orphan for ten years, and the boys spending their childhood doing minstrel routines for the family, was confirmed by Garrett Brown, the orphan in question). But they were hardly racially sensitive. For the entire run their show's theme music was Joseph Carl Breil's "The Perfect Song," the love theme from *The Birth of a Nation* (the TV version used a public domain soundalike). In a kinescope of Gosden introducing the black TV cast for the first time, he refers to actor Spencer Williams, several years his senior, as "boy." While this was standard show-people lingo for all men, regardless of age, certainly Gosden should have known how inappropriate it was to publicly refer to a black man this way (a 1932 script he wrote even had his partner declare, "I don't want nobody callin' me boy. My name is Andrew H. Brown!"). And there is the problematic use of blackface and dialect. Correll was wary of burnt cork, explaining, "in blacking up you become a minstrel, you're not a normal human being." That said, the actors appeared in publicity photos and stage shows in blackface until 1933, including their 1930 feature film *Check and Double Check*, where their pitch-black visages were grotesque in scenes among real African Americans, especially when contrasted with their dignified costar, Duke Ellington.

If hearsay is to be believed, Gosden and Correll reconsidered their position on burnt cork in 1951 when presented with the opportunity to adapt the radio show to TV. Veteran producer Fred De Cordova claims he directed a secret pilot with them in blackface but was instructed to burn the only copy when it was decided to go another direction. Instead, with the help of Flournoy Miller, the duo assembled a black cast, drawing supporting characters from their radio sitcom cast, and engaged in a nationwide search for the new leads, resulting in the hiring of Tim Moore, Spencer Williams, and Alvin Childress.

Tim Moore was born in 1887 in Rock Island, Illinois, and became enamored with entertainment as a child, spending his adolescence on the medicine show and vaudeville circuits, including a stint touring the world as a member of vaudeville act Cora Miskel and Her Gold Dust Twins. After brief sojourns as a jockey and a boxer, he returned to the stage, and by 1908 he was performing blackface comedy routines with the revered Rabbit's Foot Minstrels.

Moore was soon producing and performing in shows on the black vaudeville circuit, working with troupes like the Georgia Sunflowers, Stovall & Mack's Merrymakers, and his own Chicago Follies Company. He sometimes worked as a duo with his wife Hester (and later his second wife Gertie). In the wake of the success of *Shuffle Along*, black shows on Broadway flourished in the 1920s, and Moore was lured to New York, where he starred in numerous productions, including *Blackbirds of 1928* with Bill "Bojangles" Robinson, *Blackberries of 1932* with Mantan Moreland, and the 1931 revue *Fast and Furious*, which also featured Dusty Fletcher, Jackie (later "Moms") Mabley, Etta Moten (for whom George Gershwin had written the female lead in *Porgy and Bess*), Afro–Puerto Rican radio and film star Juano Hernández, and author-anthropologist Zora Neale Hurston (Hurston wrote four scenes for the play, including "Football Game," starring Hurston and Mabley as cheerleaders). *Fast and Furious* also featured an interpretation of *Macbeth* with Moore in the title role and Mabley as Lady Macbeth. During this period he also appeared (not in blackface) in Oscar Micheaux's 1931 film *Darktown Revue*.

After black-cast stage productions lost their mainstream audiences in the mid-1930s, Moore remained a fixture in New

York, appearing regularly at Harlem's Apollo Theater until the mid-1940s. He returned downtown in 1942 for Broadway's nostalgic vaudeville revival *Harlem Cavalcade*, produced by Ed Sullivan and co-starring Noble Sissle and Flournoy Miller. In 1947, Moore played the title role (in grotesque drag) in the low-budget race movie *Boy! What a Girl!* He then went into a brief retirement before being cast in the role that would define his legacy: the conniving Kingfish on *Amos 'n' Andy*, a character whose mannerisms he would adopt in public and promotional appearances until his death from tuberculosis in 1958.

Were it not for the eclipsing shadow of prolific black film pioneer Oscar Micheaux, Spencer Williams would likely be championed as the greatest hero of early African-American cinema. Williams was born in Vidalia, Louisiana, around 1893, and is believed to have spent time in New York City as a teen, working as a callboy for Oscar Hammerstein and receiving mentorship from Bert Williams. He fought in World War I and in the twenties relocated to Hollywood, where he worked as a sound technician on films. In 1928 he was hired to work on some of the first black talkies for the Christie Film Company's adaptations of Octavus Roy Cohen's dialect stories. Williams did continuity, some writing, and acted in these shorts, and press releases sent to black newspapers noted him as consultant on the dialect used in these films. As familiar with all aspects of Hollywood production as any black person could be at the time, contemporaries remember Williams opening a nightclub that he used as a base to conduct classes for black actors and to mentor other ambitious African Americans.

Williams continued to work as a screenwriter, actor, and consultant on B-pictures throughout the 1930s, including a series of black westerns in which he appeared (one of which, 1939's *Harlem Rides the Range*, he cowrote with Flournoy

Miller). He also wrote and starred in the first black-cast monster movie, 1940's *Son of Ingagi*.

In 1941, Williams relocated to Texas, where he partnered with a Jewish film distributor, Alfred Sack, to create content for the segregated black theaters and alternative exhibition spaces that made up the race film circuit. Williams wrote, directed, starred in, and helped produce a series of nine low-budget black-cast features that included three religious films (one of which was his masterpiece, *Blood of Jesus*), three dramas, two comedies, and a patriotic war picture. Though these films feel like the work of an independent outsider, it was his early experience as a marginal Hollywood insider that gave Williams the know-how to efficiently complete so many one-take wonders.

Williams likely had little experience on chitlin'-circuit stages, but he had no trouble orchestrating the raucous specialty numbers or coaxing solid low-comedy performances from amateur actors. His great ear and excellent sense of comedic and dramatic timing allowed him to master Miller and Lyles–style cadence, as in his comedy *Juke Joint*. He defied minstrel stereotypes not only in *Blood of Jesus*, but in *Dirty Gertie from Harlem U.S.A.* There he appears as a voodoo woman, mustache intact, recalling some grotesque minstrel-show drag costumes, but plays it completely straight, and is so frighteningly intense that there is nothing comic or absurd in the performance. "He was so convincing," Francine Everett, who played Gertie, recalled. "I didn't realize he had a mustache while I was making it."

With postwar integration hastening the decline of the race film industry, in the late forties Williams opened a vocational school in Tulsa, Oklahoma, and that's where he was when his former coworker Flournoy Miller tracked him down to offer him the Andy Brown role.

Alvin Childress had a less historic career than Moore or Williams, but he was taking a less important role. Though Amos was the heart of the radio show in the 1930s, following the show's 1943 shift to sitcom hijinks, a responsible, honest family man lost value, and scripts focused solely on the ridiculous Kingfish and Andy. Childress had been a stage actor in New York, most notably with the American Negro Theater, and was featured in a number of productions in the 1930s and '40s (including *Ham's Daughter* with Lorenzo Tucker, and the original production of *Anna Lucasta*). He also appeared in a few race films. Childress had little experience with the musical/variety/vaudeville–inspired plays Moore starred in, and he wasn't a comic actor, but in the *Amos 'n' Andy Show* he wasn't required to be. The dynamic of Kingfish as trickster and Andy as rube meant that the Amos character was reduced to sometimes narrator, occasional (and ignored) voice of reason, and frequent savior when schemes went awry.

The Amos 'n' Andy Show premiered on June 28, 1951. It was not television's first black show. A group of four black actors, including Ethel Waters and future Apollo Theater emcee Willie Bryant, had been featured on an early experimental broadcast of scenes from the play *Mamba's Daughters* in 1939; *Uptown Jubilee*, a black variety show hosted by Bryant, aired five times in 1949; and in 1950, Hazel Scott, the brilliant pianist who was married to Congressman Adam Clayton Powell, Jr., tickled ivories on her fifteen-minute show for a few months before being blacklisted by Joseph McCarthy. Also in 1950, ABC premiered *Beulah*, an adaptation of a radio show in which a black maid spins her magic to save a helpless white family (Beulah was originally played by a white man on the radio, but was played on TV by the rotating all-star cast of Ethel Waters, Hattie McDaniel, and Louise Beavers). But *Amos 'n' Andy* was the first network series with an all black-cast. And, with its brilliant performers and good writers (including Correll, Gosden, Connelly, Mosher, Bob Ross, who later worked on *The Andy Griffith Show*, and legendary screenwriter Hal Kanter) it was one of the funniest shows the young medium had yet seen.

Amos 'n' Andy adapted the loud, wacky, full-cast sitcom format the radio show switched to in 1943 and bore little resemblance to the sensitive serial episodes of the show's artistic peak. It was a broad, raucous comedy about the outrageous hustler Kingfish trying to get the best of easily duped Andy, usually involving a preposterous con job. One typical episode has Kingfish opening a letter addressed to Andy from a coin dealer revealing that his lodge brother is in possession of a rare nickel worth $250. Kingfish determines to "preform a nickelectomy" by wearing a ridiculous doctor's costume, decorating his office as a medical lab, and convincing Andy that he recently completed a correspondence course in "doctorin'." The faux-physician has his new patient take off his pants and put on a blindfold. Then he steals the coin from Andy's pocket. By the time Andy gets wise, Kingfish has already mistakenly used the nickel in a drugstore payphone attempting to call the coin dealer. Kingfish then persuades Andy to pry the phone from the wall, and the ensuing elaborate slapstick is only halted when a black plainclothes detective arrests them. In court their shyster lawyer Calhoun makes a quick exit after realizing the black judge hearing the case disbarred him several years earlier, and the duo is about to plead "slightly guilty" when Amos comes in and explains the situation. The judge determines that there was "more stupidity involved here than criminal intent" and releases the defendants with a threat of harsh punishment if they are ever caught tampering with another pay phone. In the court hallway Andy immediately attempts to call the coin dealer, depositing the coveted nickel, which angers Kingfish who storms off. A broadly smiling Andy then tells the operator he dialed a wrong number and triumphantly has his nickel returned.

Williams, Moore, and the talented cast expertly brought nonsensical narratives like this one to life, building upon the legacy of the characters' creators. Though Correll and Gosden were initially very involved with the show, their influence diminished after Gosden and Spencer Williams feuded over the portrayal of Andy Brown. "We couldn't come together on this use of dialect," Williams later told *Ebony*. "[Gosden] wanted me to say 'dis here and dat dere' and I just wasn't going to do it. He said he ought to know how *Amos 'n' Andy* should talk [but] I told him I *ought* to know how Negroes talk. After all, I've been one all my life."

Years after Jackie Robinson had made his Major League Baseball debut with the Brooklyn Dodgers, and President Truman had given the executive order to desegregate the Armed Forces, Americans on both sides of the integration issue were well aware that this progress signaled the dawn of a new era. Thus, 1951 was an inopportune time to launch a high-profile program based on the work of blackface minstrels, and *Amos 'n' Andy*'s minstrel roots would be quite evident. Facial expressions were exaggerated, jokes were stagey and loud, and despite Williams's dispute with Correll (who never returned to the set), the minstrel dialect was detectable, especially in the stilted southern speech of vaudeville veteran Moore. His malapropisms were ridiculous: "Everything's legiterate." "Not only do I deny the allegation, but I resent the allegator." "I gon 'splain it to you . . . fust the atom splits into what dey call the monocle, and den the monocle busts and breaks down into what dey call neutron, po'tron, fig newtons and mo'rons."

Of course, being an Atomic Age minstrel show, some adjustments were made. The most significant tweaks for television (beyond the reduced dialect) were in the décor and attire. Nick Stewart (who brought his Stepin Fetchit impression to the show, playing the perpetually confounded janitor Lightnin') recalled that in addition to butting heads over dialect, Williams insisted that everything be clean and sharp. Amos himself was a complete overhaul from the 1930s, speaking with less dialect, dressing in a proper taxi uniform (in contrast to the raggedy attire seen in radio promo photos), driving a pristine taxi (as opposed to the jalopy), and living in a lovely home with a perfect family. He was unquestionably intelligent and thoroughly respectable. While Amos was confused by simple arithmetic on early radio episodes, on television he calmly assists his befuddled buddies with their income taxes. In another episode, appearing on behalf of his ne'er-do-well associates at one of their many court appearances, a black judge praises Amos, calling him "one of our prize citizens."

That black judge typified another noteworthy development. While the radio show focused on the class contrast between Amos and Andy's situation and Ruby's black middle-class family, the TV show exclusively displays the black middle and upper classes and featured scores of dignified black professionals as secondary and tertiary characters. In this TV Harlem, blacks worked in law (as judges, lawyers, process servers), law enforcement (as police officers, police lieutenants, federal agents), government (a highway commissioner, IRS agents), banking, hotel management, medicine, journalism, and business. Their dignity, wealth, and taste apparently trickle down, as every home in Harlem is beautiful, with nice furniture, art, and décor. Deadbeat Kingfish has as roomy and classy an apartment as upstanding Amos, and he and Andy suffered from thoroughly middle-class problems, woes that most African Americans could only dream of: securing family inheritances, flipping large parcels of real estate, and dealing with uranium investments. Even jokes about being broke managed to be bourgeois: poor Kingfish couldn't afford to buy his wife both a fur coat *and* a fancy dress to attend a society function.

But to the show's critics the bad outweighed the positive. Kingfish's ridiculous dialect, dishonesty, and joblessness did not jibe with the political climate. Slow-witted Lightnin' was doing a routine a decade past its expiration date, and in Kingfish's shrewish, loud wife (played by Ernestine Wade) a negative black stereotype was being perfected and given an enduring name to sign alongside Sambo's, Tom's and Zip's: Sapphire. The NAACP (which had made only mild protests during the radio reign, such as quietly urging the show in 1931 to amend a storyline implying northern tourist camps were segregated) was advocating cancellation before the premiere. At the NAACP's 1951 national convention, the delegates unanimously approved a resolution condemning the show and began organizing protests aimed at its sponsor. For the next two years Executive Secretary Walter White worked to recruit allies in this fight to pressure CBS and the show's sponsor, Blatz Beer, to end the production. NAACP officer and future executive director Roy Wilkins (two decades removed from lauding the radio *Amos 'n' Andy*'s "universal appeal," and who still admitted that the radio show, "while objectionable did have some very human elements to it") damned the sitcom as "pure burlesque" and feared the power of the new medium. "The visual impact is infinitely worse than the radio version. . . . To millions of white children, who are learning about life, this is the way Negroes are."

These critics may not have been in the majority. Editorials

and letters in the black press, a great deal of anecdotal evidence, and one scientific poll suggest that not all black Americans shared the NAACP's position (only 18 percent according to Advertest Research, as opposed to 80.8 percent supporting the show). Many blacks simply liked seeing blacks on TV and found the show funny. When Moore and Williams were at their best, the show was, and still is, funny, even to racially sensitive eyes. "One of my favorite pastimes," scholar Henry Louis Gates wrote in 1989, "is screening episodes of *Amos 'n' Andy* for black friends who think that the series was both socially offensive and politically detrimental. After a few minutes, even hardliners have difficulty restraining their laughter. 'It's still racist,' is one typical comment, 'but it was funny.'" It was also no more cartoonish than its competition. The Kingfish was as realistic as *The Honeymooners*'s Ralph Kramden or *I Love Lucy*'s Ricky Ricardo.

The improvements Spencer Williams implemented may have made things worse in the eyes of the show's middle-class critics. "Tidy scenery and tidy characters on the video screen," wrote Melvin Ely in his history of the show, *The Adventures of Amos 'n' Andy*, "made it more difficult for the middle class black viewer to indulge in a comforting response—writing off the character's foibles as products of lower class origins." One fascinating theme emerges from the NAACP's memos and letters written against the series. The character that most offended NAACP members was not the no-good Kingfish, who used the minstrel-show antics Tim Moore learned in 1900, nor was it Lightnin', channeling Stepin Fetchit circa 1929. The villain was Johnny Lee's crooked lawyer character Algonquin J. Calhoun. The show's greatest crime was that (to quote an NAACP executive) "the Negro lawyer is portrayed in a most unfavorable, professional light." In a letter to NAACP members, Gloster Current, the director of branches, wrote that on the show lawyers were shown to be "slippery cowards, ignorant of their profession and without ethics." That it was only Calhoun, and not the many dignified lawyers who appeared as secondary characters, that fit these descriptions was moot. Black professionals simply would not tolerate their caste being maligned on the only black show on television.

Whether the protests were effective is difficult to determine. Sponsors may have felt some heat (after *Amos 'n' Andy* no network show with a black lead found a steady sponsor for over a decade), but it seems like a myth to say the NAACP got *Amos 'n' Andy* canceled. The show was a modest commercial and critical success in its first season, ranking number thirteen in the ratings. But in its second season an unwise scheduling decision typical of early TV damned it to low ratings (it ran biweekly, alternating with an anthology show). While CBS officially stated, "The network has bowed to the change in national thinking," the show was likely taken off the air as much for lackluster performance as it was due to the NAACP's campaign. Also, cancellation neither ended production nor got the show off the air. More episodes were filmed to put together a syndication package, and as reruns played on over 200 stations, the show was seen by far more people than in its initial run. A subsequent NAACP campaign finally got the show removed from syndication, but not until 1966.

Despite the NAACP's agenda, which perhaps erred on the side of middle-class defensiveness, and despite the incredible talent showcased on the program, ultimately demands for *Amos 'n' Andy*'s cancellation seem appropriate. As brilliant as Moore was, he was so much a product of the nineteenth-century minstrel shows he was weaned on, and the early twentieth-century medicine tent and black vaudeville circuits that followed, that he simply should not have been on television at the dawn of the civil rights era. The best example may be the most warmly remembered episode of the series, "The Christmas Story," a television update of a perennial radio favorite.

Starting in 1940, the *Amos 'n' Andy* radio show began a tradition of having Amos recite the Lord's Prayer to his daughter Arbadella as a bedtime story, simplifying the traditional language, using subdued dialect (" 'Thy Kingdom come, thy will be done, in Earth as it is in Heaven.' That means, darlin', as we clean our hearts of all hate an' selfishness an' fill our hearts with love, the good, the true an' the beautiful, then this earth where we are now, will be jus' like Heaven"). This prayer resonated with listeners, and was re-created by the television cast in 1952, the recitation becoming Alvin Childress' favorite moment of the show (and a rare showcase for the actor). The entire episode takes on a different tone than usual, with Andy becoming a three-dimensional person genuinely distressed about not having enough money to buy Arbadella the doll he promised her (a black baby doll from an upscale, all-black department store). Although the episode features some of Williams's best comic work on the series as the store's flustered Santa Claus, the general mood of the show is sober and weighty. Even the coon character Lightnin' has a serious conversation, contributing to Andy's melancholy by injecting joke-free pessimism. But Moore, the over-the-top, cartoonish relic, was incapable of dialing it down, and his character is only seen in a two-minute clownish cameo, independent of the plot, and incongruous with the episode's tone. If his shenanigans couldn't even be incorporated into a serving of earnest schmaltz, how could they possibly be aired alongside news of legal challenges to the Topeka school segregation policies, or the Cicero, Illinois, race riot where over 600 National Guardsmen and policemen had to protect a single black family from thousands of violent whites? Tim Moore was a man from another era, and though he stands as one of television's first comic greats, his big break came at a terrible time for such antics.

After the show's cancellation, the cast tried to make money touring in character, but CBS threatened to get an injunction against them, further embittering the actors, as they felt that they were the only victims of the NAACP's protest (television was too young to have worked out reasonable residual deals, so the lucrative reruns yielded them little money). Moore and Williams returned to retirement, and Childress kept plugging away, making occasional cameos on black-cast sitcoms until his death (he presided over two weddings on *Sanford and Son*). Gosden and Correll remained on the radio until 1960, playing records between banter for the last six years on *The Amos 'n' Andy Music Hall*. Hurt by the protests that surrounded the television show, they retreated from the public, rarely giving interviews. They made one last attempt at a minstrel revival in 1961 by revamping routines from the *Amos 'n' Andy* sitcom on a short-lived prime-time cartoon, *Calvin and the Colonel*. The implied inhumanity of blackface was removed because here the dialect voices emanated from a bear and a fox.

Amos 'n' Andy was a TV show that was very funny, but when it debuted was a time to get serious. And the show's gifted performers were superb students of the black minstrel tradition, but they unfortunately were showcasing that scholarship during a decade when that tradition undermined their chances for success. Perhaps the last word on the subject should be given to the man who spent the better part of the subsequent half-century moving black representation on television away from Andy Brown's confoundedness and Kingfish's coonery.

On a 1971 episode of the *Dick Cavett Show*, Bill Cosby was asked to share his thoughts about *Amos 'n' Andy.* The comic reflected at length on race relations in America, and the role of entertainment in influencing opinion, concluding, "I liked *Amos 'n' Andy.* I did not see them as ignorant blacks. But see that's a different way that we accept certain things. I mean there's different routines that I can tell on a stage to an all black audience that I cannot tell on television, wouldn't allow it, because there are some white people who would laugh at it, '*Yeah*, that's them, and that's why they ain't gonna get the so far from the so on.'

"So [the show] *had* to be taken off," Cosby continued, "although I enjoyed it. In the confines of my own home I might say [*in dialect voice*] 'Yeah, Brutha Andy,' we might do the so forth and the so on. But we don't want the white people laughing at it."

Jimmie Walker as J.J. Evans on *Good Times*.

CBS/PHOTOFEST.

6.

DYN-O-MITE

How Cosby Blew Up Black Minstrelsy, and J.J. Put It Back Together

THE FAILURE OF *The Amos 'n' Andy Show*, and the perception that the NAACP was poised to pounce upon any negative representations of African Americans, forced television to recognize that it had a "Negro Problem." Over the next sixty years the medium sometimes addressed the issue, but never for long, as minstrelsy revivals either snuck in the back door of well-meaning programming or presented themselves so shamelessly and loudly that protests could hardly be heard over the noise. Television networks, during the brief minstrelsy dry spells, alternately ignored or addressed the supposedly shameful fruits of the black minstrel traditions, either keeping black faces off the air or putting only the most dignified ones in front of a camera. But time and time again, black minstrelsy proved too powerful (and commercial) a legacy to deny, and decade after decade critics have found themselves dusting off shopworn accusations of coonery and buffoonery.

In the immediate wake of *Amos 'n' Andy*'s demise, TV's initial reaction was to go cold turkey. There were no narrative television series with black leads during the subsequent dozen television seasons (*Beulah* had been canceled in 1952). Which isn't to say that black faces disappeared from TV screens. Viewers were thrilled by history's greatest baseball players (by 1959 all teams had integrated), and rattled by powerful news footage of the demonstrations, speeches, and riots associated with struggles for civil rights. On sitcoms African American characters still appeared, but they were pushed to the margins, playing maids, handymen, and valets to white leads. Hollywood veterans like Stepin Fetchit clone Willie Best (on *My Little Margie* and *Trouble with Father*) and *Amos 'n' Andy* alums Lillian and Amanda Randolph (on *The Great Gildersleeve* and *Make Room for Daddy*, respectively) found steady, if not always dignified, work. Of the many performers occupying these updated house-slave roles, the only one who regularly demonstrated agency or enjoyed significant story lines was Eddie Anderson. During the lengthy, sporadically scheduled run of *The Jack Benny Show* (1950–1965), Anderson played Benny's sidekick Rochester, a role he'd held since joining Benny's radio show in 1937. Despite an affected vocal style that would have been cringe-worthy from a white minstrel's painted lips, Anderson was presented as an equal and a friend of Benny, more often than not getting the upper hand through cleverness.

In addition to the opportunities for black comics, there were a handful of one-shot black-cast episodes of dramatic anthology series, featuring stars like Sidney Poitier, Harry Belafonte, and Ethel Waters. Some of these specials, like the nineteenth-century elocutionists, opera singers, and serious Shakespeareans whose careers paralleled and intersected with classic minstrel shows, challenged absurd sitcom stereotypes by presenting dignified, well-acted classics (William Marshall as *Othello*, Ossie Davis as *The Emperor Jones*). As the sixties dawned, black actors occasionally had guest appearances on drama series when current events suggested racial or social issues as plot devices.

One network series with a black lead debuted in this era. *The Nat "King" Cole Show* faced two serious problems during its troubled eleven-month run in 1956 and 1957. The first was that some southern affiliates refused to air a black show, even a nonnarrative musical showcase. The second was that despite being very popular in large urban markets, the show's overall ratings were fairly dismal. Cole, a sophisticated, charismatic crooner, and his guest stars (Belafonte, Ella Fitzgerald, Mel Tormé, Tony Bennett) were hawking too highbrow a product to the lumpen masses. In a year when audiences were either worked up by Elvis on variety shows, or pleasantly lulled by Snooky Lanson's bland ballads on *Your Hit Parade*, the elegance and maturity of Cole's show fell flat. It probably didn't help that Cole was a black artist who broke the mold of minstrel- and vaudeville-trained performers, never courting audiences with manic tap dancing, broad comedy, or wild singing. Despite NBC offering huge advertising discounts, the fears of southern boycotts and the low ratings left the show sponsor-free and Cole bitter. Certain that advertising agencies could have tried harder or been more creative finding sponsors, he put the blame on them. "I was the Jackie Robinson of television," he wrote in *Ebony*. "After a trailblazing year that shattered all the old bugaboos about Negroes on TV, I found myself standing there with the bat on my shoulder. The men who dictate what Americans see and hear didn't want to play ball. [Madison Avenue] still thinks it's a white man's world. . . . They control TV. They govern the tastes of the people."

Despite the failure to get black-cast shows on the air, as Cole explained, variety shows continued to "scramble all over each other to sign Negro guest stars to help boost the ratings of white stars." Eventually the aspect of black minstrelsy most often revived on American television would be the dominant one: comedy. But during the mid-fifties through the mid-sixties the variety sections of minstrelsy and black vaudeville were showcased. The exciting dance routines of yore were updated by acts like the Treniers and the Nicholas Brothers. "Authentic" Negro folk music and spirituals were represented by acts like Bo Diddley and Mahalia Jackson. And the Motown artists' sophisticated blend of black and white popular music traditions may have been the most interesting musical miscegenation since nineteenth-century minstrel shows.

But by the mid-sixties, with the March on Washington, the Civil Rights Act, and Malcolm X's assassination in the rearview mirror, several liberal-minded producers were ready to fill Beulah's and Kingfish's long vacant positions with a new, improved Negro. Turning to a model being perfected in cinema by Sidney Poitier, they decided to go beyond mere mortals, and introduce Super Negroes. And despite it being his first acting gig, the man that producer Sheldon Leonard chose to fill this role first would emerge as the most active crusader for black dignity in the medium's history. William H. Cosby Jr., would dedicate the next four decades to muffling the echo of *Amos 'n' Andy*.

On 1965's *I Spy*, Bill Cosby was cast as Alexander Scott, an American secret agent posing as the trainer of Robert Culp's character Kelly Robinson, a Caucasian spy posing as a professional tennis player. Cosby fit the role for several reasons. The youthful comic had an athlete's build. He was an accomplished college jock, who broke into comedy by spending his summers working New York clubs before returning to the athletic fields of Temple University in his native Philadelphia. He was also ideal because he had developed a stage persona and material that white audiences found to be race-neutral, leading to successful appearances on *The Tonight Show* and *Ed Sullivan*. With his clean-cut good looks, comforting personality, and dignified demeanor, Cosby's Scott was the prototype for African American television characters for the rest of the decade. A black teacher on *Room 222*, a black electronics expert and super spy on *Mission: Impossible*, and most strikingly, a glamorous nurse looking like a black Barbie doll come to life on *Julia*, all avoided any charges of stereotypes, minstrelsy, or negative imagery by being flawless beings with perfect English, perfect posture, and perfect relationships with white coworkers. This frictionless integration of foible-free Super Negroes was promised to last for centuries, as foretold by the presence of *Star Trek*'s gorgeous black lieutenant, Nyota Uhura. Describing his motivations for presenting these paragons, and taking responsibility for an earlier gig, *Julia*'s producer-writer Hal Kanter explained, "I really owed to my black colleagues some sort of apology for a lot of things we had done on *Amos 'n' Andy*."

Cosby, as the first black lead of a nationally televised drama series, shouldered the weight of establishing TV's Sepia Superman prototype. Though some attribute it to his being a novice actor, Cosby wisely played Scott as somewhat stone-faced, putting aside his comedy background to avoid any inference of clownishness. Though he rarely jokes around on the show, the magnetic charm and likability he developed on stand-up stages served him well. The show also made it clear from its first scene that the Cold War trumped the race war, and Scott was an Afro-American who put American before Afro. The premiere opens with Scott shaking his head in disgust as he watches a film of Elroy Brown (Ivan Dixon), an Olympic star, invoking slavery as he denounces America, exhibiting the arrogance and defiance many Americans associated with Muhammad Ali, who had recently made his embrace of the Nation of Islam public (this was three years before Tommie Smith and John Carlos's defiant Black Power salute on the Olympics medal stand). Producer Leonard insisted "race was not a factor" in casting Cosby, and that even with a black lead the show "had more sponsors than we need." It still seems significant that the initial appearance of TV's first black hero shows him denigrating an "uppity" African American.

Overall, however, Cosby's character was not overwhelmingly compromised. While Poitier's cinematic Super Negro sacrifices himself to help white nuns, white blind girls, and white students, Scott and Robinson are on equal footing, alternately rescuing each other, and occasionally trading blows. And though the international spy scenario conveniently meant that Cosby would never knock around white Americans, the fact that so many of the Asians on the show were Caucasian actors in makeup meant TV's first black hero got to frequently beat up whites (albeit ones in "yellow face").

The show was a moderate success in the ratings, and Cosby became an instant TV icon, beating out costar Culp to win the Emmy for Outstanding Lead Actor in a Drama Series for all three seasons of *I Spy*. Over the next forty years Cosby was able to do whatever he wanted on television, exerting behind-the-camera creative force to craft black characters whose dignity, morals, and at times wealth deliberately countered TV and film representations he found objectionable. He starred in over a dozen series, including numerous sitcoms, four kids' shows, two variety shows, revivals of Groucho's *You Bet Your Life* and Art Linkletter's *Kids Say the Darnedest Things*, and countless specials.

Cosby's follow up to *I Spy* was *The Bill Cosby Show* (1969–71), a sitcom about Chet Kincaid, a thoughtful gym teacher at an integrated urban high school. The show's first scene has Kincaid jogging in a college sweatshirt, so that before a line of dialogue is spoken he is already established as the antithesis of

Stepin Fetchit: speedy and educated. But as his aforementioned quote about *Amos 'n' Andy* illustrates, Cosby has mixed feelings about the complicated legacy of minstrelsy. In one episode, Kincaid is ashamed of his elderly relatives, played by black vaudeville veterans Moms Mabley and Mantan Moreland, in full chitlin'-circuit glory. Ultimately he realizes that his embarrassment over their old-fashioned ways, loud comical bickering, and love of hog jowls is more his problem than theirs.

His biggest hit of the 1970s was the children's cartoon *Fat Albert and the Cosby Kids*, based on his stand-up routines about his youth. This show also made some nods to Cosby's covert respect for his comedy ancestors. *Fat Albert* featured a junkyard clubhouse and scrap-iron inventions that recall Amos's makeshift jalopy. And though he is balanced against Cosby's dignified cartoon version of himself as a child, the character Mushmouth (also voiced by Cosby) not only speaks in a variation of Lincoln Perry's "audible pantomime," but his name was borrowed from a minstrel character from the popular 1920s comic strip *Moon Mullins*. The cartoon also echoed blackface by having some black characters voiced by whites in an awkward approximation of urban dialect. That, however, was an issue of thrift, not minstrelsy—the cartoon was so low-budget that Lou Scheimer, the Caucasian head of the notoriously cheap Filmation studio, had his wife, child, and himself record supporting characters' voices.

But Cosby's grandest success came in 1984 with the debut of *The Cosby Show*. Playing Cliff Huxtable, the patriarch of an intact, upper-middle-class, African American family, Cosby had a showcase for his well-developed improvisational skills. Playfully flirting with his wife, lovingly (yet gruffly) keeping his children in line, and reminiscing with his parents, Cosby was able to use his jazzy verbal flow to create an original character.

Cliff Huxtable not only defied the two-dimensional black figures usually seen on screen, but also challenged the schmaltzy sentimentalism of most domestic sitcoms, as demonstrated in this scene where Cosby confronts his son Theo (played by Malcolm-Jamal Warner) over falling grades:

MW: Dad, I thought about what you said and I see your point.

BC: Thank you, thank you.

MW: But I have a point, too.

BC: Make your point.

MW: You're a doctor and mom's a lawyer, and you're both successful and everything, and that's great. But maybe I was born to be a regular person and have a regular life. If you weren't a doctor I wouldn't love you less, because you're my dad. And so instead of acting disappointed because I'm not like you, maybe you can just accept who I am and love me anyway . . . because I'm your son. *(studio audience applauds)*

BC: Theo . . . *that's the dumbest thing I've ever heard in my life!* No wonder you get D's in everything! Now you are afraid to try because you're afraid that your brain is going to explode and it's going to ooze out of your ears. Now I'm telling you, *you are going to try as hard as you can!* And you are going to do it *because I said so!* I am your father. I brought you in this world and I'll take you out.

The Cosby Show is one of the most popular series in television history. The top-rated show for five consecutive seasons (*All in the Family* and *American Idol* are the only other series to achieve this), it only finished below the top five in its eighth, and final, season. But with that triumph of black bourgeois broadcasting came criticism. Scholar Henry Louis Gates Jr. argued that this Reagan-era vision of black wealth "reassuringly throws the blame for black poverty on the impoverished." And others, reacting to Cosby's long track record of comedy and characters that white audiences found nonthreatening, were harsher. *The Village Voice* said Cosby "no longer qualifies as black enough to be an Uncle Tom," and *New York* magazine dismissed the show as "*Leave It to Beaver* in Blackface." Years later, after Cosby improvised a harsh diatribe about the state of black youth at a 2004 NAACP ceremony (known as "the pound cake speech," because after creating a scenario where police shoot a black child who stole some pound cake, Cosby places the blame on the child and his family, not the police), Michael Eric Dyson wrote the book *Is Bill Cosby Right? (Or Has the Black Middle Class Lost Its Mind?)*. Dyson impressively countered Cosby's conservative contentions, less impressively attacked Cosby personally (using *National Enquirer* stories as evidence), and boldly contended that throughout his lengthy career, the comic had "avoided race with religious zeal."

To argue that Bill Cosby's comedy is nonracial or to paint him as an Uncle Tom figure appeasing white audiences is to ignore the history and essence of his act. Though it is hard to imagine that in the 1960s doing racially charged political humor could be the cowardly route, when Cosby began doing stand-up, the influence of Dick Gregory and Lenny Bruce created an atmosphere in which a black comic could get easy laughs just by mentioning race. His earliest comedy conformed to those expectations. When he made a decision to focus on broadly appealing storytelling, he was challenging, rather than selling out to, white expectations. More important, regardless of content, Cosby's stage persona (a hip raconteur and oral historian with a trickster streak) fits squarely into African American performance traditions. Furthermore, he certainly saw his cool, rhythmic improvisations as a response to the black jazz music he revered, his verbal construction and nonsense word punctuations combining aspects of scat singing and Max Roach's drumming rhythm. Cosby's comedy was always markedly African American.

As far as avoiding racial topics, that also seems false. Cosby always discussed race in interviews, even if it was to explain why he didn't make it central to his performances. "Negro groups like the Deacons or the Muslims," he told *Ebony* in 1965, "all are dedicated to the cause of civil rights, but they do their job in their own way. My way is to show white people that Negroes are human beings with the same aspirations and abilities that whites have." If he wanted to avoid race, he would not have hosted the 1968 special that castigated Lincoln Perry, on which Cosby seems to simmer with contempt as he discusses the history of racism in America. Though he didn't write the script, his dire tone and embrace of the show's sometimes radical content (it ends with footage of a black separatist preschool indoctrinating children with Black Power philosophy) argues against his actively avoiding racial issues. (Ironically, the writer who won an Emmy for that show was Andy Rooney, who would be suspended from his *60 Minutes* commentator job in 1989 for racist rhetoric.) More jarring was a 1971 TV special, *Bill Cosby on Prejudice*, featuring Cosby sitting in an empty studio, improvising offensive insults for every race or religion he can think of, illustrating the senselessness of prejudice with overkill ("Niggers is a pain in the neck, too," he grumbles between cigar puffs). Though the powerful show (which had a second life in high school classrooms) is primarily focused on its message and Cosby's jazzy comic improvisations, its most memorable element may be the minimalist costume: Cosby's eyes and nose are surrounded by stylized whiteface makeup, exploiting the discomfort contemporary audiences feel when faced with blackface.

Though the characters he portrayed in movies and television rarely confronted overt racism or voiced didactic black pride lessons, his countermeasure to *Amos 'n' Andy* buffoonery went beyond instilling stoic "Super Negro" dignity. Afrocentric work by Varnette Honeywood and other artists and black-themed books fill both Chet Kincaid's and Cliff Huxtable's homes. Posters of black icons like Miles Davis and Frederick Douglass are seen on the Huxtables' walls, along with an anti-apartheid sticker that NBC unsuccessfully tried to get Cosby to remove. Appearances by numerous black Hollywood and jazz veterans on *The Bill Cosby Show* and *The Cosby Show* functioned as tributes and history lessons about African American cultural heroes.

Ultimately, most of Cosby's TV work was about black pride, even when racial subjects were not central to the plots. The underlying themes of most of his creations were uplift and positive modeling, traditional hallmarks of social activists who challenge the stereotypes and foolishness of the black minstrel tradition. Thus, it was ironic that his 1960s television trailblazing would lead to the floodgates of mass-market minstrelsy opening so wide that only his tremendous triumph in the 1980s could contain the waters.

In his 1983 book *Blacks and White TV*, a social history of African Americans on television, Professor J. Fred MacDonald titled his last chapter "The Age of New Minstrelsy, 1970–Present."

MacDonald, who often suggests that positive and negative racial images are absolutes, may have been overstating, but, after the perfection of Julia and Chet and Lieutenant Uhura, it's easy to understand how jarring it must have been to see two shows, premiering less than four months apart, turn the minstrelsy-denying Super Negro TV trope inside out.

The first show premiered on September 17, 1970, and starred Lincoln Perry's old friend Flip Wilson. The fact that the star of *The Flip Wilson Show* genuinely considered Perry a friend was significant. When Wilson quipped in a 1968 issue of *Laugh-In Magazine* that he attributed his success to his "good luck autographed picture of Stepin Fetchit," he was aware that it sounded like a punch line to a joke about obsolete minstrelsy, but it wasn't. Wilson was preparing his special with Lincoln Perry at the time of the interview, and years later proclaimed his admiration, offering, "Step had perfect timing . . . his humor was only insulting if you were uptight."

Not being afraid of the black minstrel tradition would serve Wilson well on his variety show. On his semicircle stage (its shape an echo of the minstrel-show formation) Wilson presented broad comedy with his signature characters Reverend Leroy prattling on like the "stump speech" in a traditional minstrel show, and Geraldine in absurd drag that harkened back to minstrelsy's hulking blackface faux-women. "Not since *Amos 'n' Andy* had television portrayed blacks in such stereotypic ways," MacDonald wrote.

But Flip Wilson's appeal lay in humanizing rather than the dehumanizing that occurs with broad stereotypes in both blackface comedy and mediocre sitcoms. Though the sassy, loud Geraldine may have had hints of Sapphire, she was far more three-dimensional than Julia. With her loyalty to her boyfriend Killer, her strong sense of humor and personal style, and her thrilling confidence, this man may have been playing the most nuanced black female character TV had yet seen.

Wilson's other secret weapon was likability. People wanted to be his friend. Even when Wilson played a character employing vernacular street talk, he utilized quiet, clipped tones and punctuated it with theatrical laughs, making his tough-guy voice less threatening than his regular voice. "In a time of Black Panthers," *Life* magazine wrote, "he has taken the threat out of the fact of blackness." While such a quote would have been an insult in *Ebony*, *Life* meant it as both a compliment and a prediction of success.

That prediction came true. The show was number two in the annual ratings, the cover of *Time* declared him "TV's First Black Superstar," and the man who grew up destitute in foster care with sixteen siblings became a rich, American Dream poster child (remarkably, he'd negotiated to own the rights to the series). Wilson's success not only paved the way for generations of black comics to crossover to mainstream audiences, from Jimmie Walker to Chris Rock to Dave Chappelle, but his comic cross-dressing foreshadowed the wear-a-dress-for-success careers of Eddie Murphy, Martin Lawrence, and the man who topped *Forbes*'s 2011 list of "Entertainment's Highest Paid Men," Tyler Perry.

But a different seventies show ultimately had even more impact on the future of blacks on TV. And it was a show all about whiteness. Premiering in January 1971, *All in the Family* (based on an English show, the BBC sitcom *Till Death Do Us Part*) featured Carroll O'Connor as Archie Bunker, a racist, socially conservative, blue-collar guy from Queens negotiating a post–civil rights, post-Woodstock world. What made the show so daring was that it gave its liberal producer Norman Lear a platform to explore social issues and taboos in ways previously unthinkable on a network comedy. The show's tremendous success (it was number one from 1971 to 1976) opened the field for shows that explored poverty, racism, and social issues (including the spinoff show *The Jeffersons*, and the spinoff of a spinoff, *Good Times*). That success also had a great impact on black-cast productions because it gave Lear and his producing partner Bud Yorkin carte blanche, and the subsequent shows with black leads they got on the air included *Carter Country*, *Diff'rent Strokes*, *Grady*, *One in a Million*, *Palmerstown*, *Sanford Arms*, *704 Hauser*, and *What's Happening!!*

Despite Lear's liberal agenda, his primary commitment was to comedy, and thus his shows were often loud and coarse—so coarse, in fact, that they were frequently associated with minstrelsy. "Compared to some of the buffoonish comedies that feature all-black casts on TV today," *Chicago Tribune* columnist Clarence Page wrote, "Amos 'n' Andy look downright sophisticated." While Bunker himself revived some minstrel tropes (malapropisms, wearing blackface for his lodge's minstrel show), it was his boisterous black rival on *The Jeffersons*, the cakewalking George Jefferson, who, as Donald Bogle noted, "seemed an update of the exaggerated comic coon." *Diff'rent Strokes* featured adorable black kids adopted by a wealthy white widower, recalling images of black children as entertaining Topsy figures. Nineteenth-century "mammy" characters were invoked by the plus-sized matriarchs on *What's Happening!!* (and the non-Lear-Yorkin shows *That's My Mama* and *Gimme a Break!*). But the breakout star was undoubtedly James Evans Jr. aka J.J. aka Kid Dy-No-Mite aka the Face of the New Minstrelsy.

The reason J.J., played by comedian Jimmie Walker, stands out so boldly is that of all the seventies black-cast shows, his program, *Good Times*, held the most promise to bring issues of cultural and political relevance to the screen. Created by black writers, cast with socially conscious actors, and set in a Chicago housing project, *Good Times* told the story of the Evans family and their struggles against the pressures of poverty. The household is led by Florida Evans, loosely spun off of actress Esther Rolle's character of the same name from the *All in the Family* spin-off *Maude*. On that show Rolle reluctantly took the role of a domestic hoping to address past screen stereotypes. When offered *Good Times*, she refused unless the producers altered the show's proposed single-mom scenario and added a dignified father figure (played by John Amos). J.J.'s youngest sibling Michael is presented as a politicized black radical, and while some critics argued that having a child espouse Black Power infantilized the movement, he is always accurate and eloquent when pontificating about cultural bias in school testing, the Founding Fathers' ownership of slaves, and "the stress and frustration of ghetto life." Police harassment, political corruption, gang violence, and busing were issues addressed on early episodes.

But just as the cartoonish Kingfish ultimately erased the loving, striving Amos, Walker's character, not Rolle's, came to define *Good Times*. The tall, lanky comic made an unforgettable impression striking absurd poses, wearing a ridiculous red union suit, and howling "*Dyn-o-mite!*" With his giant teeth-baring grin, wide eyes, clownish clothes, and dialect-reminiscent black English ("don't be fixin' me nothin'"), Walker mugged his way into America's heart and into the black TV Hall of Shame. As he did with George Jefferson, Bogle compared J.J. to an "old style coon figure," adding that he "didn't seem to have a serious thought in his head." Sociologist Herman Gray lamented that J.J. was a "kind of minstrel character . . . that robbed the show of the political bite it might have." Worse yet, Rolle was disgusted by his character, telling *Ebony*, "He's 18 and he doesn't work. He can't read or write, he doesn't think." Both Rolle and John Amos would quit the show because of the elevation of J.J.'s character at the expense of the show's more positive elements. Rolle continued to voice her displeasure with the show after leaving, and Lear went all out persuading her to return, replacing the producers, and promising to play down J.J.'s buffoonery. Rolle accepted the offer, with some skepticism. "They say they'll take some of that junk off of [J.J.] and dress him a little differently," she shrugged. "They say they'll try to make him more intelligent. Personally, I don't know how intelligent they can make him . . . you can't get blood from a turnip."

Walker's clowning was not completely without merit. He was good at exploiting the comedic geometry of his beanpole figure; he cleverly presented stereotypes in a style of humor enjoyed by contemporary black youth; and his overloud punchlines were unnatural and absurd in a way that arguably invoked vaudeville comedic history in a deliberate, interesting way. But the show was not the most prudent venue to revive these minstrel tropes. As Gates lamented, "*Good Times* represented the greatest potential, and also in my opinion, the greatest failure."

Another show that disappointed some scholars and critics (who often compared it to *Amos 'n' Andy*) was the sitcom *Sanford and Son* (1972 to 1977). MacDonald said the show revived the classic "coon character," and Donald Bogle said it sometimes seemed like "little more than a replay" of *Amos 'n' Andy* comedy bits. Most stinging was Eugenia Collier's 1973 *New York Times* article " 'Sanford and Son' Is White to the Core," which also made an *Amos 'n' Andy* comparison and argued that because "laughter can be a weapon cutting down one's self-esteem, distorting one's self-image, supporting negative values," *Sanford and Son* was one of TV's "most insidious programs."

One of Collier's points was that the show (like *All in the Family*) was based on a white-cast British show, *Steptoe and Son*. "You simply cannot substitute black characters for white, sprinkle around a little black English and think you have a black show," she wrote. While early episodes did feature rewritten British scripts, Collier underestimated the influence of the show's star. *The Cosby Show*, according to Bogle, was the first "program in which the governing sensibility—the absolute first and last word on just about every detail—lay in black hands." But before the Huxtable era, the black hands that wielded the most influence over the creative machinations of a TV program belonged to perhaps the funniest comedian America has ever produced, Redd Foxx.

Born John Elroy Sanford in St. Louis in 1922, Foxx spent his youth shuttling between that city and Chicago. In the Windy City he formed a high-school washtub musical-comedy band, and as a teen moved to New York to try to make it in showbiz as a busker and on Harlem stages. Though his dreams of singing stayed alive over the ensuing decade (he recorded some R&B records in 1946), his real reputation was earned by touring the chitlin' circuit as a comedian (early on with Slappy White as the black vaudeville-style comedy duo Redd & White). Settling in Los Angeles in the early 1950s, he caught the ear of Walter "Dootsie" Williams, whose doo-wop record label, Dooto, was ready to try its hand at "party records," naughty, sold-under-the-counter comedy discs. Foxx would go on to release over fifty LPs with Williams, over twenty more on his own labels, and many others on labels like King, Laff, and Loma, making him the most prolific figure in the history of comedy records.

His humor stood out because Foxx had developed a brilliant sense of timing and rhythm that elevated any type of joke, allowing him to do diverse sets where he could mix long stories, one liners, puns, alliterative tongue twisters, toasts, knock-knock jokes, insult humor, funny songs, and anything else he found amusing. Quincy Jones called him "the first of the *urban* black comics," meaning he eschewed the rural, slow, simple elements that had imbued African American comedy since minstrelsy's gestation. "The blackface comedian was something I strongly resented," Foxx later explained, adding, "a nigger don't need no makeup to be funny." While drawing upon the comedy prevalent on the black vaudeville circuit, Foxx added a fearless defiance, casually joking about miscegenation, racism, and other taboos.

In the 1960s, Foxx began to gain some mainstream recognition, in part because of his intimate after-hours Vegas shows, which attracted many performers and VIPs winding down after shows in the high-profile lounges. Sinatra became a fan and signed Foxx to Warner Bros. Records. Television took notice and had Foxx do cleaned-up versions of his act on talk and variety shows. In 1970 he was offered a prominent role in Ossie Davis's Chester Himes adaptation, the protoblaxploitation film *Cotton Comes to Harlem*. It was Foxx's role as a junkman in that film, mixed with a desire to repeat the successful formula of adapting a popular Britcom, that led to Norman Lear's creation of 1972's *Sanford and Son*, a show about an aged, ornery junkman living in Watts with his son.

When his show quickly rose to the upper echelons of the ratings (ranked second to *All in the Family* by its second season), Foxx began making demands, some of them material (better dressing room, a salary of "whatever Carroll O' Connor gets, plus a dollar"), but most having to do with the tone of the program. "I don't want this show to be *Amos 'n' Andy*," he insisted. Foxx cast his sitcom, against the network's objections, with cohorts from his chitlin'-circuit days, including Slappy White, Don Bexley, Skillet and Leroy, and an exotic dancer he knew from St. Louis, LaWanda Page. Plot lines and scripted jokes often took a backseat to improvised and physical humor between these veterans. Foxx and Page playing the dozens became one of the show's most popular elements.

RF: I remember your wedding, Esther . . . never forget it. Three ushers were crushed trying to help give you away.

LP: How would you know, Fred Sanford, you spent the whole night with your face over the punch bowl.

RF: Yeah, and when you took your veil off, [the groom] spent the whole night with his face over the toilet bowl.

LP: You just jealous because you didn't catch my garter.

RF: Oh, that's because when you threw it, it was so stretched out you lassoed the band.

LP: Watch it, sucka!

RF: And at the time the band was playing your song . . . the love theme from *King Kong*.

Foxx also injected autobiography into the show from the moment he was hired, naming his character Fred Sanford after his brother, making his own migration from St. Louis to Los Angeles an important part of the show's narrative, and including running jokes about the character being a frustrated vocalist. The latter led to one of the least-filtered moments of black cultural expression on a 1970s TV screen, when an episode ended with the cast improvising blues verses with B.B. King.

Like many sitcoms in the 1970s, *Sanford and Son*'s credits reads like a B'nai Brith mailing list, but between the Turteltaubs and Orensteins, the show (at Foxx's insistence) on occasion used black directors (including Stan Lathan and *Soul Train* director-announcer Sid McCoy) and black writers like Paul Mooney, Richard Pryor, and Ilunga Adell (the latter also working as story editor). Foxx strove for even more black input, confounding bosses not used to such demands, as Mooney recalled in his autobiography. "'We're having trouble finding black comedy writers,' the NBC people would say in meetings right to our black faces."

The show may have been a kind of *Amos 'n' Andy* revival, but not the kind mapped out by MacDonald, Bogle, and Collier. *Sanford and Son* turned TV's first black-cast sitcom inside out. Here was a show, like *Amos 'n' Andy*, about urban blacks running a ragtag business, but instead of relying on Spencer Williams's defense mechanism of dapper clothing and tasteful décor, Fred Sanford wore drab clothes and lived in a home sublimely cluttered with salvaged, sullied junk. Here was a show, like *Amos 'n' Andy*, about an old trickster working vocal magic, but instead of Kingfish's antiquated faux-southern dialect, Foxx's speech patterns marked him as a big-city (small-time) hustler. Instead of delivering a character built upon predetermined stereotypes, Foxx delivers a character built around his own distinct personality. Instead of the shenanigans going down in an all-black bourgeois utopia, it is made clear that Sanford and his son's world is predominantly black because that's how poverty segregates. And most important, unlike the black actors bringing white minstrels' characters to life, Redd Foxx, no matter what anyone, including Norman Lear, might have thought, was the inventor, creative force, and soul of his show.

Though MacDonald heavily focused on *Sanford and Son*, *Good Times*, and the shows of the early seventies, *Blacks and White TV* was not published until 1983. Had MacDonald written it a year later, it seems certain that he would have marked 1984, with *The Cosby Show* premiere, as the end of his "New Age of Black Minstrelsy." Both Cosby and his consultant, Dr. Alvin F. Poussaint (a professor of psychiatry at Harvard whom Cosby had hired to assure that the show's content reinforced mental health in black viewers) made it clear that presenting an intact, respectable, financially stable, loving black family was a response to the poor representations that preceded it. The disappearing parents on *Good Times*, the white savior parent on *Diff'rent Strokes*, and the single "mammy" figure on *What's Happening!!* were (temporarily) rendered obsolete by *The Cosby Show*. That show's phenomenal success seemed to prove to network executives that black-cast shows were not required to address social issues, reflect on poverty, or stick to stereotypical notions of blackness. Consequently, the resulting wave of black programming bypassed both the prideful ethnic specificity of *The Cosby Show*'s bourgeois "talented tenth" lifestyle, and the pre–*Cosby Show* black sitcom traditions of stereotypes and social messages. This was done by producing bland, cookie-cutter domestic sitcoms, indistinguishable from their white counterparts.

These included Flip Wilson's short-lived *Cosby* clone, *Charlie & Co.*, and the long-running *Family Matters*, both featuring child actor Jaleel White. On *Family Matters*, White played Steve Urkel, a black character who managed to be a cartoonish buffoon without ever referencing classic minstrelsy. It was a perfect example of color-blind conventionality. Decades earlier Sammy Davis Jr., exhausted from years of black entertainers being "expected to have *more* than whites if we're going to make it," lamented that blacks had "earned not only the right to stardom but the right to mediocrity, the right to be adequate, OK, unsensational—and still make a living in this business." With the ascension of Urkel, Davis's utopian dreams of black mediocrity had been achieved. Conditions would soon be ripe for that mediocrity to mushroom.

A warm memory for many African Americans who had televisions in the fifties and sixties is the collective excitement, calls to gather, and frantic phone-tree action that occurred whenever a black face was on-screen. A staple of *Jet* magazine was a page listing black performers appearing on television that week (both radio and television appearances were listed from 1951 to 1969, the first few years yielding only two or three per issue). By 2009, when *Jet* retired this feature, it had long since become incomplete and obsolete, as years earlier television had entered a phase of (as Herman Gray dubbed it) "hyperblackness." In the nineties and the early twenty-first century the explosion of low-budget reality and daytime talk shows put countless black faces on screen, some striving to be positive (Oprah Winfrey and several copycats and protégés, including Iyanla Vanzant and Tyra Banks), but many personifying negative stereotypes. These included criminality (on *vérité* police show *Cops*), hypersexuality and irresponsibility (*Maury*, with its infamous "Who's Your Babydaddy" on-air paternity tests), and outrageous ignorance (*The Jerry Springer Show*, which also showcased "white trash," though one recurring signifier of their low-class status was a black paramour).

In addition, the era saw an explosion of prime-time comedies featuring black casts, resulting from the rise of "upstart networks." In 1986, Fox was launched as a fourth broadcast network ("The Big Three," ABC, NBC, and CBS, had been the only major commercial TV networks since DuMont folded in 1956). Initially, Fox broadcast on weekends only, but when expanding their schedule in the early nineties they realized that because blacks were voracious TV consumers (the Nielsen market research company has long reported that African Americans watch more television that any other segment of the population, up to 44 percent more than nonblacks), catering to them was a quick way to build a large audience. *In Living Color, Roc,* and *Martin* were early successes for the network. In 1994, Fox invested in Black Star Communications to take advantage of minority-owned business tax breaks and circumvent FCC ownership limits, making Fox's black bloodline legal as well as cultural.

The WB and UPN networks were launched in 1995, hiring black Fox employees and making them executives. Their early offerings included the WB's *The Parent 'Hood, The Jamie Foxx Show,* and *The Wayans Brothers,* and UPN's *Homeboys in Outer Space, Malcolm & Eddie,* and *The Secret Diary of Desmond Pfeiffer* (the latter a quickly canceled farce about a black servant in the preemancipation Lincoln White House). By 1997 twenty-one prime-time network shows had black lead characters. In 1998, Jordan Levin, head of development for the WB, admitted that blacks were "a built-in audience that is open to trying new services," and that wooing them was part of the network's start-up plan. Once established, both Fox and the WB dropped their black shows in favor of programs that appealed to white youth, who advertisers consider a more upscale demographic. UPN continued black programming until it merged with the WB in 2006 to become the CW network.

The low comedy on these shows offended some black viewers (rapper-pundit Chuck D called UPN the "United Plantation of Negroes," and director Spike Lee declared in 1997, "I would rather see *Amos 'n' Andy*; at least they were just straight-up Uncle Tommin'"). Others were offended by low production values. Donald Bogle complained that these shows "appear thrown together. They're not well written. They're not well directed. You feel for the actors."

Bogle's assessment was accurate enough to make Chuck D's and Spike Lee's complaints somewhat moot. Few of these shows were original enough to either revive or challenge the minstrel tradition in notable ways. Despite rare exceptions (*Roc* was a melancholy dramedy cast with theater actors; *Girlfriends* was an exploration of class and value differences among African American women), these largely unambitious shows focused on young men who were as clownish, horny, and easily confounded as their white counterparts on mainstream sitcoms. Though Marlon Wayans certainly played the role of the bug-eyed, mugging fool on *The Wayans Brothers*, the pedestrian writing and production felt more offensive than the stereotypes. Cognizant of charges of minstrelsy (the show's title sequence featured the brothers violently rejecting a white director's theme song: "We're brothers, we're happy and we're singing and we're colored"), Wayans defended his TV shenanigans by lamenting that "if a black person does some physical comedy, [he's] considered a buffoon."

Even when shows directly challenged the minstrel tradition, low production values made good intentions fall flat. In

"I'm O'Tay, You're O-Tay," a 1996 episode of *The Parent 'Hood*, an adolescent meets resistance when he decides to honor Buckwheat (the postpickaninny character from the 1930s *Our Gang/Little Rascals* films) for his Black History Month project. The show's closing speech, arguing that talented black actors historically forced to take demeaning roles deserve respect, was undermined when delivered by an untalented black actor.

On these programs the legacy of minstrelsy was also addressed in broader ways. Many shows went the Bill Cosby route, taking pains to place characters in respectable, bourgeois careers; the father on *Moesha* owns a Saturn auto dealership, the protagonists on *Sparks* are attorneys (more Cochran than Calhoun), the young characters on *The Jamie Foxx Show* are ambitious employees at a black-owned hotel. One of the most popular programs, the high-school-based sitcom *The Steve Harvey Show*, always emphasized its characters' dignity (Harvey and sidekick Cedric the Entertainer dressed well, worked hard, and lovingly mentored the show's young urban characters).

The other historic precedent these shows followed were those of the race-film industry. Unlike the seventies black-cast shows that aimed for diverse viewership, these programs understood niche demographics and addressed an audience that was predominantly black. Shows like *Girlfriends*, *The Steve Harvey Show*, and *The Parkers* (starring future Academy Award winner Mo'Nique) were incredibly popular with African Americans and virtually unknown by whites (in the Nielsen ratings, *The Parkers* was by far the number-one show in black households at the same time that it ranked dead last in white homes). At one point the WB had a 586-percent higher black viewership than white viewership. Because these productions (a number of them developed and executed by black producers and directors like Stan Lathan, Robert Townsend, Topper Carew, and Winifred Hervey) were aware of this, the shows often have a direct dialogue with their black audience, showing little concern for white audience recognition. There were jokes about nuances of black hair care, references to "high yella" skin complexion, mentions of the black middle-class youth club Jack and Jill, pop culture citations of *Right On!* magazine, or singers with limited crossover appeal like Teena Marie or Jerry Butler. So while mediocre black sitcoms were nothing new (the lower echelon of Bud Yorkin productions in the 1980s and *Family Matters* made sure of that), what was fresh was that these shows played directly to black audiences who were willing to trade lower production values for targeted material.

Just as expectations of black spectatorship allow Spencer Williams's performance in *Blood of Jesus* to defy the negative aspects of minstrelsy, comics in these shows seem unburdened by the weight of stereotypes. Mo'Nique never invokes the Mammy-inspired matriarchs of seventies sitcoms, instead playing her plus-sized parent character as a glamorous, sexualized trickster. Martin Lawrence faced charges of minstrelsy in his work before and after the sitcom *Martin* (his breakout role as emcee of HBO's *Def Comedy Jam* earned acrimony from Cosby, who called it "a minstrel show," and his much-maligned movie role as a prosthetic mammy inspired the 2009 Smith College course "Minstrel Shows from Daddy Rice to *Big Mama's* [sic] *House*"). Yet there is a sense of freedom and shamelessness, rather than pandering, in his sitcom's manic mix of low comedy, stereotypes, Sapphire-esque females, hypersexuality, and grotesque drag. The cartoonish show (with bright-hued sets and clownish caricatures that suggest a hip-hop–era Frank Tashlin production) was profoundly sexist and crude, but seemed to create an alternative universe where minstrel tropes could be revived without any acknowledgement of their legacy of appeasing white audiences.

The only predominantly black-cast show on the upstart networks that successfully aimed for and earned a significant mixed audience was the 1990-to-1994 sketch and variety show *In Living Color*, produced by Keenen Ivory Wayans (assisted by an army of siblings). Not coincidentally, that was the only show that left no doubt that it was knowingly reviving and subverting minstrel-era stereotypes. There were malapropisms from would-be intellectual inmate Oswald Bates, and skits like "Homeboy Shopping Network," in which ignorant, incompetent thieves hustle stolen goods. Yet their contrarian streak had them recast black clowns and hobos as empowered figures, never shuffling or bowing their heads to whites or upper-caste blacks, but rather challenging them. Damon Wayans's character Homey D. Clown refused to do funny dances: "Degrade myself? I don't think so. Homey don't play that." And in the Brothers Brothers skits, in which uptight folksingers don't know they are black, the show turned around minstrelsy's roots with a virtual whiteface performance (later brought to two disparate extremes in Dave Chappelle's white supremacist skit and the Wayans' literal whiteface comedy *White Chicks*). Discussing the show's philosophy with comedy historian Darryl Littleton, Shawn and Damon Wayans explained, "I think we helped broaden black comedy. Still keeping it black, but making it accessible to the masses . . . not Massa, masses."

When UPN and the WB became the CW network in 2006, they continued airing two UPN black sitcoms, *Girlfriends* and *The Game*, until canceling them in 2008 and 2009 respectively (*The Game* migrated to the cable channel BET, becoming the network's all-time highest-rated series). With the backing of

Fox, some of the abandoned affiliates became the MyNetworkTV network, but this time the formula of courting black viewers to build a foundation was no longer viable. New digital methods for collecting viewership data had suggested that black and white viewing habits were less disparate than previously believed, although some minority advocacy groups have disputed these results. A wave of broadly appealing, unedgy shows like *American Idol* and *Dancing with the Stars* further bridged the gap between racialized viewing habits. During MyNetworkTV's three-year existence (2006–2009) it launched only one black-cast sitcom, and their projections for that show's success were not based on expectations of segregated audiences. This show, *Under One Roof*, was a vehicle for a man who had become the biggest star on cable television the old-fashioned way. He did it by being the most blatant practitioner of televised black minstrelsy since 1953.

Many reality shows have featured black participants (token angry black men on MTV's sexy-strangers-in-a-house experiment *The Real World*, sassy divas on *The Real Housewives of Atlanta*), but there is one notable exception. The popular dating series *The Bachelor*, in which a harem of beautiful women compete to win a marriage proposal from a handsome man, has showcased a white bachelor in (so far) all sixteen seasons, with almost every competing woman also being white (as were the title characters in all eight seasons of spin-off *The Bachelorette*).

The wheels on the bus of progress in this particular desegregation issue went into motion with a very unlikely Rosa Parks in September 2004 when cable channel VH1 premiered the third season of their reality series *The Surreal Life*. The show was an absurdist parody of *The Real World*, in which a mansion was filled with an incongruous mix of bizarre celebrities like televangelist-puppeteer Tammy Faye Baker, porn star Ron Jeremy, and dwarf actor Verne Troyer. Over the course of its six seasons, the series cast several black housemates, including rappers MC Hammer, Da Brat, and Pepa. The third edition featured a single African American, William J. Drayton, Jr., better known as Flavor Flav. Drayton had risen to prominence in the late 1980s with Public Enemy, a militant, political-minded, hyperserious hip-hop group. In that context Flavor Flav, with his bugged-out eyes, comically oversized hats, and signature dance (a staccato variation of a stoop-shouldered shuffle) defied the minstrel tradition by emerging as a dangerous contrarian rather than a harmless buffoon. Hip-hop historian Marcus Reeves refused to accept his foolishness at face value, dubbing him the "Clown Prince of Irony." Despite Flavor Flav's outrageousness, the African American folk icon he invoked was much closer to the still-revered trickster than to the now-shameful Sambo or Zip Coon.

But under the klieg lights of reality TV, the same act, the same hats, the same ostentatious jewelry (including ornate gold-tooth caps and a full-sized wall clock worn on a necklace), and the same outsized smiles and laughs devolved into something uncomfortably familiar. The breakout star of the show (a star shining so bright that VH1 quickly launched two spin-offs for him, *Strange Love* and *Flavor of Love*) was not electrifying audiences because he brought something new to the screen, but rather because he brought something very old to TV that hadn't been presented so shamelessly since Kingfish last tried to put one over on Andy Brown.

Criticism of this behavior was muted as Drayton clowned his way through the first two series, where he often worked as a comedy duo with Brigitte Nielsen, an equally cartoonish white actress. But that changed when VH1 launched a black-cast parody of *The Bachelor*, in which an army of rowdy, tattooed, foul-mouthed black women literally fought over a man of dubious desirability (prior to his reality-show renaissance Drayton had spent time in jail for domestic violence, drugs, and weapons charges). Not surprisingly, critics were vocal about a show where Flavor Flav, the self-proclaimed "Black-chelor," spoke in dialect, gobbled fried chicken, and bulged his eyes while fondling scantily clad women.

In Valerie Palmer-Mehta and Alina Haliluc's essay "*Flavor of Love* and the Rise of Neo-Minstrelsy on Reality Television," the scholars note that Drayton's "expressions mirror the performance of Sambo minstrel characters," to the point that "compared [to] *The Bachelor*, Flavor on *Flavor of Love*, and black masculinity by extension, emerge as the deviant other to an idealized white masculinity." African American studies professor Mark Anthony Neal told the *Washington Post* that "it's very easy to see this as the second coming of Sambo." On black-themed blogs and Web sites, critiques were less subtle. Bossip used the phrase "minstrel monstrosity"; Notes of This Native Son said Drayton was "setting the black race back with his modern day minstrel show." And *The Root* celebrated Black History Month by including Drayton on a list of "Black Folks We'd Like to Remove from Black History." Chris Rock joked that "in order for black people to truly reach the Promised Land, Flavor Flav has to be shot." Drayton himself never directly answers any of these charges (in his autobiography he says he was upset by Rock's joke, but never mentions what inspired the comic to say it). The closest he's come to addressing charges of buffoonery is this third person self-description: "He's a clown and all the kids that go to the circus love clowns."

In addition to the show being legitimately outrageous in its revivals of ancient stereotypes and its negative portrayals of black women, the other major reason *Flavor of Love* earned such extraordinary ire from cultural critics was that it was an incredibly popular show among whites and blacks. The first season's finale had almost 6 million viewers, twice as many as had ever watched a show on VH1; the second season's finale drew 7.5 million viewers. *Variety* declared it "the most-watched episode of an original basic-cable series among 18-to 49-year-olds—possibly ever," noting that "one out of every three black viewers watching TV" that night was admiring Drayton's golden grin. The true testament to its popularity was that VH1 virtually reinvented itself as the *Flavor of Love* channel. One contestant, Tiffany "New York" Pollard, was given a spin-off dating show, *I Love New York,* plus two subsequent nondating series, and two contestants from *I Love New York* hosted *Real Chance at Love*. A white version of *Flavor of Love—Rock of Love—* was launched, with 1980s rock band Poison's clownish vocalist Bret Michaels in Drayton's role. A contestant from that show hosted *Daisy of Love*, and contestants from all of the shows united for two other series, *Charm School* (a self-improvement show) and *I Love Money* (a game show).

The fact that most of these shows continued without Flavor Flav (Drayton left VH1 for *Under One Roof*) may indicate that rather than his seemingly outmoded minstrel posturing, *Flavor of Love*'s success was due to the more timeless racial stereotypes that permeated many of the series. These include criminality (flurries of fistfights), fertility (on his last episode Drayton proposes to his pregnant girlfriend), and inhumanity (the contestants are presented as crude and animal-like to the point where one drunken woman is shown defecating on the floor). Considering *Rock of Love*'s first finale had 5.4 million viewers, race-neutral misogyny could also be the magic ingredient (though *Flavor of Love's* sexism has *Amos 'n' Andy* echoes: unlike the mostly demure ladies on *The Bachelor*, Flav's women exhibit a shrillness that recalls the Sapphire stereotype. Drayton, who renames all the contestants, even dubs one brawling bachelorette "Saaphyri").

Any doubts about why VH1's parent Viacom appreciated Flavor Flav were answered on August 12, 2007, when VH1's sister station premiered *The Comedy Central Roast of Flavor Flav*. Barely a year after Comedy Central aired the "Lost Episode" of *Chappelle's Show* featuring the minstrel-themed "Racial Pixies" sketch that convinced Dave Chappelle to walk away from his contract, the network produced a high-profile special featuring Drayton (dressed in an outrageous purple suit and a gigantic toy crown) surrounded by white comedians bombarding him with cruel, racist jokes, many of them directly referring to the shame he brought black America with his millennial minstrelsy. Greg Giraldo called him a "horrible embarrassment to black people" who looked like a "turd with teeth." Carrot Top made a watermelon joke. Jeffrey Ross said, "you remind me of my uncle . . . my Uncle Tom," and that he set African Americans back twenty years, theorizing, "when white people watch your show they say 'that guy's hilarious'; when black people watch your show they say, 'I hope no white people are watching this right now.'" Throughout all of this Drayton bared his gold teeth in a gigantic smile as he histrionically laughed, clapped, and stomped at every jibe.

Katt Williams, a black stand-up comedian virtually unknown to white audiences, but at the time selling hundreds of thousands of DVDs to African Americans, was hired to emcee the roast. His account of his experiences during the event became a staple of his 2008 stand-up tour (*Billboard* declared it the top-grossing comedy tour that year). Despite requesting a script in advance, Williams said he was not provided one until dress rehearsal. Jokes were written for him and the other black guests (rappers Ice-T and Snoop Dogg), and only the blacks were required to show up for the rehearsal. Upon reading the jokes (including one in which he called Drayton a monkey), Williams realized the script was "racist like a 1946 newspaper" and that the show was to be the "Crispity, Crackly, Crunchety Coon Hour." Because of the money and contract commitment, Williams reluctantly did the show despite his shame. Williams claims the white comics seriously upset Drayton's children during the taping, but after the show Drayton was in excellent spirits, thrilled about everything. Baffled by this, Williams asked how he could take such abuse in stride. Williams recalled Drayton saying that sometimes it is worth it to "go back on the porch and hold up the lantern," concluding, "I don't give a fuck what they think, they got to pay me, boy*eee*!"

A publicist for Drayton denied this happened (in response to a *New Yorker* writer, who summarized Drayton's alleged statement as "the mantra that has cheered up controversial black comedians since the days of minstrelsy"). Discussing the televised roast with *Sister 2 Sister* (a black women's magazine that has championed the female stars of *Flavor of Love*), Drayton declared, "That roast was one of the most funniest things that I could ever do in the history of my life . . . all these people are doing is playing the dozens."

The truth likely lies somewhere between Williams's contention that Drayton was slyly, consciously exploiting the medium's hunger for degrading minstrelsy and Drayton's insistence that the roast's friendly ribbing was a validation of brotherhood comparable to a beloved neighborhood ritual. But whatever the motivations, the results—several years of TV stardom and a revived career—would certainly please his predecessors. The talented actors of *Amos 'n' Andy* had their exits expedited by agitated activists, and their earning abilities hampered when their former employer forbade them from capitalizing on their TV fame. But Drayton was embraced and fully supported by a network that seemed unfazed by its critics. Unlike Lincoln Perry, bitter over television opportunities he thought lost and stolen by "Lost, Stolen, or Strayed," Drayton got the sitcom he coveted, even if it only lasted a few months.

But most significantly, the phenomenon of *Flavor of Love* proved that the war between black performers embracing the minstrel tradition without irony and the performers, pundits, and activists dedicated to the death of minstrelsy can never be decisively won. White children weaned on *The Cosby Show* grew up to love *Flavor of Love*, and then went out and voted for Obama. Many of the same black viewers who religiously watched *Flavor of Love* hooted in disapproval during Williams's onstage dissection of Viacom's drubbing of Drayton. The contradictions and duality inherent in the TV public's warm embraces of both Cliff Huxtable and Flavor Flav prove that our cultural biology is complex. As complex as the interactions between "neutrons, po'trons, fig newtons and mo'rons."

Ethel Waters and Sammy Davis, Jr., in *Rufus Jones for President*, 1933.

7.

THAT'S WHY DARKIES WERE BORN

How Black Popular Singers Kept Minstrelsy's Musical Legacy Alive

ALTHOUGH THE BLACK MINSTREL SHOW went into decline in the 1890s and was essentially replaced by vaudeville in the early twentieth century, many of its most vital elements remained alive and well for decades. And one of those is the minstrel song. Songs that were firmly in the minstrel tradition enjoyed great success among both blacks and whites until well after World War II.

Practically every great black singer of the first half of the century performed such minstrel-like material; and even in the postwar period the tradition was kept alive by some of America's most popular black entertainers. These performers could have easily refused to sing such numbers—after all, there were plenty of alternatives available—and some of them successfully avoided them for the most part. But a host of other mainstream black performers kept the image of the "happy darky" down on the plantation alive and kicking until the civil rights revolution finally rendered it obsolete. Why did black singers perform these songs?

To answer this requires us to look briefly at the entire story of twentieth-century minstrel songs. But case histories are useful as well. Through a close examination of two exemplary songs written in the early 1930s—"When It's Sleepy Time Down South" and "Underneath the Harlem Moon"—and the black men and women who performed them, we can see the wide variety of approaches such songs inspired.

These songs are just two out of hundreds that essentially expressed what filmmaker and poet Marlon Riggs called "the fantasy of happy darkies in their proper place." While technically not minstrel songs, they share many of the features of their predecessors, in particular their central theme—the goodness of the South and the innate happiness of black folk. "Happy darky" songs were wildly popular, and black singers such as Louis Armstrong, Paul Robeson, Ethel Waters, Louis Jordan, and Ray Charles played an important part in their success. The stories of these songs and singers will help elucidate the surprising resilience and eventual demise of the American minstrel song.

When the traditional minstrel show all but died at the end of the nineteenth century, minstrel songs were supplanted by coon songs, which continued and expanded the tradition. The protagonists of coon songs were almost universally black rural buffoons; they loved watermelon and chicken, dice and razors, women and drink. The coon was not just any black man: he was a complete stereotype and a paragon of misbehavior. Coons were out to have a good time, damn the consequences.

Musically, coon songs were quite like minstrel songs, but they featured syncopation, thus marking them as "black," whether written by blacks or whites. The lyrics were always comic—there were very few sad, tragic, or sentimental songs among them. In other words, this was clearly happy music and, therefore, it was also escapist.

The first coon songs were published in 1880, and they became a full-fledged craze five or six years later. Over six hundred of them were published in the 1890s. Their popularity persisted through about 1910, and by 1920 the genre had more or less disappeared. During its height, however, the most successful songs sold millions of copies (in sheet music, of course, the recording age being in its infancy).

Perhaps the most popular coon song, "All Coons Look Alike to Me," was the work of Ernest Hogan, an immensely popular black entertainer; but plenty of other prominent black composers also penned coon songs, among them Sam Lucas, Sidney Perrin, Bob Cole, and, as mentioned earlier, Bert Williams.

What differentiated coon songs from their minstrel-show antecedents was the characters' proclivity for criminality. The razor was seldom seen or mentioned in the antebellum minstrel show; it was a constant in coon songs. "Four things you'll always find together," ran Williams and Walker's "The Coon's Trade Mark": "A watermelon, a razor, a chicken and a coon!" Coons were given to stealing, gambling, and hustling, not to mention fighting. There was even plenty of gunplay, as exemplified by the encounter of two gun-toting "real bad coons" in "He's Up Against the Real Thing Now," with lyrics by Edward Furber, a black writer, and music by Bert Williams: "I carved dem in de East, and I shot dem in de West, but I'm up against the real thing now." For the coon, life was a constant adventure.

Using the same logic applied earlier to explain the appeal of the minstrel show, the appeal of coon songs to black Americans seems clear: these songs painted a picture of masculine liberation completely opposed to the actual condition of blacks of the era. Blacks no longer lived on plantations, under the thumbs of slaveholders; now they lived in big cities, under the thumbs of the police. The vices they bragged about in song had to match the nature of their new oppressors. Instead of liberating themselves from slaveholders with indolence, gluttony, and laughter, they liberated themselves from the police with stealing, hustling, and adventure. (This liberation would, of course, be echoed by the hip-hop music of a hundred years later.) And hand in hand with this came a newfound sexual liberation. Minstrels were safe; coons, being dangerous, could also be dangerous sexually. Perhaps the most extreme example is a white-authored song called "The Mormon Coon," in which the narrator, a black polygamist, brags about all his women, including several white ones. But a more typical example is George Walker's "The Hottest Coon in Dixie," whose lyrics were written by the great black poet Paul Laurence Dunbar—here the coon's sexual power is implicit in the word "hottest" rather than spelled out.

The conventional explanation for the popularity of coon songs is that these images of violent, sexual, dangerous black men justified the segregation and oppression of an era of lynchings and peonage. But this doesn't explain why so many coon-song performers and writers were black. And it's easy to turn this argument on its head. For the protagonists of these songs emerge *happy* and *triumphant* rather than getting punished, as would be expected in music used to justify oppression. The images promulgated by these songs could have been liberating for *all* listeners, for by simply putting on blackface, *anyone* could be a "coon."

It is hardly coincidental that the birth of the blues was concurrent with the popularity of the coon song. Both feature overt masculinity; both celebrated violence, criminality, and sexuality; both were lively and syncopated. To say that the blues was derived, through coon songs, from minstrelsy may raise more than a few eyebrows; and in truth the blues is far more rooted in black folk traditions—and in the reality of black life. But the continuum of black music is incomplete without including the coon song as an essential, if vanished, element.

Concurrently with the demise of the coon song, a host of new songs were written for white blackface actors like Al Jolson, whose hits "Waiting for the Robert E. Lee" (1913) and "My Mammy" (1918), among dozens of others, resurrected nineteenth-century minstrel-show portrayals of black Americans. The former is particularly heinous, with its description of happy darkies "humming and swaying" and its chorus of "watch them shuffling along"—Mickey Rooney and Judy Garland sang it (in blackface!) in the 1941 film *Babes on Broadway*; Louis Jordan, Dean Martin, and dozens of others recorded it; and it kept rearing its ugly head throughout the twentieth century.

At the same time, songs of southern nostalgia, a mainstay of the minstrel tradition, never failed to be popular. They were sung from at least an implied point of view of an ex-slave longing to return to the plantation, typified by James Bland's "Carry Me Back to Old Virginny," with its happy slaves and kind masters. Out of this tradition came songs written by white Tin Pan Alley songwriters that on their face had little or nothing to do with slavery—"Georgia on My Mind," "Stars Fell on Alabama," "Alabamy Bound"—but whose roots were firmly in the "carry-me-back" tradition. These songs may ostensibly have been about missing the South for its warmth and sweetness, but they were simply the latest songs in a long-established tradition that the songwriters respected, and that went over well with white audiences, who liked a touch of sentimental nostalgia and enjoyed the idea of the South as an American paradise.

The fact that these songs are still popular and widely sung can be somewhat bewildering for anyone who knows their origins.

The 1920s and '30s were the heyday of this type of song, many of which did indeed feature happy "darkies" in the South: "Black Bottom," "The Birth of the Blues," "Alabam' Banjo Man," "Away Down South in Heaven," "Pickaninnies' Heaven," "There's a Cabin in the Cotton," "Is It True What They Say About Dixie?" (and, of course, the answer song "Yes It's True What They Say About Dixie"), "I Haven't Mentioned Mammy," "I'd Love to Fall Asleep and Wake Up in My Mammy's Arms," and "Pickin' Cotton," in which "There's a beat, there's a measure for each cotton row; they make work seem a pleasure, dancing as they go." Then there were equally pernicious songs about lascivious black women—"Sweet Georgia Brown," "Pretty Quadroon," "Louisville Lou," "Mah Lindy Lou"—and randy black men—"Romeo in Georgia," "Lovin' Sam (The Sheik of Alabam')," "Georgia Gigolo," "Dapper Dan," "Charleston Charley." A number of these songs had very long lives—"Sweet Georgia Brown," a perfect portrait of a female "happy darky," is one of the most durable standards of the last hundred years, kept alive as the theme music for the Harlem Globetrotters, the basketball team whose black vaudeville-inspired clowning has been entertaining audiences since the era when these songs were written.

A pale moon shines on "darkies" playing banjos, "crooning songs soft and low," and then dancing all night. "Take me back where I belong—how I'd love to be in my mammy's arms," the singer confesses. All in all, "When It's Sleepy Time Down South," written in 1930 but with lyrics that seemed a hundred years old, is trite, false, and overtly racist.

Yet Louis Armstrong recorded it close to a hundred times and played it at almost every concert from 1932 on—probably several thousand times in all. He even made a "soundie" film of it ("soundies" were short films made for viewing through a coin-operated machine) in 1942, in which he sat on a hay bale dressed in a plaid shirt and straw hat, while Nick "Nicodemus" Stewart was doing his Stepin Fetchit imitation and eating a turkey drumstick, a big lazy river rolling by in the background.

And Armstrong was far from the only black performer connected to this song. In fact, "When It's Sleepy Time Down South" was composed by Clarence Muse, a black actor, and Leon and Otis René, black songwriters from Louisiana, who gave it to Armstrong in 1930; he recorded it in April 1931, and a slew of other versions followed. Mildred Bailey, a white singer, performed it with the Paul Whiteman Orchestra—their version reached number six on the *Billboard* charts in November. In the movie *Safe in Hell* (released in December), Nina Mae McKinney, a black actress who played a Caribbean hotel owner (Muse played the porter), sang an imitation of Armstrong's version while serving dinner to her white guests. Ethel Waters performed it too, and beautifully, though she characteristically gave a twist to the lyrics: after singing "folks down there live a life of ease," she gives that line the lie by singing, "when mammy falls down upon her poor tired knees" (in her version, the "darkies" aren't quite as happy).

Even more puzzling to modern-day listeners, Paul Robeson, an actor and singer who was most famous for his roles in *The Emperor Jones, Show Boat*, and *Othello,* also recorded it in 1931—the year of the near-lynching of the Scottsboro Boys, nine innocent black teenagers accused of a rape in Alabama. Violence was endemic in the South, especially against blacks, who had no rights that anyone was compelled to respect. Yet the idyllic "Sleepy Time Down South" was written by blacks, performed by blacks in a Hollywood movie, and recorded by three of the most famous black singers of the day—including Robeson, a former All-American football player and politically engaged Broadway star who might be expected to know better.

Robeson had no actual connection to the rural South, having been raised in New Jersey and having worked in New York and Europe. But in 1928 he sang "Ol' Man River" in *Show Boat*, playing a part that was written with him in mind, and became, for his largely white audience, a rural southern Negro. In keeping with this image, he also recorded several actual minstrel songs, as well as a large number of spirituals.

Robeson recorded "When It's Sleepy Time Down South" in 1931. But at the same session he also recorded an even more astonishing song. "That's Why Darkies Were Born" was written for Kate Smith to sing in the Broadway revue *George White's Scandals of 1931*; at first glance, it appears to be the most reprehensible of the racist songs of the decade. It seems to urge blacks to work hard, be happy, and "accept your destiny": "Someone had to pick the cotton, someone had to plant the corn; someone had to slave and be able to sing—that's why darkies were born." Sam Dennison, in his book *Scandalize My Name*, a history of black imagery in American pop music, calls it a "gross horror of misplaced sympathy that can only be considered as among the worst songs ever written on the subject of black religion." But Robeson sang it with just as much earnestness and dignity as he put into the well-known spiritual "Go Down Moses." His classically trained basso profundo invested everything he sang with weight, seriousness, and depth.

How can we explain this? At the time, Robeson was outspoken in his declarations of racial pride. He espoused sympathy for southern blacks, who, under the systems of sharecropping and peonage, were still essentially enslaved. He had strong communist sympathies, which he did not keep hidden, that were a result, in part, of his rage at how white Americans treated blacks. Yet here he was singing songs that seemed to defend the continued oppression of his race.

Robeson, like Armstrong, never explained why he sang such songs, and nobody seems to have thought to ask him. But music historian Will Friedwald has written an excellent justification of this seemingly strange phenomenon. Like "Ol' Man River," "That's Why Darkies Were Born" "presented the black man in a way that the multiethnic Tin Pan Alley could relate to—casting the 'colored' race in the same role as the Jews in the Old Testament. To take up the black man's burden meant to shoulder both the suffering and the moral and religious obligations of the rest of the world." Both songs have the same somber undercurrent: life is hard for blacks, even painful, but the river keeps flowing toward the Promised Land. And that's the same message one finds in spirituals.

Perhaps "That's Why Darkies Were Born," then, can be read not as a justification of slavery but as a portrait of blacks as Christ-like—they suffer, they endure, and they will eventually save the world. The song's last line is "Someone had to stoke the train that would bring God's children to green pastures."

Robeson had given his first solo recital in 1925, at which he had sung only "Negro songs and spirituals." By 1931 practically every single song he had ever recorded was either a spiritual, an actual nineteenth-century minstrel song, a black folk song, or a song written about black people. He largely avoided popular songs that had nothing to do with his race. It would appear that for Robeson, almost all songs about blacks, whether written by whites or not, functioned like spirituals.

This also helps explain why Robeson sang "When It's Sleepy Time Down South": he gave everything he sang an air of spirituality. The "dear old Southland" becomes an imagined place of spiritual succor, the equivalent of the spirituals' "promised land." There's a melancholy in Robeson's version that simply isn't in the song as written.

But this was a very different conception of "Down South" than that of the song's primary interpreter—and, one surmises, its composers.

Louis Armstrong grew up not quite as removed from the rural South as Robeson—although he was raised in New Orleans, he had a feeling for country life, having spent over a year at the Colored Waif's home on the outskirts of that city and a few weeks in a small Louisiana town called Houma. But these were a far cry from the "dear old Southland" of the song, an imagined place of leisure and pleasure. And in contrast to Robeson's reading, for Armstrong the succor of the Southland was physical rather than spiritual. When he sang, he evoked a possibility of liberation, since "folks down there live a life of ease." The songwriters had put into the lyrics what they and Armstrong might have envisioned as paradise—a place where "darkies" could "dance till the break of day" and then fall asleep in Mammy's arms. Yes, it's a fantasy of infantile regression with anachronistic imagery originating in racist ideology. But for Armstrong, as for the composers, it was no less potent for all that. There was nothing calculated about Armstrong's love for this song—it was genuine. Here was a place he could go to in his music, a heaven/haven away from the frenetic life he led, and he went there as often as he could.

It's no coincidence that the song was written in 1930 and recorded in 1931, during the Great Depression, when blacks who had come North from the South were discovering that life wasn't necessarily easier than it had been in their old hometowns. In fact, in his first recording of the song, Armstrong begins with some banter with his pianist, Charlie Alexander, evoking the Great Migration: "How long you been up here, boy?" "Oh, I been up here 'bout, about a year and a half." "A year and a half? Well, man, I been up here a long time myself. I'm goin' back home."

Yet it's hard to imagine that in the year of the Scottsboro Boys' trials the injustices of "Down South" could be utterly forgotten. Where else, then, could this "Sleepy Time" heaven be found in reality?

Nowhere else but in the minstrel show. Yes, "When It's Sleepy Time Down South" functioned as an exercise in southern nostalgia, but since it was common knowledge that no such plantation scene had ever existed except in fiction, it also functioned as an exercise in *minstrel-show* nostalgia—an evocation of a showbiz rather than an actual plantation heaven, as Laurence Bergreen suggests in his excellent biography of Armstrong. The song effectively celebrated American entertainment itself.

With this in mind, the "soundie" that Armstrong filmed appears in a new light. Nicodemus Stewart's eyes widen when he sees the turkey drumstick. He's too lazy, at first, to go get it, but when he gets it, he does a slow loping dance, and he falls asleep cradling it in his arms. What is this but a reenactment of a minstrel show? True, there's no blackface involved, but it's very clear that this is being filmed on a set, not in the actual South, and there's no explanation of why a turkey drumstick should appear in the middle of the night. This is nothing but traditional showbiz, which had been very good to Louis Armstrong. "When It's Sleepy Time Down South" was, at least in part, his tribute to it.

But Armstrong suffered for his indulgence of minstrelsy. Not only did he insist on playing songs like this, he was known for his large grin and grimaces, his deep hoarse chuckle, and his "aw shucks" demeanor. Making the white folks laugh was essential to his performances. The beboppers roundly criticized him for his "plantation image," in Dizzy Gillespie's words. He was "tomming," according not only to them, but to the generation of more militant blacks who followed. Armstrong fought back, attacking bebop even more fiercely than the beboppers had attacked him. Nobody could make Armstrong ashamed of his minstrel roots. In 1949 he donned blackface and became the Zulu king in New Orleans's Mardi Gras parade, fulfilling a long-cherished dream. His embrace of the minstrel tradition was now complete.

At a 1951 recording session, he sang the song as written for the first take, but for the second was asked to change "darkies" to "people." He turned to Gordon Jenkins, the conductor, and growled, "What do you want me to call those black sons-of-bitches this morning?" The fact that he often made some substitution for "darkies" after that did not reflect his own preference, which was made clear by the fact that he kept playing the song at almost every performance for the rest of his life.

While "Sleepy Time Down South" never even mentioned city life, another song of the era took an almost opposite approach. "Underneath the Harlem Moon" was Mack Gordon's first hit.

Gordon was a Polish Jew, originally named Morris Gittler, who had come to the United States in 1908 at the age of four. In 1932, having appeared in vaudeville and written songs for the *Ziegfeld Follies of 1931* and the all-black revue *Fast and Furious*, he decided to pen a song that played upon the current vogue for southern nostalgia songs, but was set instead in Harlem. His lyrics were pure racist malarkey.

The song's verse, which was rarely if ever performed, asks if you're missing the South, with its candy yams and Virginia hams, its sunny skies and "mammy's pies." It then reassures the listener that "the South is in your own back yard." The chorus abruptly shifts to third person, and describes a Harlem where "Creole babies walk along with rhythm in their thighs," feet, lips, and eyes; where there's no cotton to pick; and where the cabins have been replaced by Lenox Avenue penthouses. "They just live on dancing," Gordon tells us, "they're never blue or forlorn. 'Tain't no sin to laugh and grin—that's why darkies were born." Joe Rines, a white Boston bandleader, helped popularize the song, and it became a huge hit, with at least eight different versions on record.

Of all the racist songs of the early 1930s, perhaps none were as colorful as "Underneath the Harlem Moon"—or as demeaning. The others all portrayed blacks in the bygone South, romanticizing or making fun of a group of people whose dignity had already been severely compromised by poverty and abuse. But "Harlem Moon" explicitly caricatured the most sophisticated corner of contemporary African American society, making it seem plantationlike. So what should we make of the fact that at least half of the people who performed "Underneath the Harlem Moon" in the 1930s were black themselves?

The Washboard Rhythm Kings did it. So did Don Redman

and His Orchestra, with vocals by Harlan Lattimore (billed as "the colored Bing Crosby"). So did Fletcher Henderson and His Orchestra, with Katherine Handy (W. C. Handy's daughter) on vocals. Ethel Waters performed it in the movies. The Brown Sisters did too. Even Billie Holiday wrote, in *Lady Sings the Blues*, that she used it to audition for a spot in a Philadelphia theater. It appears that black artists *liked* this song. Their performances are fast and funny, full of unfeigned enthusiasm and joy. Did they completely overlook the racism of its lyrics?

The Washboard Rhythm Kings', Harlan Lattimore's, and Katherine Handy's versions are pretty straight lyrically, but they all really swing. Only Handy makes a couple of minor word changes, replacing "laugh and grin" with "guzzle down gin."

The Brown Sisters were a Los Angeles trio who performed with Ethel Waters and were clearly influenced by the white New Orleans–based trio the Boswell Sisters. "Underneath the Harlem Moon" is their only recorded performance, from the 1938 short film *Harlem Revue*, which despite its title is set on a ship, and also features black comedians in blackface speaking dialect. The Brown Sisters perform it in sailor suits behind a piano that one of them is playing; the camera is stationary, as are their bodies—all the animation is in their spirited voices, faces, and rhythm. Near the end they add a surprising lyric that appears nowhere in the original song: "Ain't no sin to take off your skin and dance around in your bones!" Were they negating the racial aspect of the song by removing their skin? That might seem the logical conclusion, even if they were simply quoting the chorus of the 1929 hit "'Tain't No Sin."

By far the most radical version is Ethel Waters's, which

appears in a short film called *Rufus Jones for President* starring Sammy Davis, Jr., as a seven-year-old whose mother, played by Waters, dreams he gets elected president. After Waters sings her monster hit "Am I Blue?" to the assembled black senators, one of them objects—"You've got all the senators goin' to sleep around here! Let's give them somethin' to wake them up!" Waters goes right into it.

First off, she changes "they" to "we" throughout. Then she changes "darkies" to "we schwartzes." "You may call it madness" becomes "white folks call it madness," and Lenox Avenue becomes St. Nicholas Avenue. And then she really goes to town, supplying brand-new—and brilliant—lyrics for the last half of the song. Now the Harlemites have exchanged bandannas for Parisian hats, going barefoot for shoes and spats, being Republican for being Democrats, picking cotton for picking numbers. "We just laugh, grin, let the landlord in—that's why house rent parties were born," she sings. When they're feeling bad, the Harlemites in Waters's lyrics drink gin and puff reefers, which give them enough courage to take on anything from traffic to policemen. She ends the song on a note of spirited defiance: "Don't stop for law or no traffic when we're rarin' to go, underneath the Harlem Moon!"

By revising the lyrics, Waters completely changes the meaning of the song. In the original version, Harlem was, for nostalgic listeners, a good plantation substitute. Now, Waters's Harlemites have left the plantation completely behind for something a whole lot better. It's an incredible act of reclamation, changing racism to triumph. And it dates from 1933, only a year after the song's debut. "Underneath the Harlem Moon" would become something of a theme song for Waters, who frequently performed it onstage, though she never recorded it on a disk.

Black performers didn't necessarily like all the songs they performed. In many cases they sang songs because they were popular with a white audience. But some also performed them for all-black audiences. For example, *Harlem Revue* was a race movie, made by blacks for blacks, so the popularity of "Harlem Moon" among whites was not a factor for the Brown Sisters.

There are three other reasons black artists might have performed songs like these. First, "Underneath the Harlem Moon" was a celebration of Harlem, however couched in racist metaphors and analogies; and blacks had good reason to celebrate Harlem, the locus of the Harlem Renaissance, in those days. This was something black entertainers could relate to. (Needless to say, this reason doesn't apply to "Sleepy Time Down South.")

Second, blacks were so inured to minstrel imagery by this point that it may have been like water rolling off their backs. Nowadays these songs' blatant racist imagery strikes everyone who comes across it as unspeakably awful. *New York Times* critic Ben Ratliff is horrified by Handy's performance of "Harlem Moon," which he quotes in his guide to the 100 most important jazz records; *Rolling Stone*, reviewing a later version, wrote of it that "every line contains some of the most blatant racial typing ever set down in song." But back in 1932 it was simply par for the course. Racist or not, these songs could be a lot of fun to sing.

Lastly, and most important, these artists weren't just performing straight versions of these songs, like the white folks were. With the exception of Paul Robeson, they were jazzing them up. Ethel Waters and Louis Armstrong did it best, Lattimore hardly at all, with the others somewhere in between.

But what Waters did is a perfect example of signifying, and the variations in tempo, emphasis, and spirit that these other artists introduced constitute a measure of signifying too. For by jazzing up songs, performers present them with a wink and a shrug.

Thirty-eight years later Randy Newman engaged in a "white" kind of signifying when he recorded a slow, lovely, seductive version of "Underneath the Harlem Moon" on his second album, *12 Songs*. It closed side one. The other side began with "Yellow Man," which is equally racist malarkey penned by Newman himself, followed by a satirical version of "My Old Kentucky Home," the Stephen Foster minstrel number. Newman's point was unmistakable: he was singing racist and demeaning songs in order to upset his listeners. It seemed that everyone who listened to "Underneath the Harlem Moon" became uncomfortable. As Greil Marcus wrote in *Mystery Train*, "Here [Newman] was, a struggling singer whose only possible audience would be urbane, liberal rock 'n' roll fans, and he was unveiling . . . the charms of racism." (Newman would go on to write many even richer evocations of American racism, among them "Sail Away," "Rednecks," and "Short People.")

And that points out another, broader difference between how whites and blacks have approached racism in music. Whites use irony, and there's no better example than Newman. They make white racism seductive, thereby problematizing it. Blacks, on the other hand, tend to keep things close to home, performing racist material either with humor and defiance, like Waters, or with unfeigned nostalgia, like Armstrong. Their "signifying" is more sly and playful than ironic.

But a few years later a black performer came along who

expertly combined these seemingly opposite approaches of defiance and nostalgia, and turned racist imagery into huge hits.

After the 1930s, songs about "happy darkies" became less prevalent. Some prominent African Americans continued to sing them, though, and none were more successful than Louis Jordan.

Jordan had performed with his father in the Rabbit's Foot Minstrels, and was heavily influenced by Mantan Moreland and Bert Williams, according to his biographer John Chilton. As one of the saxophone players in Chick Webb's band in the 1930s, Jordan would frequently steal the spotlight with his antics, leading his colleagues to call him Stepin Fetchit behind his back.

By the 1940s, Jordan had become the country's most popular black entertainer, and he did so by indulging in a variety of minstrel stereotypes, including chicken-stealing in "Ain't Nobody Here But Us Chickens," faux dialect in "Is You Is Or Is You Ain't My Baby," and the lazy, drinking, stealing, chicken-loving preacher in "Deacon Jones." He even recorded "Waiting for the Robert E. Lee" and frequently performed preacher routines onstage. Few performers of his era so clearly reveled in the minstrel tradition, and it was one of the keys to his triumph: Jordan is still considered the greatest practitioner of the African American comic song, and his songs have been revived again and again, most notably in the hit Broadway musical *Five Guys Named Moe*. According to Friedwald, the key to Jordan's success was that he "affectionately savage[d] all the institutions of African American life: family life, business, education ('Teacher, Teacher'), the law, and even the church."

The minstrel tradition, like for so many others, presented Jordan (who wore immaculately tailored suits and came across in interviews as an intellectual) with an alter ego who could get crazy and unconstrained.

It's interesting to compare Jordan's minstrel shtick with that of James Baskett, who became the first African American man to be awarded an Oscar (albeit an "honorary" one) after he sang "Zip-a-Dee-Doo-Dah" in Walt Disney's 1946 film *Song of the South*. A "happy darky" song par excellence, complete with the malaprop "satisfactch'll," it was covered by, of course, Louis Armstrong, but also by the Jackson 5 and Sun Ra, who both emphasized the song's nonsensical fun rather than its "happy darky" message. There was no signifying in Baskett's original version—there wasn't even any swing. While Jordan was outrageous and untamable, Baskett played the submissive "darky" to the hilt.

Louis Jordan's attitude toward the minstrel tropes he trotted out was, like both Armstrong's and Waters's, one of indulgent humor. But while Armstrong and Waters both took a laid-back approach like that of the black Hollywood stars of their era, Jordan was as manic as could be. With his wide grin and bulging eyes, he could have been mistaken for a minstrel caricature were it not for his amazing suits and the fact that he never stopped moving. Despite the words of his songs, here was no *plantation* darky—Jordan was *big city* through and through.

Previous performers in the black minstrel tradition had also been this manic—think of Stepin Fetchit's transformation from ultraslow to maniacally speedy as soon as he hears the word "chicken"—though unhurried performers like Bert Williams and Mantan Moreland were more the norm. Jordan also likely patterned himself after Cab Calloway, who sang similarly comic songs and jump blues with big smiles and frenzied energy. Calloway, however, performed very few minstrel-like songs.

But Jordan's conversion of the minstrel-song tradition from easygoing swing to electric excitement—of plantation conventions into big-city jive—was pivotal, for it led directly to the birth of rock 'n' roll.

While rock 'n' roll for the most part steered clear of the minstrel song, Ray Charles, in 1957, signified on Stephen Foster's "Old Folks at Home" by making it into "Swanee River Rock (Talkin' 'Bout That River)," scrubbing the song of all reference to plantations, "darkies," or banjoes. Quickly covered by white rockers Brenda Lee and Billy Lee Riley, the song exemplified rock 'n' roll's approach to minstrelsy. Absolutely anything from the past could be fodder for a rock 'n' roll song, but it had to be made new, wiped clean, and injected with youth and vigor. As a movement whose foundation was a multiracial youth market, rock 'n' roll had to appeal to black and white teenagers of the 1950s, who in the main were either ignorant of minstrelsy altogether or saw it as something they'd rather forget. By the '60s, rock had adopted folk music's disgust with phoniness, and what could be more phony than wearing blackface and singing songs about a hundred-year-old make-believe land?

Charles, however, moved away from rock quite quickly, and took a more sentimental, pop approach to other "happy darky" numbers, among them James Bland's minstrel song "Carry Me Back to Old Virginny" and the 1927 Bing Crosby number "Mississippi Mud," on his 1960 album *The Genius Hits the Road.* Once again he entirely scrubbed these songs clean of "darky" references, making them into simple songs of nostalgia for the South—surely a genuine sentiment for this southern-born man. Yet due to their sentimental, string-laden interpretation, they remained minstrel numbers through and through—the implication lingered, even if the words were no longer offensive.

Perhaps Charles's most minstrelish moment came in 1975, when he covered Randy Newman's "Sail Away." Written from the point of view of a slave trader enticing "little wogs" to come to America, the land of promise, Newman's song was a masterpiece of irony, on the surface appearing to be a simple patriotic ditty—"It's great to be an American," Newman sarcastically sang. Unfortunately most other singers who performed the song, including Linda Ronstadt, Etta James, Gladys Knight, and Ray Charles, completely missed the irony and sarcasm, deleting the "little wog" and treating the song as if it were "God Bless America." Charles also seemed to be praising watermelon and buckwheat cake with complete sincerity, and instead of singing "We will cross the mighty ocean," he sang "Lord, won't you please help us cross this mighty ocean" in a pure gospel tone. Here was Ray singing about the virtues of America from the point of view not of the slave trader, but of the slave. On the other hand, "Sail Away" closed an album that began with a spirited and especially pessimistic cover of Stevie Wonder's protest song "Living for the City," to which Charles appended a brief and vivid catalog of one black man's contemporary misfortunes. Maybe he hadn't missed the irony after all—maybe he was just complicating it. He never gave any indication of his thinking.

At any rate, compared to what had preceded him, Ray Charles's latter-day minstrel-like performances were relatively innocuous. For the rise of the civil rights movement had brought about a complete turnaround in the subject matter of black song. "Happy darky" material was no longer acceptable; black pop singers wanted to sing about what blues singers had always sung about: real life. Throughout the 1960s, singers ranging from Nina Simone to James Brown introduced songs about racial injustice and black pride, building on the folk music movement of the early 1960s, which had decried racial injustice. Black minstrel–tradition performers such as Bill "Bojangles" Robinson, who had been lauded in 1930s songs, were now pitied, as in Jerry Jeff Walker's 1968 hit "Mr. Bojangles." For a twenty-year period, approximately from 1960 to 1980, American popular musicians and their critics rarely invoked minstrelsy.

But with the rise of hip-hop, all that was about to change.

Logo for the short-lived Flav's Fried Chicken in Clinton, Iowa. JOE FASSLER.

8.

EAZY DUZ IT

How Black Minstrelsy Bum-Rushed Hip-Hop

WHEN CRITICS COMPARE RAP MUSIC to minstrelsy it is never meant as a compliment. Gangsta rappers got dubbed "the Amos and Andy of the 1990s." "Wiggers" (white rappers and fans who speak in black dialect and feast on black culture) are branded millennial Jolsons. Lil Wayne is called "Stepin Fetchit in the flesh." Though these parallels are flawed, rap's detractors are not completely off track. For hip-hop, the rhythmic street poetry that emerged in the seventies and became a cultural juggernaut in the eighties, has enjoyed as lively a dialogue with the black minstrel tradition as any art form in the last fifty years. Some rappers address their theatrical ancestors by signifying and critiquing. Before he eschewed irony for reality-TV glory, Flavor Flav was one of several prominent comic rappers who recontextualized black minstrelsy, radicalizing it by becoming jesters in the courts of revolutionaries. Other artists, particularly the wave of southern rappers that took over hip-hop in the twenty-first century, explore low comedy, clownish antics, dialect, and stereotypes with a shamelessness rarely seen in the wake of the civil rights movement. Though hip-hop has proven a diverse and flexible form that makes generalizations impossible, one theme has reemerged decade after decade: audiences eat it up when rappers boldly present low, lurid, taboo, criminal, and stereotypical facets of black culture. Anyone who'd seen a Billy Kersands performance or a Rabbit's Foot revue could have told you that a century ago.

Though they have little to do with the *black* minstrel tradition's hip-hop legacy, it would be remiss to discuss hip-hop and minstrelsy without briefly examining the phenomenon of white rappers, who are seen as metaphorically putting on blackface. The first white superstars of hip-hop, the Beastie Boys, seemed to deliver a wink with their wiggery, but other acts mimicked black culture, cadences, and style without irony. Black fans and fellow rappers openly accepted some of these acts, notably 3rd Bass. The respect bestowed upon Michael "MC Serch" Berrin, that group's main writer, was demonstrated by Spike Lee casting him in the minstrelsy critique *Bamboozled*, and by the hip-hop gadflies from *ego trip* magazine choosing him as host of their reality TV competition *The White Rapper Show* (on which one finalist used the abolition-themed rap name John Brown). Some acts, like Vanilla Ice, drew less respect from black audiences. And some, like the all-white group Young Black Teenagers, who released a single called "Proud to Be Black," were just confusing.

A number of Caucasian hip-hop fans also update Norman Mailer's "White Negro" concept by adopting exaggerated versions of hip-hop–influenced African American speech, dress, and mannerisms. Chuck D of Public Enemy (a group that helped produce and promote Young Black Teenagers) often stated that rap music's influence on young white listeners would ultimately challenge racist institutions. "Rap is teaching white kids what it means to be black," he told *Spin* in 1990, "and that causes a problem for the infrastructure." But with the revolution still pending, hearing Opie spew Ebonics can be cringe-inducing. However, it is a cringe of embarrassment for the wayward wigger rather than a cringe of pain that contemporary audiences experience when encountering images and recordings of white minstrels in pitch-black makeup doing racist dialect. While nineteenth- and early-twentieth-century white performers consistently paid lip service to their admiration for the carefree, naturally musical Negro, that imitation is not comparable to the one contemporary kids perform. Even if one accepts (as scholar Eric Lott argues) that a twisted sense of respect and love was involved in nineteenth-century theatrical racial impersonation, they did not go as far as changing everyday street clothes and speech patterns. Although today's incautious copycats may still be engaging in degrees of stereotyping, dehumanization, and essentialism, they seem to be doing it with (imprudent) earnestness, and without acknowledgment of minstrelsy's problematic legacy.

A handful of black hip-hop artists have explicitly acknowledged and messed with this legacy. The group KMD (first known for collaborating with 3rd Bass and now best known as the launching pad for the eccentric masked rapper MF Doom) addressed minstrel stereotypes in their song "Who Me?" in which they challenge the absurdity of the physical attributes portrayed in blackface makeup and racist caricature ("Lips and eyes, dominant traits of our race, does not take up 95 percent of one's face"). The song's music video featured a Sambo mascot (a dancing seven-foot pitch-black–costumed character) interacting with the young rappers. Their 1993 album *BL_CK B_ST_RDS* went unreleased for years because Elektra Records objected to the cover art featuring that Sambo mascot being lynched. In 1992, the L.A. group Pharcyde released the song-skit "It's Jiggaboo Time" ("when you rappin' for the money, it's jiggaboo time . . . You're rappin' for the white man, it's jiggaboo time . . . Show me them teeth baby . . . could you bug your eyes out just a little bit?"). North Carolina rap trio Little Brother's 2005 LP *The Minstrel Show* featured wide-grinning rappers on the cover. The album framed its songs in skits that critiqued contemporary black pop culture in the context of a televised minstrel show (on the UBN, or "U Black Niggaz" network, a riff on the black audience programming of UPN). One rapper even had a minstrelsy-related alias: Rashaan Jackson, who appears on Pharcyde and Eazy-E albums, went by Buckwheat (alternately Bucwheed). There was also a Florida rap group named Buckwheat Boyz whose song "Peanut Butter Jelly Time," coupled with an animation of a dancing banana, became an Internet sensation.

But overtly referencing minstrelsy for its cultural weight, comic elements, and shock value involved far less commitment than the comic rappers who drew upon the black minstrel tradition when forging their identities, challenging codes of cool that many rappers lived (and several died) by. No rapper embraced and contorted the minstrel buffoon caricature like William "Flavor Flav" Drayton. Though during his reality TV days Drayton's eye-buggin', wide-grinnin', foot-shufflin', dialect-barkin' ways earned him harsh criticism and a scarlet "C" (Google "Flavor Flav" + "coon" and get 90,600 results), the same mannerisms had met with an opposite response in the late eighties and early nineties. His mugging read as subversive and ironic in Public Enemy, a group whose music sounded so imposingly serious that comic relief felt like a necessity.

Formed in Long Island around 1982 when Carlton "Chuck D" Ridenhour and producer Hank Shocklee joined forces with Drayton while they were all deejays on Adelphi University's radio station, Public Enemy combined heavy, severe-sounding production techniques and Chuck D's staccato bass vocals to make even songs about cars and black fraternities sound hazardous and political on their 1987 debut LP *Yo! Bum Rush the Show*. But when 1988's *It Takes a Nation of Millions to Hold Us Back* shifted the subject matter to rage, revolution, and Black Power rhetoric, the brilliance of Drayton's clowning became apparent. Instead of sexy girl dancers or b-boys breakdancing on stage, Public Enemy had a pseudo-paramilitary unit called the S1Ws (Security of the First World) perform stiff military maneuvers behind the group. Public Enemy performances would have been far less palatable if the focus were solely on drill routines and the stone-faced Chuck D. By drawing upon eye-bulging mugging, broad buffoonish humor, and outlandish attire—all racially charged, low-comedy techniques with centuries-long proven track records—Drayton was guaranteeing that their concerts would be *shows*.

But more significantly, Drayton made his buffoonery seem dangerous. Though a slight, strange jester may have seemed harmless on his lonesome, the composition of Public Enemy gave the impression that he was a valuable soldier in this intimidating army. The line between revolution and revelry was blurred—before some shows a stoic S1W, in full camouflage and facemask, would stand silently on stage for long minutes, stripping down to reveal himself to be a wildly dancing Drayton when the gig began. That Drayton's teeth-baring grins and herky-jerky jigs revived negative stereotypes felt like an intentional call for racial unease, a recontextualizing reminder of the racism the group was reacting to. On the back cover of 1990's *Fear of a Black Planet*, the group, including several S1Ws, is seen in a war room studying a globe and world map as Chuck D presumably formulates a strategy for revolution. Everyone is paying rapt attention or taking notes except for Drayton, who stares directly at us with an ominous toothy smile. This marriage of black nationalism and bug-eyed blackface comedy tropes was not unprecedented: Jimmie Walker, prior to catching flack for his minstrelish mannerisms on *Good Times*, was the "official" comedian for the Black Panther Party, doing numerous benefits and events. But what felt new for the hip-hop generation was the idea that a ludicrous clown, by associating himself with more traditional models of masculinity and menace, could equal the badassness of his grimacing brothers.

Though no other comic-relief rapper drew upon the black minstrel tradition with the specificity of Drayton, others exploited stereotypes and reveled in comic absurdity. Digital Underground's "Humpty Hump" character (portrayed by Gregory Jacobs) was a trickster endman, relaying nasal one-liners through a rubber nose. Marcel "Biz Markie" Hall, with his slack-jawed mugging, gaudy outfits accentuating his girth, and slow, marble-mouthed speech, was the most blatant clown in the hip-hop circus, shamelessly delivering unfiltered buffoonery. Hip-hop's most dangerous joker was Russell Jones aka Ol' Dirty Bastard of Staten Island's Wu-Tang Clan, who played the histrionic, stereotype-flaunting fool to his sober-ensemble-act allies. "Wu-Tang is real serious, we're always in deep concentration," bandmate Jason "Inspectah Deck" Hunter explained, "and he's the dude who would show up and fart in the middle of all of it." Jones balanced his theatrical eye-bugging by flaunting more menacing stereotypes, like criminality (two years in jail for drug offenses), irresponsible fatherhood (he failed to pay child support, and did little to dispel reports that he had thirteen children, though he actually had seven), and welfare leaching (his first solo album cover featured his purported public assistance I.D. card, and he once had MTV film him picking up his food stamps in a limo).

The most frequently invoked link between rap music and minstrelsy involves a subgenre that describes activities far more felonious than food-stamp hustling. When Stanley Crouch gets curmudgeonly, when Spike Lee identifies the "21st Century version of a minstrel show," or when congressional hearings on the dangers of stereotypes in rap music are conducted, the critics usually keep it "gangsta." It is not surprising that they would attack gangsta rap, an easy target that proudly delivers (to children, among others) graphic violence, misogyny, and profanity.

But equating these tales of violence, anger, and retribution with nineteenth-century tap-dance-peppered comic variety shows symbolized by broad, clownlike smiles is clearly problematic. Self-identified "gangstas" legitimately earn many loathsome labels, including poor role models, unrepentant potty-mouths, calculating capitalists, dirty laundry–airers, and bad boyfriends. But they are not minstrels, at least not by any historical definition. Examining how and why that word has became one of the harshest insults and accusations these rappers bear is key to understanding the inflammatory contemporary usage of the M-word.

"Gangsta rap" can be used as a very broad term (at a 2007 congressional hearing on "Stereotypes and Degrading Images," Congressman Bobby Rush implied that all hip-hop falls into two categories: negative gangsta rap and positive conscious rap) or an extremely narrow one (critic Nelson George argued that only four acts—N.W.A., Eazy-E, Dr. Dre, and Snoop Dogg—qualify as gangsta). So it seems worthwhile to establish a definition before confronting its critics. Gangsta rap is a subgenre of hip-hop often featuring remorseless lyrics about violence and crime (frequently concerning the drug trade), and often including misogyny and coarse language (some of which draws from the vernacular of pimp culture). In itself this style and content is far from new or revolutionary. "Stagolee," a folk song about a black outlaw done in the African American "toast" style of oration, is a clear precedent. In the early 1970s, toast-inspired, rhythmically spoken, murder-and-pimping-themed performances were most famously done by Rudy Ray Moore (aka Dolemite), and most artfully executed on the 1973 LP *Hustler's Convention* by Lightnin' Rod (Jalal Mansur Nuriddin of the Last Poets). By the mid-1980s, when rap music's commercial and artistic leaps forward coincided with the rise of (and public fascination with) crack cocaine, gangsta rap's cultural moment had arrived.

Technically the first important gangster-themed rap song is 1984's "Drag Rap" by the Showboys, a novelty single about 1930s gangsters, using the theme music from the TV show *Dragnet* (a minor release at the time, it gained prominence when it was sampled in bounce music, a New Orleans style of party rap). But Philadelphia rapper Schoolly D is credited with birthing gangsta rap with his regionally popular 1984 single "Gangster Boogie" and his better-known 1985 recording "P.S.K. What Does It Mean?" (It meant Park Side Killas, a local street gang.) Ice-T used the latter as a prototype for his 1986 B-side "6 in the Mornin'," bringing crime-themed hip-hop to Los Angeles, where it would wildly procreate.

Eric Wright, an ambitious L.A. drug dealer known as Eazy-E, assembled the defining gangsta rap act, N.W.A. (Niggaz With Attitude), in the mid-80s. The group released its first record in 1987 and became superstars with the release of *Straight Outta Compton* the following year. N.W.A. became the prototype that defined for aspiring gangstas not only vocal and musical style, but also fashion and, perhaps most important, demeanor.

In lyrics and interviews Eazy-E and lyricist O'Shea "Ice Cube" Jackson claimed to be reporting on reality, but despite the rise in violent crime associated with the crack cocaine trade, clearly N.W.A. was engaging in hyperbolic fantasy. The songs "Straight Outta Compton" and "Natural Born Killaz" *both* open with a protagonist on a multigun murder spree involving a shotgun, a semiautomatic firearm, and a pistol (the ante is upped on the latter, in which he "ain't hesitatin'" to do "decapitatin'"). Eazy-E's song "Nobody Move" describes an elaborate bank robbery (which includes a hostage situation, a murder, a showdown with police, and the rape of a transsexual) as if it were a casual, everyday event. Their closest thing to a cautionary song, "Dopeman," describes the misery of addicts while farcically glamorizing the gold-bedecked, fancy-car-driving dealer, who has "bitches sucking on his dick, 24-7."

N.W.A.'s gangsta theology, laid out lyrically as the "Ten Commandments of the Hip-Hop Thugster," involves murder (in six of the Commandments), sex ("Always gotta fuck outta wedlock/I like it when the pussy goes snap crackle pop"), and anarchy ("Fuck any brainwashing man-made law"). These scriptures established a gangsta church that opened its pews to generations of hip-hop royalty, including Tupac Shakur, Geto Boys, Biggie Smalls, Raekwon, 50 Cent, Rick Ross, Clipse, Lil Wayne, and countless others. If themes of drug dealing, violence, and misogyny define gangsta rap, few non–Fresh Prince rappers over the last quarter century have not dabbled with or dived into the art form (and even Fresh Prince's "Parents Just Don't Understand" includes grand theft auto and statutory rape).

Which explains the concerns of parents, politicians, the

black middle class, and the Feds (who helped N.W.A. cement their outlaw status when F.B.I. executive Milt Ahlerich imprudently sent the group's label a letter of concern about their song "Fuck tha Police"). What it doesn't explain is why gangsta rappers seemingly became synonymous with minstrel-show performers in the eyes of their critics. The most prominent foe of gangsta rap, Dr. C. Delores Tucker of the National Political Congress of Black Women, called rappers "the new Stepin Fetchits" and the "Amos 'n' Andy of the 1990s." Writer Stanley Crouch bluntly stated that gangsta rap was "contemporary minstrelsy." A scathing editorial in *Billboard* lamented that "what white folks have always believed about black men is just what the work of Ice Cube, N.W.A., and other gangsta rappers confirms today. The chicken-thieving, razor-toting 'coon' of the 1890s is the drug-dealing, Uzi-toting 'nigga' of today."

Except that he isn't. Drive-by shootings and crack dealing are not the equivalent of the petty theft of chickens and melons portrayed in traditional minstrelsy, and the razor in a minstrel show was usually a punchline, not a threat of visceral violence. Gangsta rappers fundamentally do not fit into the mold of nineteenth-century minstrels. The prototypical gangstas from L.A. dressed relatively conservatively, did not dance or shuffle, trended away from the comic, and rarely smiled, let alone toothily grinned. They were not lazy, sloppy, poorly attired, or slow-witted like Sambo. In fact, they were the opposite: sharp-witted, business-minded, prolific recording artists. Their costumes were always neat and new, yet in contrast to the minstrel-era dandies, were less flashy than much of rap's prior attire. N.W.A.'s uniform—black jeans, crisp t-shirts, Starter-brand jackets, and black baseball-style caps (often bearing Oakland Raiders logos)—was partially inspired by gang wear, and specifically adapted from the look N.W.A. member Lorenzo "MC Ren" Patterson was wearing during the band's formation. Hardly ridiculous or flamboyant, this was far more low-key than the precedent: the punk/comic book/Afro-futurist-inspired outfits seen on early New York acts like Grandmaster Flash and the Furious Five.

The gangsta rapper is not Zip Coon, foolishly failing to navigate urban modernity because his attempts at whiteness fall flat. Not only is his attire subdued, save for occasional gold chains, but the only whiteness he overtly strives for is capitalism's riches. He presents himself not as a clueless urban buffoon, but as a savvy traveler in his city's segregated territories. Most strikingly, he is not presenting himself as harmless, which is an underlying theme of the stereotypes invoked in classic minstrelsy (though gangsta rappers are relatively harmless to white listeners, as they mostly fantasize about black-on-black crime).

Some minstrel-gangsta parallels exist. "Coon song" lyrics sometimes mention revolvers and razors. Both feature "criminality," the broadest of stereotypes if it includes fruit theft and mass murder. But fundamentally, comedy is at the heart of minstrelsy, and gangsta rap is certainly not light, goofy, and funny, though it does not eschew comedy entirely.

Gangsta rap's ability to present itself as fundamentally serious while sometimes engaging in the comic demonstrates hip-hop's complicated relationship with humor. Had Eazy-E followed his own instincts, N.W.A., and perhaps all subsequent gangsta rap, would have traveled down a more foolish path that would have been easier to place in the tradition of classic minstrel humor. Hip-hop journalist Harry Allen noted that his "absurd sense of humor [and] bilious style . . . made Eazy—a short, little man—carry on like the hip-hop Danny DeVito."

His first solo album, 1988's *Eazy-Duz-It*, like some of N.W.A.'s earliest songs, features self-deprecating lyrics, and even a dice-playing scene. But Eazy-E wisely yielded to his collaborators, writer-rapper Ice Cube (with his dire lyrics) and producer Andre "Dr. Dre" Young (with his urgent backing tracks), allowing them to set a more threatening tone that came to define gangsta rap.

N.W.A. was not devoid of humor. The mock trial that opens their most infamous song, "Fuck tha Police," has shades of minstrel comic Pigmeat Markham's signature "Here Comes De Judge" routine (Dr. Dre, swapping out advanced degrees to become Judge Dre, announces "Ice Cube take the muthafuckin stand . . . do you swear to tell the truth the whole truth and nothin' but the truth so help your black ass?"). After leaving N.W.A. (and becoming a solo artist responsible for some of the most nihilistic gangsta rap ever penned) Ice Cube eventually had his grandest success writing and producing *Friday*, a film in which he and comedian Chris Tucker spend much of the picture sitting on the porch performing comedy routines that would be recognizable to fans of the blackface vaudeville duo Miller and Lyles. "I'm not serious 24 hours a day," he explained to journalist Ira Robbins. "I have a sense of humor."

But the inclusion of snatches of comedy in gangsta rap does not determine the genre's character, because as a rule, all hip-hop uses comic elements as tools without transforming its tone. One foundation of hip-hop is "the dozens," the African American street game of insults and boasts, especially its punchline-based rhythm. The humorously amplified boasts of the street toast tradition are also ubiquitous in rap lyrics (Rudy Ray Moore, the pioneer of recorded toasts, appears on albums by Eazy-E, Snoop Dogg, 2 Live Crew, Big Daddy Kane, and others). Rappers frequently use ridiculous metaphors and similes and absurd pop culture references without compromising the weight or power of a song. "Jesus Walks" by Kanye West and Rhymefest is still considered a powerful statement of religious faith despite the line "The way Kathie Lee needed Regis—that's the way I need Jesus." Sensitive emo rapper Drake in no way compromises gentle, romantic lyrics like, "no makeup on, that's when you're the prettiest" by following it with the declaration, "I can make your pussy whistle like the *Andy Griffith* theme song." Along those lines, hypermasculine gangsta rappers never worry about being transformed into clowns or buffoons because they garner a few laughs. Despite humorous elements, gangsta rap ultimately (to quote a lyric that appears in Dr. Dre's "Fuck Wit Dre Day," Tupac's "Hit 'Em Up," Spice 1's "Three Strikes," Wu-Tang Clan's "Brooklyn Zoo," Geto Boys' "Ain't with Being Broke," Soopafly's "O.G. 2 B.G.," M.O.P.'s "Heistmasters," and B.G. Knocc Out & Dresta's "Real Brothas") "ain't no motherfuckin' joke."

However, many critics are unlikely to weigh the comedic nature of historic minstrelsy when reviving the term: for contemporary audiences feelings of discomfort, pain, insult, and shock may overwhelm any instinct to chuckle when surveying classic blackface material, so they can't be faulted for not associating minstrelsy with comedy. The contemporary use of the term seems to draw on only certain aspects of the black minstrel tradition: lowbrow African American performances of stereotypes for an audience that includes whites. Current usage suggests that this applies even to stereotypes like the violent brute and the sexually aggressive "buck" figures, characters that certainly were a part of white prejudice against blacks but were intentionally left off most minstrel-show stages. Overly sexualized women with no agency became a central theme in gangsta rap videos, which critics still equated with minstrelsy, despite the typical minstrel presentation of a desexed version of black womanhood.

Stanley Crouch all but admitted that his use of the term didn't fit the minstrel prototype when he categorized gangsta rap as a "minstrel update." The new characters he identified were "Threatening Sambo. Cursing Sambo. Whorish tramps who get cases of the wiggles any time money is mentioned." This redefinition was echoed by Reverend Al Sharpton, who referred to the "gangsterized thug Uncle Toms that entertain whites' worst opinion of black folks."

This concern with the white gaze, and fears about catering to the prejudiced expectations of whites, seem to be at the heart of this new definition. As this music enjoyed incredible mainstream success (N.W.A.'s first proper album went double platinum without airplay, and their follow-up was number one on *Billboard*), the performers often found themselves playing to massive stadium crowds. In the Midwest and Europe these seemingly all-white audiences would sing along every time the lyrics referenced "nigga." This led many critics to accuse the rappers of intentionally kowtowing to white prejudices for profits. While rap's rampant capitalism and tales of guiltless drug slinging indicate that an "anything for a buck" mantra is no source of shame, the form and content of gangsta rap was clearly not determined solely by white expectations. The market research firm Mediamark did find out that white consumers made up between 60 and 75 percent of hip-hop sales in the 2000s, but that figure corresponds to the racial breakdown of the U.S. population (in the 2000 Census, 75.1 percent of Americans identified as white). Even though an Idaho Ice Cube concert may have skewed Caucasian, urban black teens and adolescents have closely followed hip-hop artists' careers from the genre's inception, and most of the artists are certainly aware that white audiences craving "authenticity" are guided (as they are in fashion, music, and dance) by the desires of black teens. Thus, gangsta rappers exploiting stereotypes of criminality, brutality, and hypermasculinity (again, not terms one associates with Bert Williams or Stepin Fetchit) are directing their tales toward black audiences as much as, or more than, white ones.

There are several possible explanations for the revamped definition of "minstrelsy." One is simply a matter of evolution: as a century passes, and minstrelsy becomes a hazy concept (in part because offensive minstrel imagery is excised from old movies, TV shows, and cartoons), a new definition, less informed by precedent, takes form. Some confusion may also have arisen from the importance given to *The Birth of a Nation* in contemporary discussions of the portrayal of blacks in popular culture. This 1915 film featured whites in blackface portraying violent and sexually rapacious thugs who at other times behave just like minstrel-show performers, thus giving rise to a false equivalency between these characters and those of the minstrel stage. The stereotype of the malevolent and violent black male has ancient roots, and the cultural impact of the Nat Turner rebellion of 1831 made it practically inescapable in America. *The Birth of a Nation* was wildly successful in enshrining that stereotype. However, unlike that film, the minstrel show proper rarely featured threatening blacks.

Thus, based on historical amnesia and confusion, "minstrelsy" has been redefined to mean any behavior that invokes demeaning black stereotypes for a white audience, whether these stereotypes were seen in actual minstrel shows or in other contexts. Spike Lee and Stanley Crouch were raised in an era when black pride was reflected in the music that inspired them, not only in the highbrow jazz they both love, but in popular music as well, with James Brown preaching "Soul Power" and Motown artists demonstrating class and comportment. Thus, they seem disturbed to see black art fall beneath the standards they hold for their people's creative work and dismayed to hear music that they feel demeans black manhood rather than dignifying it. To present undignified blackness seems to be akin to appearing in blackface clown makeup in their eyes.

There is another significant reason for reviving terms like "sambo," "coon," and "minstrel." Studying the harshest critics of gangsta rap suggests that whether or not the accuser believes the comparison is accurate or important, those terms are invoked in hopes of shaming the subject into altering undesired behavior. Though many critics have legitimate concerns about tapping into a shameful past, others use "blackface" strategically, name-checking Sambo and Coon as vicious snaps in a game of the dozens. In attempting to shame young African Americans who engage in language so coarse and negative that Ice Cube proudly claims "the nigga ya love to hate" as a kingly title, they have reached back to what may be the only insults that might still have sting. In going into battle against the gangstas, they weaponized the word "minstrel."

Many of gangsta rap's foes consider the objectification of women in music videos the genre's most objectionable aspect. Congressional hearings were devoted to the subject, countless editorials addressed it, and a rowdy academic conference at the University of Chicago centered around it. Yet even in this context, the M-word was frequently invoked. Certainly black women were (by law) dehumanized and perilously fetishized in the nineteenth-century, but this was not a convention of the minstrel stage, and the near-pornographic imagery in rap videos obviously doesn't hearken back to mainstream entertainment from the 1800s. That this blatantly unminstrelish aspect of gangsta culture was at the forefront of so much criticism brings into question whether or not gangsta rap's critics actually believed this was a minstrelsy revival.

C. Delores Tucker, an African American civil rights activist who served as secretary of state in Pennsylvania and campaigned vociferously against gangsta rap from the early nineties until her death in 2005, seemed less passionate and invested in her charges of minstrelsy than in any other aspect of her criticism, yet she pointedly included passive-aggressive references to Amos and Andy in her discourse on the music. Tucker (who had the misfortune of having a profanity-rhyming last name, and unsuccessfully brought suit against Tupac for emotional distress when he lyrically addressed her by her full name, followed by "you's a motherfucker / Instead of trying to help a nigga you destroy a brother") was not concerned with stereotypes or clownishness; she was obsessed with young women and children at risk. So when she halfheartedly invoked minstrelsy while advocating for black girls, it was tactical.

Similarly, when Al Sharpton said gangsta rap was "the new way of Stepin Fetchit," he enunciated Lincoln Perry's alter-ego's name with streetwise gusto that suggests he believes the kids will hear him and not like it. Sharpton, Tucker, and others used names and language associated with minstrelsy—Minstrel, Coon, Sambo—to catch the ears of their community's youth, using some of the last words that contained any shock value in the post-gangsta-rap sea of profanity.

But this tactic doesn't seem to have been successful. Though rappers and hip-hop journalists counterattacked gangsta rap's critics (particularly Tucker, whose age, credentials, and motives were questioned), none of the artists seemed to have been particularly perturbed by the M-word, C-word or S-word. The fact that N.W.A.'s debut sold 2 million copies without radio airplay suggests that the press generated from criticism and protest was actually invaluable.

Perhaps the most powerful parallel between blackface minstrelsy and gangsta rap has to do with how uncomfortable and offended both art forms made many thoughtful people. Familiar, queasy feelings, previously associated with seeing red-lipped racist caricatures on a 1920s jar of "Nigger Head Oysters," watermelon-eating orgies in nineteenth-century Edison films, or clips of blackface would-be rapists in *The Birth of a Nation*, bubbled up when outlandish gangsta rap music videos hit the airwaves. It is this feeling, more than any historical links to burnt-cork stage plays, that accounts for Spike Lee saying, "if you look at a lot of gangsta rap videos, that's a . . . 21st century version of a minstrel show." Or Crouch claiming "minstrel images now dominate us again in the form of gangsta rap videos." Or hip-hop writer Faraji Whalen calling the music video show *Rap City* "a seemingly never-ending parade of escaped slaves who have somehow found their way to a Bentley dealer and a gun show. . . . Amos n Andy ain't got nothing on these boys."

It is notable that one of the most prominent black critics of gangsta rap, Bill Cosby, made harsh, sometimes cruel attacks on rappers and black youth that drew upon numerous stereotypes yet never specifically invoked minstrelsy. Cosby (who recorded proto–hip-hop funk records in the sixties and seventies, and launched the career of Charles Wright and the Watts 103rd Street Rhythm Band, a funky act that became so associated with Los Angeles hip-hop that when Eric "Eazy-E" Wright died many obituaries erroneously claimed Charles

Wright was his father), was not against rap on principle. In his 2004 *Fat Albert* movie, Cosby's characters love rap music (though they're shocked by the profanity) and in 2009 Cosby oversaw the release of a conscious rap album by a group he named the Cosnarati (he did not rap on it). He hated gangsta rap and blamed that music for proliferation of "the n-word" and profanity in black youth culture. Yet in the tour, media appearances, and book that followed his infamous 2004 "pound cake" speech (in which he publicly showered harsh words on black youth), Cosby never compares the "lower economic people who are not holding up their end," or artists and fans engaging in "black thug fantasy" to minstrel performers. A reason he avoided that tactic may have been revealed in 2008 when he took a trio of black comedians to task for making racial jokes about Barack Obama. He called the comedy routines "minstrel time," and with the same sense of shaming that critics of gangstas used when invoking blackface, he added, "those three guys are minstrels without having to put on the makeup." However, he quickly backtracked, not in deference to the contemporary comedians, but in deference to Cosby's comedic predecessors.

"I'm doing minstrels a disservice," Cosby reflected, "because some of the minstrel jokes at least showed a little more thought."

Gangsta rap's popularity eventually faded, no thanks to its critics, though its influence remained. Dr. Dre, one of the genre's architects, went on to mentor and produce the wildly popular, frequently violent hip-hop of Eminem and 50 Cent. But despite the sales triumphs of Dre's protégés, in recent years the lion's share of rap sales, radio play, and, some would say, innovation has come not from hip-hop's traditional capitals (New York and Los Angeles) but from the American South, courtesy of artists like Lil Wayne, T.I., and OutKast. Many of the southern rappers who found themselves atop the hip-hop heap basked in bold, irony-free incorporations of the comic, the absurd, the stereotypical, and the southern, all adding up to the broadest, most shame-free embrace of the black minstrel tradition in popular culture seen in over half a century.

Perhaps these countrified, comical, contemporary southerners have faced fewer charges of minstrelsy than the original gangstas because critics were frustrated in their own quixotic antigangsta campaigns. But it may also be because the standouts from the region provided their critics with far more contemporary crises to deal with than the revival of nineteenth-century antics. The first southern rap stars, 2 Live Crew, proved so profane that obscenity laws were rewritten on their behalf (resulting in scholar Henry Louis Gates testifying in court that the Floridians were drawing not upon minstrelsy, but rather upon oral traditions dating back to Africa). In Houston the codeine-inspired, molasses-slow remix style of Robert "DJ Screw" Davis did not inspire invocations of Stepin Fetchit sloth, but did help popularize recreational use of prescription-strength cough syrups to the point that pharmacies nationwide changed security policies. Fellow Texans the Geto Boys, despite recalling minstrel and vaudeville variety segments by showcasing a dancing dwarf, earned their criticism by featuring lyrical explorations of mental illness and pathology so violent that Senator Bob Dole railed against them in his failed 1996 presidential campaign, and Geffen Records refused to distribute their major-label debut.

But looking past the smoke of the sex, drugs, and violence, southern rap appears to fit more squarely in the black minstrel tradition than its East and West Coast cousins. From its inception, hip-hop from the "Dirty South" embraced low comedy, raucous festivity, and century-old rural stereotypes in ways that were taboo for too-cool coastal crews.

The foundation for southern hip-hop was laid in the mid-eighties by Luther "Luke Skyywalker" Campbell, whose Miami-based 2 Live Crew became rap's first Confederacy-state commercial success. Creating outrageous songs more concerned with party functionality than radio play, the group was overtly comic, with little concern for cool or tough posturing. DJ Mr. Mixx, a member of 2 Live Crew, summarized, "We was Eddie Murphy, Redd Foxx, Richard Pryor, just as a rap group."

Campbell established southern rap's aesthetics on two fronts. Artistically he created coarse, simple, repetitive song structures, a formula that has been revisited by southern rappers for a quarter century. Unlike East Coast rap's oratorical nimbleness ("flow") or West Coast rap's narrative drive, southern hip-hop values vocal prowess less than the ability to make the party jump, as it recognizes its role as social music for a populace that values gatherings, hospitality, and communal space. In contrast to the East Coast audience for a song like "Lean Back" by New York's Terror Squad (a theoretical dance track with a chorus declaring, "my niggas don't dance"), southern rap never shames its audience (or its rappers) for moving something.

Some southern party dances have shuffles, jumps, and arm movements that recall steps done in minstrel shows. This reflects direct lineage more than a revival. Unlike black artists mimicking whites pretending to mimic blacks (as with minstrel dialect comedy), William Henry Lane, aka Master Juba, the nineteenth-century minstrel dancer credited with establishing the style that became popular in shows, learned many of his moves from amateur black mentors prior to joining the circuit. Lane's version of the buck-and-wing dance from the 1840s became the buck dance, which was performed on minstrel stages around the world (and can be seen in the 1903 silent film *Buck Dance*). That stylized tap dance survived throughout the 1900s and was kept alive in New Orleans in a version done by Second Liners at parades. And this in turn eventually developed into a black club dance that inspired *Buck Jump Time*, the regionally popular debut record of Byron "Mannie Fresh" Thomas. His production work for Cash Money Records helped redefine hip-hop, and establish Dwayne "Lil Wayne" Carter as one of pop music's most powerful artists. Lane's chain of influence, which links him to contemporary southern hip-hop, is unbroken.

Campbell also built southern rap through his entrepreneurial example. By running all aspects of his record label, he paved the way for DIY moguls like Percy "Master P" Miller and DJ Screw to start their empires at the selling-records-out-of-a-trunk level. This allowed recordings to include unfiltered black vernacular that may have been compromised in a white-owned, shareholders-beholden corporate structure, and also rewarded pandering to the lowest common denominator in a way that likely kept lurid subject matter and stereotypes at the fore. Because of this black distribution and production model, these recordings, by author Nelson George's accounting, are "not the vision of white men in suits [but are instead] pungent products of the black male imagination."

The use of vernacular (dubbed "Country Grammar" by rapper Nelly) reveals another parallel between minstrel-era oration and southern hip-hop. Contemporary rappers' theatrical use of regional slang brings to mind the absurd faux-black dialect of minstrel-show performers. Rappers like Juvenile, Gucci Mane, and David Banner stylize their drawls. Exaggerated pronunciations that rarely occur in natural conversation are emphasized, with words like "here" and "there" becoming "*hurr*" and "*thurr*" in the mouths of emcees from New Orleans, Atlanta, and St. Louis. Rappers like Field Mob's Shawn "Kalage" Jackson employ what writer Roni Sarig called an "overstated, minstrel-like delivery" with phrases like "I luv'ded you."

"Southern rap lyrics are full of hyper-regional slang," Ben Westhoff explains in his book *Dirty South*. "Formal rap structures and metaphor-heavy rhymes are often forsaken in favor of chants, grunts, and shouts." Some critics consider these grunts and the exaggerated pronunciations to be a dumbing down of hip-hop's oratory traditions, analogous to minstrelsy's malapropisms. Wu-Tang Clan's Robert "RZA" Diggs posited that southern rappers lagged behind emcees from his region because they "evolved later than us," and were still "frying fat back in the kitchen." But their use of slang has more to do with regional pride than historical dialect comedy, and the lyrical minimalism is a strategy employed so as not to bog down pumped-up festivities with excess verbiage, not a sign of stupidity.

One symbol that has stood as shorthand for minstrel imagery for over a century—a black male showing off a wide toothy grin—was revived and ornamented when "grills" became de facto accoutrement for successful southern rappers. While New York rappers like Flavor Flav and Just-Ice sported gold, jewel-encrusted dental caps prior to southern rap's ascendancy, the trend reached a tipping point in the early 2000s when adapted by trendsetters like Atlanta's Lil Jon and Houston's Paul Wall (who runs a successful side business manufacturing the jewelry). Grills evoked minstrelsy more vividly than any other aspect of southern rap culture, primarily because they encouraged oversized, unnatural teeth-baring smiles. The unusual jewelry also brings to mind Zip Coon's antics of futilely attempting to appear urbane by spending money unwisely (Wall sells grill sets for $10,000, and in 2009, Lil Wayne told talk-show host Jimmy Kimmel that his choppers cost $150,000). The foolishness is compounded when one considers the health risks involved: prior to his 2010 incarceration for weapons possession, Lil Wayne required eight root canals and a number of implants to repair the teeth that deteriorated under his deluxe dentistry.

However, unlike his northern brethren, Lil Wayne is not ashamed of looking or acting wild or foolish. He became a pop music superstar in the late 2000s by embracing the bizarre with unusual musical productions featuring froglike vocals that make even violent content seem unthreatening. Between his comical compositions and extreme appearance (in addition to his ornate teeth, his often-shirtless body and face are covered with hundreds of tattoos) it's understandable that some perceive buffoonery in Lil Wayne's public persona. "He, essentially, validates the centuries-old lies told about Blackness as a racial demerit," cultural critic Tolu Olorunda wrote on AllHipHop.com. "Lil Wayne is the epitome of a twenty-first-century Minstrel. Stepin' Fetchit in the flesh. He bucks, coons, and shines, for the shillings tossed his way." Olorunda was angered by a song featuring Lil Wayne's joyful description of preparing ("whipping") cocaine that used the imprudent metaphor "whip it like Kunta Kinte," referencing the slave from the book and miniseries *Roots* who was lashed and dismembered for his insolence. Despite his (cannabis-aided) heavy-lidded eyes, Lil Wayne defies the slothful Fetchit caricature—one of the defining aspects of his public persona is a manic, seemingly drug-fueled work pace that has resulted in almost thirty full-length albums and mixtapes in a decade. But Olorunda's reaction has little to do with the specifics of the Stepin Fetchit character and more with Lil Wayne's shamelessness: he embraces the low, the criminal, the clownishly absurd, and the stereotypical, and he does it as pure entertainment, with little concern for imparting lessons or any "uplift" beyond raising the coffers of his Young Money crew. Like many of the great black minstrel and postminstrel-show performers in the late nineteenth and early twentieth centuries, Lil Wayne is not (as Olorunda charges) kowtowing to white audiences, but instead crafting the best, lowest, most outrageous material he can without being embarrassed that white people see it.

Lil Wayne's appearance and mannerisms were also attacked in the harshest accusation of southern hip-hop minstrelsy to date (though it came from a critic with a horse in the race). The Internet video *Eat Dat Watermelon* by New York rapper Nas opens with a *Star Wars*–style scroll blaming the degradation of hip-hop culture on "the corporate world . . . ridiculous dances, ignorant behavior, and general buffoonery." Nas predicts the future of hip-hop by having comedians Nick Cannon and Affion Crockett wear the jewelry, clothing, and hairstyles favored by southern rappers, and don blackface makeup, including prominent red and white cartoonish lips. Playing their hip-hop beat on a gold banjo, the duo (named "Shuck N Jive") grunts like Lil Wayne while doing a shuffle dance and holding slices of watermelon, endlessly repeating the lyric, "Eat dat watermelon, eat dat watermelon, eat dat watermelon, sho' is good!" At one point a close-up shows diamond-encrusted grills taking a huge bite of melon. The short song (about ninety seconds) ends with a blinged-out watermelon, with diamonds spelling out the coon rappers' names, exploding as Nas (not in blackface) shakes his head and laments, "Yo check it all, this is Nas, and if that don't stop, hip-hop is dead" (the last three words were the title of the album he was promoting, making the video more a controversy-courting commercial than an unfiltered political statement).

Nas's 2008 video was also striking because it was two years late. In 2006 the ascendency of simple, repetitive southern rap singles, coupled with the emergence of YouTube as a method for breaking underground, DIY, budget-free acts (like Atlanta's Soulja Boy), opened the door for comparisons between Southern rap and blackface. In the wake of Memphis's Three 6 Mafia's televised performance in advance of winning an Oscar for "It's Hard Out Here for a Pimp" from the film *Hustle and Flow*, Stanley Crouch wrote that "a minstrel show interrupted the Academy Awards." Later that year Byron Crawford, an online columnist for the hip-hop magazine *XXL*, declared that "record labels are rushing out to sign the most coon-like negros they can find," resulting in a wave of acts that "can only be viewed as an outright and purposeful embrace of minstrelsy." He dubbed this new trend "Minstrel Show Rap."

Crawford's article targeted three specific acts. The first was a St. Louis rapper named Jibbs who had a pop-rap hit record that year with "Chain Hang Low," which borrowed its melody and lyrics from the children's song "Do Your Ears Hang Low?" a cleaned-up version of "Do Your Balls Hang Low?" a soldier's song dating back to at least World War II. That melody was borrowed from "Turkey in the Straw," which started life as one of the best-known minstrel-show songs, "Zip Coon." Crawford accusingly pointed out the song's distant minstrel lineage as if that were irrefutable evidence that Jibbs was a willfully self-degrading twenty-first-century Sambo. Though it is seductive for both damners and praisers of the black minstrel tradition to point out a composition's minstrel ancestry as significant, since Jibbs (fifteen years old at the time of the recording) probably couldn't trace the song's lineage further back than neighborhood ice-cream trucks playing the melody, this work's connection to blackface stagecraft was likely unintentional.

Crawford's second target (a Yankee) was DJ Webstar, a producer who realized that tunes about black youth dances could become viral video sensations. Webstar's mind-numbingly repetitive song drew millions to YouTube to learn to do the "Chicken Noodle Soup," as demonstrated by youngsters doing the energetic dance. The scant lyrics to the song don't abjectly invoke minstrel stereotypes (other than referencing poultry), but anyone who has seen an early Edison Company film of black children doing the dances associated with Topsy/pickaninny characters will find the shuffling, arm-flapping jig familiar.

But by far the most interesting figure in Crawford's would-be hall of shame was Ms. Peachez. As portrayed by husky aspiring comedian Nelson Boyd, Peachez is a sassy, aggressive, wig-wearing diva who (as seen in her YouTube videos) spends her days cooking soul food for packs of dancing children, cackling blunt, catchy lyrics about southern pride and country cuisine, and negotiating the rural backwoods and black-owned neighborhood businesses of Shreveport, Louisiana.

In the breakthrough video "Fry That Chicken," Peachez is operating an open-air restaurant of sorts in a rural dirt patch, with the skeletons of rotting shacks providing the real estate to attach a cardboard, handwritten sign reading "PEACHEZ GETTO FRIED CHICKEN." As her press-on-nail-bearing fingers batter, massage, and do puppetry with raw chicken carcasses, Peachez raps, "I got a pan, and I got a plan, I'm-a fry this chicken in my hand." Surrounding Peachez's grease-spattering skillet are a swarm of young black children, singing, dancing, and licking fingers as they voraciously gobble up her wares.

Even if one sets aside the grotesque drag (which was an element of some minstrel shows, but has a complicated history in black and white American comedy), it would be hard to tally up the stereotypes recycled from minstrel-era sources, especially when taking into account the follow-up video "From Da Country," with a supporting cast that included Uncle Shorty, a toothless midget attacking a huge slice of watermelon, and Chickenhead, a dancing rapper in a chicken suit. Crawford is left speechless by this video, calling it indefensible, then foregoing descriptive critiques. He lets a quote from one of the video's thousands of racist YouTube comments demonstrate how damaging and humiliating he feels these images are: "Ms Peachez is suing the man that filmed this because . . . this was a private family reunion and not a rap video," the anonymous commentator wrote. Other critics were willing to get more specific.

"The most disturbing part is the prominent role children play in the video," wrote columnist Jabari Asim for the *Washington Post* Web site. "More than a dozen young people—most of whom look no older than 12—cavort to the beat while deliriously stuffing themselves with chicken flesh and sucking rapturously on the bones . . . [*The Birth of a Nation*] seemed mild when compared to 'Fry That Chicken.'"

LA Weekly columnist Ernest Hardy saw more promise in it. "Ms. Peachez' shtick is almost performance art—a knowing embrace of stereotypes, a dead-on replication of rap's state-of-2006 beats. It's also an unabashed celebration of things many black folk still have shame around: Southern-ness, countriness, faggotry and ingenuity born of poverty . . . a hodgepodge of cultural pride and internalized racist stereotypes."

After discovering Peachez's secret identity and tracking down Boyd, as well as Peachez's producer Dale Lynch, Ben Westhoff found that the participants claimed to subscribe to neither their critics' nor their defenders' schools of thought. "The video was pure innocence," Lynch explained; "it had nothing to do with coonery, no negative vibe at all . . . We're used to seeing stuff like that in the south. We eat fried chicken! We eat watermelon!" Boyd also denied that his comedy was intentionally exploiting or parodying minstrel stereotypes. "I'm from the country," he shrugged, "that's how we do." Which is certainly the right thing to say considering the flack the gangstas caught for their alleged minstrelsy, and is perhaps sincere in the sense that it's likely that neither Boyd nor Lynch are schooled in minstrel-show history, and may have never even seen the 1950s *Amos 'n' Andy* sitcom. But they certainly know they are playing with taboo subjects, drawing on time-proven black comic traditions, and clowning in a low, ridiculous manner. Ms. Peachez is doing what minstrels have always done—they act happy, free, and silly; they purvey demeaning stereotypes without giving a hoot; and they provide both themselves and their audiences with laughter and liberation.

But regardless of the why-they-did behind the how-we-do, they didn't do for long. Peachez had a relatively popular follow-up ("In the Tub," a parody of 50 Cent's "In Da Club," in which Boyd raps in an outdoor metal tub in a junk-filled rural yard), but by 2007 the mojo was fading. *Getto Bar B Q* (in which Peachez has made her business mobile with a run-down school bus, modified with smokestacks, spinner hubcaps, and chicken cages) was more outrageous than the debut. But despite raising the stakes (Boyd raps about grilling a live rat, and there are confounding shots of black youth pouring barbeque sauce on their feet) this video garnered less than 10 percent of the views of "Fry That Chicken," 412,606 at this writing, compared to 4.5 million. Despite Byron Crawford's claims, no record label rushed out to sign this "coon-like negro," and Boyd and Lynch dissolved their partnership, retiring the character. Ultimately diminishing returns, not social criticism, closed the Peachez Getto Fried Chicken franchise.

But the long-term commercial failure of today's most preposterous perpetrator of minstrel plantation comedy tropes neither ended nor discredited the practice of celebrating black southern stereotypes. And anyone quick to dismiss the rough-edged Peachez as a low-class anomaly should note that some of the South's most critically revered, intellectual rappers also went this route. Kentucky's Nappy Roots recorded *Watermelon, Chicken & Gritz*, Atlanta's Goodie Mob (now known as the launching pad for Thomas "Cee-Lo Green" Calloway) saluted "a heaping helping of fried chicken," and the promo copies of the first OutKast album came with a set of dice. While it's conceivable, though barely credible, that the team behind *Fry That Chicken* had no idea people would take offense, undoubtedly Cee-Lo, André 3000, and their conscious cohorts chose to explore the cuisine, patois, virtues, and vices of the American South with full knowledge that many of their bourgeois brothers and sisters would prefer that this laundry go unaired. But southern pride wouldn't let that be, and just as Williams and Walker trumped Caucasian blackfacers in the 1890s by dubbing themselves Two Real Coons, southern rappers with drawling flow, buck-jump-inspiring chants, and soul food for fuel may very well have overtaken their northern neighbors by doing it how they do.

The secret ingredient in this success gumbo seems to be the

one that was left out—shame. Raucous comedy, clownish demeanor, rural cuisine, exaggerated expressions, and "dirty laundry" can all be drawn from both real-life experience and theatrical traditions developed in the days of burnt cork. But codes of dignity and masculinity, inner struggles caused by Du Boisian "double consciousness," and spoken and unspoken mandates to uplift the race have pressured generations of black artists to keep these themes and inspirations in check. Perhaps, like the contemporary revelers on the New Orleans Zulu floats, today's rappers can let loose and have fun because their generation doesn't bear the weight of the cultural memories of the civil rights and Black Is Beautiful eras. Or perhaps the freedoms their forebears fought for have allowed them to experience artistic freedom so broad that taboo buffoonery is again on the table. Whatever the reason, the most shameless hip-hoppers have proven one thing: they do not require their critics to redefine minstrelsy. They can do fine redefining it themselves.

Surprisingly, despite the triumphs of minstrelsy-embracing southern rappers, it is in the Midwest heartland rather than the heart of Dixie where one finds definitive proof of the failure to curtail stereotypical behavior by crying "*Minstrel!*" After his TV glory days ended in 2008, William "Flavor Flav" Drayton (the man most consistently called "coon" in contemporary culture) returned to the hip-hop world that spawned him, touring and recording with Public Enemy. Always open to new revenue streams, in 2011 Drayton proved truth to be more ridiculous than fiction when he opened a real-life restaurant called Flav's Fried Chicken in the predominantly white town of Clinton, Iowa. The FFC logo (which appeared on a towering sign, dwarfing the neighboring KFC) featured a bright, gaudy image of a

Iowa patrons enjoy Flav's Fried Chicken. JOE FASSLER.

shiny-faced Drayton grinning from ear to ear. Though it would be possible for this to look more like a minstrel-era black mascot product label, you would be hard-pressed to find any American goods in the last fifty years bearing a logo so similar to those odious artifacts. Shortly after it opened, Joe Fassler, a writer for the *Atlantic*'s Web site, cornered Drayton in the then-bustling bistro (it closed less than four months later, due in part to conflicts between Drayton and a business partner). The journalist collected a few choice quotes about the restaurateur's pride in his secret recipe and the affinity he'd developed for Clinton when Public Enemy began touring through the small city in 1987. Fassler prepared to ask Drayton how he could reconcile operating a fried-chicken joint with Public Enemy's radical politics and black empowerment messages. Of course, it's obvious how Drayton would respond: using an endman's wit, he'd crack a clever joke, he'd employ some tricksterlike misdirection, and he'd draw upon his African American comedic ancestors to simultaneously act like a hapless fool while deftly maintaining control.

Unlike the scowling gangstas that entered the game in his wake, much like the handful of overt hip-hop jesters that he counted as contemporaries, and in solidarity with the festive southern rappers who built upon his legacy, Flavor Flav understands that the comic rituals, the absurd stereotypes, and the fearless foolishness that have been a part of black comedy since the days of minstrelsy are useful tools. Perhaps the black minstrel tradition is something that can't be mentioned aloud, its name something to ignore if it's hurled your way. But if handled correctly, Flav's actions seem to declare, it's nothing to be ashamed of.

Alas, the *Atlantic* writer never got to hear Flav's mischievous nonresponse, because he never asked his question.

He chickened out.

Zora Neale Hurston photographed by Carl Van Vechten,
one of her white patrons, in New York City, April 3, 1938.

9.

WE JUST LOVE TO DRAMATIZE

How Zora Neale Hurston Let Her Black Minstrel Roots Show

ZORA NEALE HURSTON'S *THEIR EYES WERE WATCHING GOD* is the single most widely read book written by an African American. With U.S. sales totaling about 150,000 copies each year, it outsells—by a wide margin—all others, including *Invisible Man, I Know Why the Caged Bird Sings, The Color Purple, A Raisin in the Sun, Narrative of the Life of Frederick Douglass,* and *The Autobiography of Malcolm X.*

Yet when it was first published in 1937, Richard Wright, who would soon be considered one of America's greatest black novelists, damned it in no uncertain terms. His review in *New Masses* read, in part,

> Miss Hurston *voluntarily* continues in her novel the tradition which was *forced* upon the Negro in theater, that is, the minstrel technique that makes the "white folks" laugh. Her characters eat and laugh and cry and work and kill; they swing like a pendulum eternally in that safe and narrow orbit in which America likes to see the Negro live: between laughter and tears. . . .
>
> In the main, her novel is not addressed to the Negro, but to a white audience whose chauvinistic tastes she

> knows how to satisfy. She exploits the phase of Negro life which is "quaint," the phase which evokes a piteous smile on the lips of the "superior" race.

Wright's words have been more or less dismissed as the Marxist—and sexist—attack of a writer whose conception of black fiction was diametrically opposed to Hurston's. Hurston would get her revenge on Wright the following year, when she gave his *Uncle Tom's Children* an extraordinarily nasty review in the *Saturday Review*—the first book review she ever wrote. As Henry Louis Gates writes, "No two authors in the tradition are more dissimilar than Hurston and Wright."

Yet Wright's words, if taken not as a critique of the novel but as a description of it, have considerable merit. For Hurston, there was nothing the least bit wrong in "making the white folks laugh." And while Hurston never saw any good in white minstrelsy, to be associated with the black minstrel tradition might have been, to her, not only unproblematic but fitting. Hurston had been closely associated with black minstrels for years by this point, and she publicly praised performers in the tradition. And insofar as that tradition intersected with the folk traditions that blacks brought with them from Africa and developed during their generations in slavery, *Their Eyes Were Watching God* reflected it well.

This in no way diminishes Hurston's achievement. It is simply untrue that, as Wright put it, "the sensory sweep of her novel carries no theme, no message, no thought." For *Their Eyes Were Watching God* takes black minstrel traditions and transforms them into a profoundly affecting masterpiece whose sense of liberation parallels that found in those traditions.

—

As is well known, Zora Neale Hurston grew up in an all-black southern town—Eatonville, Florida—and was immersed in black folklore practically from birth. She grew up to play a prominent part in what we now call the "Harlem Renaissance," a movement of black writers—including Langston Hughes, Countee Cullen, Claude McKay, Jean Toomer, and Sterling Brown—who were explicitly inspired by black folk traditions and transformed them into artworks that appealed both to the black intelligentsia and to their white benefactors. Of these writers, Hurston was the most concerned with presenting these folk traditions in an unadulterated fashion—as her two books of folktales bear out. She also adapted them not only for fiction—as she's now most famous for—but also for drama. She explicitly recognized throughout the process that she was doing so for a mixed audience.

Almost inevitably, then, Hurston dabbled in minstrelsy in her stage works, since, as she recognized, the black folk and minstrel traditions intersect. In 1925, the year of her first play, *Meet the Mamma*, New York's theatrical productions included a blackface *Uncle Tom's Cabin* adaptation entitled *Topsy and Eva* and a musical entitled *Lucky Sambo* featuring a character named Aunt Jemima. Given this atmosphere, it's small wonder that *Meet the Mamma* reads almost like a minstrel pastiche, featuring a jungle dance, characters brandishing razors, and original songs like "Brown Skin Cora," "from way down Dixie way," who "came up North, but did not want to stay" because she missed her "good old chicken and stuff" too much. The play even incorporates the time-worn plot of an American whom the savages mistake for a god, and has the Africans brandish a "love stick" that's actually a baseball-bat-sized club.

Meanwhile, Hurston's fiction featured plenty of minstrel-show elements as well. In a scene in her short story "Sweat" (1926), one character remarks, "Thass right, Joe, a watermelon is jes' whut Ah needs tuh cure de eppizudicks"; soon the men hold a watermelon feast, interjecting such jests as "She don't look lak a thing but a hunk uh liver wid hair on it." The centerpiece of another dialect short story, "The Bone of Contention" (1929), is a courtroom scene that could have come straight out of a minstrel-show afterpiece: Jim is accused of stealing a turkey and hitting Dave over the head with a mule bone, and the lawyers get into a long, ridiculous argument about whether or not a mule bone is a weapon. Hurston often told this story at New York parties, and she would soon adapt it into a full three-act play entitled *Mule Bone* with the help of coauthor Langston Hughes.

Hurston's only Broadway play was *Fast and Furious*, an all-black review, which was produced in 1931. It starred Tim Moore, whose minstrel heritage is discussed in Chapter 5, and Jackie (later "Moms") Mabley, among others. Many of the lyrics were by Mack Gordon, who would soon write the notorious "Underneath the Harlem Moon." Hurston wrote four of the twelve sketches that comprised the review, of which *New York Times* drama critic Brooks Atkinson wrote, "In quantity and in toothsome exuberance the minstrels give full measure, [but when] the material is hackneyed, when the performers are fat and clumsy, the animalism of Negro entertainment is lumpish and unwieldy." Another critic commented on "a real frenzy of lightning-swift legs and rolling eyes." Clearly, *Fast and Furious* was viewed at the time as a continuation of the black minstrel tradition.

One of Hurston's sketches, "Lawing and Jawing," was another ludicrous courtroom scene, full of malapropisms. "Is you guilty or unguilty?" Judge Dunfumy (played by Tim Moore) asks, and then tells the lawyer, "Yo' mouf might spout lak a coffee pot but I got a lawyer dat kin beat your segastuatin'." He then turns to a girl he's taken a fancy to and asks her, "How am I chewin' my dictionary and minglin' my alphabet?" When the lawyer argues that "This is a clear case of syllogism!" and quotes eight lines from the nineteenth-century "Twinkle, Twinkle" parody that begins "Scintillate, scintillate, globule orific," the judge is convinced by the long words the lawyer uses to let his client go free.

"Lawing and Jawing" is clearly indebted to a long history of malaprop-spouting minstrel judges, which had recently appeared in *Darktown Jubilee, Africana, His Honery,* and *The Judge,* four all-black musicals of the 1920s; the tradition of wacky black judges (Dunfumy sentences one miscreant to nine years in a watermelon patch with a muzzle) was to be continued by Pigmeat Markham, Sammy Davis, Jr., and Flip Wilson (and to a degree, Judge Mathis, Judge Mablean, and their contemporary daytime court-show brethren). And, as Hurston would shortly point out in her essay "Characteristics of Negro Expression," which will be discussed more fully below, "Is you guilty or unguilty?" was a use of minstrel-stage rather than vernacular dialect: in that essay she argues in favor of the use of dialect, but distinguishes natural dialect from that of minstrels, specifying "ams" and "ises" as clear cases of the latter. In this play Hurston was reaffirming her continuity with the minstrel tradition, even as she was working hard on her study of black folklore, *Mules and Men,* whose initial draft was completed the same year.

After *Fast and Furious,* Hurston turned to what she called "a program of original Negro folklore" for her next stage show, *The Great Day,* in 1932. More a concert than a theatrical presentation, it consisted of songs and dance numbers with monologues, skits, and commentary interspersed. This show, for which no script survives, was Hurston's first real success, receiving positive reviews in New York newspapers like the *Evening Post* and the *Sun-Herald.* But for a revised version of it, entitled *From Sun to Sun,* presented the same year, she wrote a skit entitled "The Fiery Chariot" that echoes the minstrel tradition once again. Here, perhaps for the first time, Hurston presented the gullible, frightened Negro who had long been a staple of minstrel shows (and who would also appear in a number of the tales in *Mules and Men,* published in 1935). Ike, a slave, is tricked by Ole Massa into believing that God himself (played by Ole Massa in a sheet) is coming for him. He does everything he can to delay going with God, and ends up running for his life. Ole Massa is nonthreatening here, and the joke is entirely on Ike. While the story has clear roots in black folklore, it revives the same minstrel-show caricature that was providing careers for blacks in Hollywood at the time.

Wright had accused Hurston of "making the white folks laugh," and indeed, her theatrical work bears this out. But she made plenty of black folks laugh too. It often seems that Hurston never wrote a word without a mixed audience in mind. For playing to white folks was one of her literary aims from the very beginning of her career.

Hurston's first nationally published story appeared in 1924 in *Opportunity: A Journal of Negro Life,* the most important publication of the Harlem Renaissance. Called "Drenched in Light," it concerns Isis, a mischievous little girl, who runs off to a neighborhood barbecue, wearing her grandmother's brand-new red tablecloth as a shawl. She captivates the townspeople, who ignore the Grand Exalted Ruler of the Grand United Order of Odd Fellows in favor of watching her dance. The crowd includes two white men and a white woman. When Isis's furious grandmother comes after her, Isis runs away to a nearby creek, where she is found by the white folks. They ask her how to get to the Park Hotel in Maitland, and invite her into their car. As they drive past Isis's house, they stop to drop her off. The white lady asks Isis's grandmother, "You're not going to whip this poor little thing, are you?" The grandmother swears she will. So the white lady pays her five dollars to let Isis go to the hotel with her and dance for her in the red tablecloth. "I want brightness," she says, "and this Isis is joy itself, why she's drenched in light!" Hurston tells us, "Isis for the first time in her life, felt herself appreciated and danced up and down in an ecstasy of joy for a minute." The grandmother offers to comb her hair, but the white lady says, "I like her as she is." The story ends with Isis nestled against the white woman, who says, "I want a little of her sunshine to soak into my soul. I need it."

It's almost as if Hurston had written the story to validate Wright's later comments. The black girl, unappreciated by her family, performs for whites, who give her money and succor; she may appear ridiculous to her own folks, but the white folks adore her. "Drenched in Light" is a perfect parable of blacks "making the white folks laugh." Isis feels free and happy when she's performing for the whites—there's no self-consciousness or shame until her grandmother appears. In Hurston's view, "making the white folks laugh" is an act of liberation.

The story is, as Hurston's biographer Valerie Boyd points out, "almost completely autobiographical." Isis's childhood dreams correspond precisely to those Hurston details in her memoir, *Dust Tracks on a Road.* Like Isis, Hurston used to amuse white travelers and take short rides with them—without her parents' permission or knowledge. When they found out, she "usually got a whipping." Her grandmother (who bears the same name in the story as she did in real life) was particularly dismayed by Hurston's behavior. Soon two white ladies took a special interest in her after witnessing her performance of some Greek myths in school. They invited her to the Park House, the big hotel in Maitland, Florida, where they gave her candy and dolls in return for another performance. They continued to mail her clothes and books, and she has nothing but kind words to say about them in *Dust Tracks.*

Indeed, Hurston was remarkably proficient in pleasing white patrons, and rarely turned down an opportunity to cater to them, while at the same time serving her own purposes. Her education was funded primarily by contributions from white admirers, solicited by Annie Nathan Meyer, Barnard College's founder. In her letters to Meyer, Hurston even referred to herself as "your little pickaninny." She cultivated strong friendships with the men and women she referred to as "Negrotarians"—white humanitarians with an special interest in the welfare of blacks—especially Carl Van Vechten and Fannie Hurst. And her research into black traditions in Florida—research that would have an enormous impact on our present understanding of black folklore—was entirely funded by another white woman, Charlotte Mason, who paid her nearly $15,000 in the late 1920s and early 1930s, at the outset of the Great Depression, in order to deepen Mason's understanding of the "primitive" race.

This isn't to imply that Hurston studied black folklore only in order to make white folks happy. She also aimed to satisfy herself—and to make a mark in the black community as well. Juggling her white and black readers was no easy matter for Hurston. But she was committed to pleasing both.

"Making the white folks laugh" makes a later appearance in *Their Eyes Were Watching God*. Mrs. Turner is a light-skinned black woman who hates everything about blacks. "Ah can't stand black niggers," she says. "Ah don't blame de white folks from hatin' 'em 'cause Ah can't stand 'em mahself." When Hurston's protagonist Janie asks Mrs. Turner why she feels that way, she responds, "Dey makes me tired. Always laughin'! Dey laughs too much and dey laughs too loud. Always singin' ol' nigger songs! Always cuttin' de monkey for white folks."

Mrs. Turner soon starts talking about Booker T. Washington in the same terms. "All he ever done was cut de monkey for white folks. So dey pomped him up. But you know whut de ole folks say 'de higher de monkey climbs de mo' he show his behind' so dat's de way it wuz wid Booker T. . . . He didn't do nothin' but hold us back—talkin' 'bout work when de race ain't never done nothin' else. He wuz uh enemy tuh us, dat's whut. He wuz uh white folks' nigger."

Mrs. Turner's critique of Booker T. Washington—and of blacks in general—is in many ways prescient of Wright's critique of Hurston. Wright's statement that "Miss Hurston seems to have no desire to move in the direction of serious fiction" and his comment on her "facile sensuality" echo Mrs. Turner's scorn for "uh black woman goin' down de street in all dem loud colors, and whoopin' and hollerin' and laughin' over nothin'." Mrs. Turner's point of view may indeed be based on that of Hurston's earlier black critics, who not only felt she was "uh white folks' nigger" but were uncomfortable with unadulterated black folk traditions in general.

By making Mrs. Turner by far the most disagreeable person

in the novel—she only uses white doctors, only shops from white stores; she takes "black folk as a personal affront to herself"; she brags, "Ah ain't got no flat nose and liver lips"—Hurston implicitly affirms everything Mrs. Turner denies and denies everything she affirms. Clearly, for Hurston, the laughter of blacks is a good thing; by logical extension, so is "cuttin' de monkey for white folks."

Hurston's 1934 essay "Characteristics of Negro Expression," one of her contributions to Nancy Cunard's *Negro Anthology*, is perhaps the most explicit affirmation of the idea of the Negro as "primitive" ever written by an African American (though certain writings by Countee Cullen, Claude McKay, and Langston Hughes share this affirmative stance). This idea was, by then, at least twenty years old; it was the basis for the vogue for African art in the teens, Josephine Baker's career, Picasso's *Demoiselles d'Avignon*, Eugene O'Neill's *Emperor Jones*, Harlem's Cotton Club, and, in general, an abiding fascination among whites with the idea of the Negro as savage. As Valerie Boyd succinctly puts it, primitivism "was a form of racial essentialism rooted in a conviction that black people—if they'd only be their 'savage' selves—could save whites from the aridity of civilization."

Hurston's own essay begins:

> The Negro's universal mimicry is not so much a thing in itself as an evidence of something that permeates his entire self. And that thing is drama.
>
> His very words are action words. His interpretation of the English language is in terms of pictures. . . .
>
> Every phase of Negro life is highly dramatised. . . .

Everything is acted out. Unconsciously for the most part of course. . . .

Frequently the Negro, even with detached words in his vocabulary—not evolved in him but transplanted on his tongue by contact—must add action to it to make it do. So we have "chop-axe," "sitting-chair," "cook-pot" and the like because the speaker has in his mind the picture of the object in use. Action. Everything illustrated. So we can say the white man thinks in a written language and the Negro thinks in hieroglyphics.

A bit of Negro drama familiar to all is the frequent meeting of two opponents who threaten to do atrocious murder one upon the other.

Who has not observed a robust young Negro chap posing upon a street corner, possessed of nothing but his clothing, his strength and his youth? . . . His eyes say plainly "Female, halt!" His posture exults "Ah, female, I am the eternal male, the giver of life. Behold in my hot flesh all the delights of this world. Salute me, I am strength."

Hurston goes on to classify blacks into three groups: "the average Negro," who "glories in his ways"; the "highly educated Negro," who does "the same"; and the "middle class who scorns to do or be anything Negro." Hurston clearly considers herself one of the second group, "the truly cultured Negro[s]"; she has nothing but contempt for the middle-class black, who "wears drab clothing, sits through a boresome church service, pretends to have no interest in the community, holds beauty contests, and otherwise apes all the mediocrities of the white brother." (Here Hurston echoes quite clearly Langston Hughes's description of the black middle class in his influential

1926 manifesto "The Negro Artist and the Racial Mountain": "the whisper of 'I want to be white' runs silently through their minds"; her primitivist ideas were also informed by those of her former patron, Charlotte Mason.)

In this essay Hurston attempts to define an identity for her race that is entirely opposed to the previous definitions of Frederick Douglass and W. E. B. Du Bois, and the subsequent ones of Ralph Ellison, Albert Murray, and Stanley Crouch. For these writers, black Americans are dignified, thoughtful, and sophisticated; the only reason they sometimes act brutishly is because they are oppressed, not because it is in their nature. For Hurston, black Americans were truly primitive.

And this idea of black identity Hurston shared with black minstrelsy. There is little dignified, sophisticated, or elegant either in the minstrel show or in the Negro manner Hurston characterizes in "Characteristics of Negro Expression." The essay is broken into short sections entitled "Drama," "Will to Adorn," "Angularity," "Asymmetry," "Dancing," "Imitation," "Dialect"—all words that could describe the black minstrel show.

Near the end of the essay she makes this connection explicit. Rejecting both white minstrels and the highbrow entertainment of the Fisk Jubilee Singers and serious black theatrical troupes, she says, "Butter Beans [*sic*] and Susie, Bo-Jangles [*sic*] and Snake Hips are the only performers of the real Negro school it has ever been my pleasure to behold in New York." Butterbeans and Susie were stars of the Rabbit's Foot Minstrels; Butterbeans typically played a fool, with too-small clothes and floppy shoes. Hurston might have seen Bill "Bojangles" Robinson, one of the biggest black stars of Broadway and (later) Hollywood, in either or both of two shows. The printed program of *Blackbirds of 1928* depicted comic poker and graveyard scenes, and behind the chorus was a picture of a grinning child eating a huge slice of watermelon. And Brooks Atkinson wrote of Robinson's performance in the other show, *Brown Buddies* (1930): "Tap dancing is the material of his performing, but he translates it into a sort of rapture by the wild roll of his eyes and the expansive content of his beaming smile." As for Earl "Snake Hips" Tucker, he danced at the Cotton Club for Duke Ellington, illustrating the band's jungle effects, and was the first male headlining dancer who didn't do tap: instead he moved his pelvis and torso in suggestive ways. He was indeed the most "primitive" of the black dancers of his day; Ellington said of him that he was from "one of those primitive lost colonies where they practice pagan rituals and their dancing style evolved from religious seizures." Tucker may not have engaged in minstrelsy, but neither was there anything dignified about his act.

Hurston roundly despised white minstrelsy, and was sensitive to white condescension toward members of her race. It was fine for her, a black writer, to portray Negroes as primitives, but unconscionable for whites (including Charlotte Mason) to do so, for blacks alone could give such a portrayal the depth and complexity it deserved. In an essay she wrote in 1934 entitled "You Don't Know Us Negroes" (which has unfortunately never been published, though it has been quoted at length), she attacked minstrelsy and, in general, white portrayals of blacks, pulling no punches:

> The rules and regulations of this Margarine Negro calls for two dumb Negroes who chew up dictionaries and spit out grammar. They will and *must* go into some sort of business and mess it all up. . . . All Negro characters

> must have pop eyes. The only time they are excused from popping is when they're rolling in fright. . . . Most white people have seen our shows but not our lives. If they have not seen a Negro show they have seen a minstrel or at least a black-face comedian and that is considered enough. They know all about us. We say, 'Am it?' and go into a dance. By way of catching breath we laugh and say, 'Is you is, or is you ain't' and grab our banjo and work ourselves into a sound sleep. First thing on waking we laugh or skeer ourselves into another buck and wing, and so life goes. All of which may be very good vaudeville, but I'm sorry to be such an image-breaker and say we just don't live like that.

How does one reconcile this with Hurston's contemporaneous praise for Butterbeans and Susie and Bojangles Robinson? Perhaps by making three distinctions. First, black minstrelsy has merits that white minstrelsy doesn't. Second, black *expression* is distinct from black *life*: the former partakes of the primitive, of the grin and the dance, of malaprops, exaggerations, and dramatizations. Everyday black life, however, can be much more mundane—or, as in Hurston's novels, much richer. Third, the white perception of blacks can never come close to black self-perception.

But there is, perhaps, a double-standard here. As Boyd points out, Hurston objected when, on a fieldwork trip to Eatonville, a white professor she was with wanted to photograph a child eating watermelon. At the same time, however, "at a ritzy interracial party in New York, Zora had angered some of her fellow New Negroes by going straight for the watermelon. They viewed its inclusion on the buffet as a test of sorts, almost an insult, and had collectively vowed to abstain from the forbidden fruit. 'And leave all this good watermelon for the white folks?!' Zora dissented."

Ultimately, Hurston wanted to have her watermelon and eat it too.

Their Eyes Were Watching God was published in 1937, and marked the high point of Hurston's career. Hurston had been *retelling* all her life—retelling black theater and minstrel tales in *Meet the Mamma* and *Fast and Furious*; retelling folktales in *The Great Day*, *From Sun to Sun*, and *Mules and Men*; retelling her parents' life in her first novel, *Jonah's Gourd Vine*. But *Their Eyes Were Watching God*, like the best of her short stories, was *telling*. It was an entirely original concept, tracing a woman's journey from birth to middle age, and immortalizing the concomitant men she became attached to for better or worse. But more than that, it created a whole new world, a black world (with almost no whites), a world where blacks were by their very nature liberated to do and say what they wanted to. The African Americans who people *Their Eyes Were Watching God* seem to enjoy more freedom than those of any other black novel.

So it was, in a sense, only natural for Richard Wright to say that *Their Eyes Were Watching God* used a "minstrel technique," since minstrelsy also posited a world of absolute freedom, even if that world was a paradise of grinning fools. And there is one section of the novel that, while no less original than the rest, draws deeply from the black minstrel tradition. In Chapter 5, Janie and her husband Joe arrive in Eatonville. They are greeted by Lee Coker and Amos Hicks, the kind of lazy good-for-nothings typical of the minstrel show. When Joe expresses surprise that the town has no mayor, Coker explains, "Ah reckon us just ain't thought about it," and Hicks chimes in,

"Ah did think about it one day, but then Ah forgot it and ain't thought about it since then." Coker and Hicks use minstrelish malapropisms like "He's mighty compellment," "Ah'm uh son of uh Combunction," and "You just talkin' to consolate yo'self by word of mouth." Hurston makes a point through Coker: "Us talks about de white man keepin' us down! Shucks! He don't have tuh. Us keeps our own selves down." But the chapter as a whole—if one disregards the portions about Janie's relationship with Joe—would make a splendid minstrel afterpiece, with a big barbecue celebrating Joe's acquisition of the town's first streetlight, his comic speech about how the lamp is better than the sun, the singing of a spiritual, and the book's most delightful malapropism of all: "Dat chastisin' feelin' he totes sorter gives yuh de protolapsis uh de cutinary linin'."

While nothing else in the novel is quite as indebted to the minstrel show as this chapter, *Their Eyes Were Watching God* is undeniably theatrical and outrageously comic. Like those of the minstrel show, its characters are mostly lower-class, uneducated blacks; they indulge in broad gestures and exaggerated speech; they joke about mules and chickens; they stage nonsensical arguments; they embody a wide variety of stereotypes. Hurston's use of dialect, as the critic Otis Ferguson wrote in the *New Republic* at the time, "set[s] up a mood of Eddie Cantor in blackface." And the book's readers, both at the time of publication and now, certainly include plenty of white folks who enjoy witnessing the passionate, down-to-earth, unselfconscious behavior of blacks. As the *New York Herald Tribune Weekly Book Review* commented, the book presents "a flashing, gleaming riot of black people, with a limitless exuberance of humor," while the *New York Post* celebrated its "refreshingly pagan undercurrent of the joy of life and an earthy wholesomeness that is both racial and universal."

Yet two of the four prominent African American writers who wrote about the book roundly disparaged it, and a handful of less prominent black reviewers disliked it too. While the novelist and critic George Schuyler called it "one of the best novels of Negro life ever written" in the *Pittsburgh Courier* and the poet Sterling Brown gave it some faint praise in *The Nation*, Alain Locke, "the father of the Harlem Renaissance" and Hurston's former teacher, friend, and supporter, commented in *Opportunity*, "Her gift for poetic phrase, for rare dialect, and folk humor keep her flashing on the surface of her community and her characters and from diving down deep either to the inner psychology of characterization or to sharp analysis of the social background. . . . Progressive southern fiction has already banished the legend of these entertaining pseudo-primitives whom the reading public still loves to laugh with, weep over and envy. Having gotten rid of condescension, let us now get rid of oversimplification!" And then, of course, came Richard Wright's review in *New Masses*.

This decidedly mixed reception echoed that of *Mules and Men*, published three years earlier. The black critic Henry Lee Moon had given that book effusive praise in the *New Republic*. The review in *The Crisis* (the official journal of the NAACP), however, associated black folklore with minstrelsy, imputing that Hurston was "more concerned with [her] pocketbook than with the authentic life of the race." It pointed out that "those who profit from Negro primitivism have an obvious interest in preserving that primitivism," and called her a "literary climber." Sterling Brown, writing in *New Masses*, said that she portrayed her informants as "naïve, quaint, complaisant, bad enough to kill each other in jooks, but meek otherwise, socially unconscious. Their life is made to appear easy-going and carefree. This . . . makes *Mules and Men* singularly *incom-*

plete. These people live in a land shadowed by squalor, poverty, disease, violence, enforced ignorance and exploitation. . . . *Mules and Men* should be more bitter; it would be nearer the total truth."

Much the same could be said of the characters in *Their Eyes Were Watching God*—or the characters in a black minstrel show. And that was precisely Hurston's point. Through her writing, Hurston was providing a space for black Americans where they could thrive free from whites and their oppressive ways. The minstrel stage provided one such space; the Eatonville of *Mules and Men* and *Their Eyes Were Watching God* provided another.

From April 1936 to September 1937, Hurston lived in Jamaica and then in Haiti (with the exception of a two-month stay in New York City), where she wrote *Their Eyes Were Watching God*. In July 1937, seven months after finishing the novel, Hurston penned an outrageous essay entitled " 'My People! My People!' " which remained unpublished until 1995. In it Hurston attempts once more to define the essential characteristics of her race—here she enumerates seven of them.

But before laying out these characteristics, she takes a moment to jestingly lay into her old friend James Weldon Johnson, calling him "white enough to suit Hitler and . . . passing for colored for years. . . . Look at James Weldon Johnson from head to foot, but don't let that skin color and that oskobolic hair fool you. Watch him! Does he parade when he walks? No, James Weldon Johnson proceeds. Did anybody ever, *ever* see him grin? No, he smiles. He couldn't give a grin if he tried. He can't even Uncle Tom. Not that I complain of 'Tomming' if it's done right."

Here Hurston lays out her essential (if unstated) claim: the behaviors that respectable blacks are ashamed of when they encounter lower-class blacks are the *essential* black behaviors. And none of these behaviors runs counter to those displayed on the black minstrel stage. The *grin*, which writers like Johnson and Wright assiduously avoided, Hurston here reclaims as the nonpareil Negro act.

Hurston divides the remainder of her essay into seven sections, each devoted to one characteristic of "My People." The first is an inability to agree about anything. The second is a tendency to use "six big words where one little one would do." Her examples include "distriminate" for "slander" and "bodacious" for "entire." The third is a constant focus on the present with no sense of consequences. The fourth is a test: Put two piles of money on the table, $1,000 and $1.25, and leave the room. If a man enters and takes the dollar and a quarter, he is "My People," since he would never take more than that. The fifth is the "recognition of the monkey as our brother." Hurston doesn't elaborate much on this, but lets readers draw their own conclusions. The sixth is a love of imitation, a subject she had already dealt with at length in "Characteristics of Negro Expression." But here she applies imitation to ambition: Blacks want to imitate whites by proving that they can do anything that a white person can. The last characteristic is: "My People love a show. We love to act more than we love to see acting done. . . . We just love to dramatize."

Obviously, not all of these characteristics exactly pertain to minstrelsy. But Hurston clearly approves of the minstrel show's love of malaprops, parody, and exaggeration.

Hurston's essay is very funny, written with tongue firmly in cheek. But her points are at the same time forcefully expressed. She is not being satirical here. No matter how extreme her remarks may seem, she wants to get at an underlying vision. And that vision is that blacks are *indeed* different (culturally) from whites, and in many of the same ways that they've been characterized as such by whites.

Hurston's 1942 autobiography, *Dust Tracks on a Road,* includes a chapter with almost exactly the same title as this essay. But while it borrows a few lines from it, its conclusion is entirely different. "If you have received no clear-cut impression of what the Negro in America is like," Hurston writes, "then you are in the same place with me. There is no *The Negro* here. Our lives are so diversified, internal attitudes so varied, appearances and capabilites so different, that there is no possible classification so catholic that it will cover us all."

In this book Hurston definitively turns her back on the minstrel tradition. In recounting her life story, she says not one word about a single play she ever wrote. No mention is made of her collaboration with Langston Hughes or her stint on Broadway with *Fast and Furious*; no mention is made of Butterbeans and Susie, Bojangles Robinson, or Snake Hips Tucker. Hurston's publisher may have forced her to make these cuts, but either way, these are astonishing omissions, for they imply that she had finally learned to be ashamed of what she had never before been ashamed of. And never again would Hurston write favorably of the black minstrel tradition or include minstrel-like characters in her published work.

By the 1950s, Hurston had practically vanished from the face of American arts and letters. Her books were out of print and she could find no publisher willing to take a chance on her new ones. Ralph Ellison had written that Hurston had contributed "nothing" to African American literature; now it looked like he had been proven right. The condemnation she had endured at the hands of Wright, Brown, Locke, and Ellison—all of whom rightly saw her as a proponent of the black minstrel (or, in Ellison's words, "burlesque") tradition—had relegated her to oblivion. And her public opposition to desegregation certainly didn't help matters. "By 1955," writes M. Genevieve West, one of the most perceptive Hurston scholars, "her reputation was in ruins."

Tragically, Hurston did not live to see her vindication, which began almost immediately after her death in 1960. *Their Eyes Were Watching God* was reissued in 1965, and by 1971 it had become, according to the scholar Mary Helen Washington, "an underground phenomenon, surfacing here and there, wherever there was a growing interest in African American studies—and a black woman literature teacher." Perhaps the turning point was Alice Walker's 1975 *Ms.* magazine essay "In Search of Zora Neale Hurston," which described Walker's search for Hurston's unmarked grave, or Robert Hemenway's 1977 biography, which, according to West, "did more to stimulate Hurston's recovery than any other single text." By 1979, Harvard law professor Randall Kennedy was calling Hurston "the leading lady of black American letters between 1920 and 1950" in the *New York Times Book Review*. Her critical rehabilitation was complete.

It was also extreme. Rarely in the history of literature has a writer been so disparaged during her life and so praised in the years afterward. Usually rediscovered writers had been simply forgotten; but Hurston had been deliberately *erased*. And the primary reason for her erasure lay in her allegiance to the black minstrel tradition.

That tradition, however, had nothing to do with her revival in the 1970s. With the exception of *Mule Bone,* her plays were not collected and published until 2008, and writers have tended to ignore or minimize the significance of her theatrical work and her love of black comedy. Where the word "minstrel" is used in reference to Hurston, it's always paired with at least an implicit denial of Richard Wright's charge.

But Wright was on the money. Zora Neale Hurston did indeed use "the minstrel technique that makes the 'white folks' laugh," and she never apologized for it. Her conception of black identity and, therefore, of black literature depended in part on the intersection between the black minstrel and the black folk tradition—in other words, the use of black folklore to make white folks laugh. For in that intersection, she found a space of absolute freedom and joy.

Tommy Davidson and Savion Glover as Sleep'n Eat and Mantan in Spike Lee's *Bamboozled*.

NEW LINE CINEMA/PHOTOFEST.

10.

NEW MILLENNIUM MINSTREL SHOW

How Spike Lee and Tyler Perry Brought the Black Minstrelsy Debate to the Twenty-First Century

THE SCREEN HAS NEVER SEEN AS BOLD, as powerful, or as angry a response to the black minstrel tradition as Spike Lee's 2000 feature *Bamboozled*. The movie is a vehement damnation of black minstrelsy, a presentation of some of the art form's best moments, and, perhaps most valuably, a vividly illustrated catalogue of some of the greatest hits, misses, and embarrassments of American cinema's adoption of the form. In the years since its initial release *Bamboozled* has introduced fresh eyes and minds to shocking images and practices, and provided students of this complicated cultural history a useful tool to spark discussion, debate, and scholarship. It would be impossible to thoroughly study black minstrelsy and its impact on contemporary culture without lingering on this mesmerizing work.

The Atlanta-born, Brooklyn-reared Shelton "Spike" Lee emerged in the 1980s as one of the most original and prolific voices in American film, and he has directed (and often written, produced, and appeared in) an average of a new narrative film or documentary each year for over a quarter century. His first theatrically released feature, 1985's *She's Gotta Have It*, introduced Lee's highbrow-lowbrow hybrid of artsy film-school aesthetics and keep-it-real populism. The low-budget, highly profitable independent feature also sparked a new wave of black filmmaking, both independent and studio-financed, that has been sustained to the present day. Lee's trademarks became the overt messages of a "race man," an approach to scriptwriting and actor collaboration that resulted in debate-sparking ambiguity, and a branding of himself as a regular guy (sports fan, casual dresser, slang-slinger) who can still maintain the gravity, and high ground, of an *artiste*. This dichotomy leads to some contradictions, as Lee may challenge black consumerism in his texts while moonlighting as a director of effective TV commercials ("you know we love some new sneakers and I'm guilty—I have helped sell a couple. . . ."). While 1989's *Do the Right Thing* is his most important film, and 2006's *Inside Man* is his biggest hit, his most ambitious, original, and angry film was a low-budget, high-concept, self-declared satire that confused black and white audiences alike.

A difficult film that takes several viewings to appreciate, *Bamboozled* unsurprisingly met with critical and commercial indifference upon its theatrical release. But the ensuing decade has seen the film earn the respect it deserves. *Spike Lee*, in the the Pocket Essential series, declares it "Spike Lee's most powerful film." *Salon* calls it a "near-masterpiece." And in the documentary *The Making of "Bamboozled,"* New York University professor Clyde Taylor corrects anyone who doesn't realize it is "Spike's best film."

Bamboozled tells the story of Peerless Dothan (Damon Wayans), who has reinvented himself as Pierre Delacroix, an uptight dandy with an oddly affected accent who finds himself in the uncomfortable position of being the only African American writer-producer at CNS, a struggling television network that features black programming. After being dressed down by Dunwitty (Michael Rappaport), his over-the-top Wigger boss ("I probably know niggers better than you, and don't go getting offended by my use of the quote unquote N-word, I have a black wife and two biracial kids so I feel I have a right; I don't give a goddamn what that prick Spike Lee says . . ."), Delacroix and his assistant Sloan Hopkins (Jada Pinkett-Smith) come up with a subversive plan. They recruit two homeless buskers, Manray and Womack (Savion Glover and Tommy Davidson), and rebrand them Mantan and Sleep'n Eat (borrowing names from minstrelsy-inspired movie actors Mantan Moreland and Willie "Sleep 'n' Eat" Best). The performers are to star in *Mantan: The New Millennium Minstrel Show*, a television production that overtly revives minstrel-era entertainment and stereotypes, including blackface makeup, a plantation setting, watermelon patches, and tap-dancing pickaninnies. Delacroix's original plan is to create an explosive production that will expose his racist boss and get Delacroix out of his contract. When the show becomes a hit, sparking a blackface fad across the nation, Delacroix is seduced by success. He soon becomes as guilty of exploiting racism as his bosses or his nineteenth- and twentieth-century predecessors. The show's success enrages black activists, particularly the dimwitted, pseudo-revolutionary rappers the Mau-Maus (led by Sloan's brother, Julius, portrayed by Mos Def), who eventually kidnap and assassinate Manray (over a live web feed; the Mau-Maus are subsequently slaughtered by the police). Delacroix, driven to madness by the circumstances, is found in blackface by Sloan, slumped over in his office, surrounded by collectible racist knickknacks. While forcing him to watch a montage of offensive Hollywood images ("Look at this shit, look what you contributed to . . ."), Sloan avenges the deaths of her brother, her friend Manray, and her integrity by shooting Delacroix. He passively accepts his fate, his life eking away as a series of clips of blackface white actors, African

American minstrel comics, racist cartoons, and dancing pickaninnies fills the screen, underscored by a poignantly mournful Terence Blanchard composition.

***Bamboozled* was not** the first narrative film of the black cinema boom Lee helped launch that addressed the legacy of minstrel-era black screen stereotypes. Robert Townsend's 1987 comedy *Hollywood Shuffle* tells the tale of a black actor discovering that the film industry only offers blacks roles that perpetuate negative stereotypes. The movie features a series of comic vignettes. In the funniest sketch, "Black Acting School," a slothful Stepin Fetchit caricature finds himself in the middle of a slave melodrama, his brainless, marble-mouthed non sequiturs clashing with the overemoting and dynamic actions of his fellow runaway slaves. While the point of the sketch (the pathetic limitations of black celluloid representation) is expertly executed, it shouldn't be lost that the Fetchit character's jokes draw laughs. This is not merely because the informed audience recognizes a ridiculous and offensive stereotype, but also because the sketch revives the winning comic inventions of Lincoln Perry (whose film comedy often relied on his being the only cartoonish character in a more serious film, making even the dynamic juxtaposition in this scene more revival than revelation). *Hollywood Shuffle*'s audience is laughing at "Stepin Fetchit" because Stepin Fetchit *was* funny.

Unlike *Bamboozled*, which manages to indict past and present performers, black and white spectators, and guilty parties at every level of media production and consumption, *Hollywood Shuffle* has a myopic focus. Its concerns were not with the dangers and legacy of negative stereotypes or their impact on audiences, but specifically their effects on opportunities for actors.

Helaine Head's 1992 family film *You Must Remember This* and Cheryl Dunye's 1996 indie dramedy *Watermelon Woman* both addressed the mental pain and frustrating limitations black performers and directors faced in early-twentieth-century Hollywood. Neither film was concerned with challenging the broad impact of minstrel-era stereotypes, both focusing instead on the contemporary rediscovery of that era's black film images and on the humanity of forgotten performers. The closest any creators have come to matching Lee's levels of anger or audience discomfort were visual artists like Kara Walker, with her sickening silhouettes of *Uncle Tom's Cabin*–esque figures engaging in shocking behavior, or Michael Ray Charles, whose beautifully repulsive revivals of nineteenth-century racist imagery helped inspire Lee's film (Charles was a consultant on *Bamboozled*). At its best, however, *Bamboozled* trumps even the strongest works by Walker and Charles because Lee is able to showcase heartbreakingly fragile humanity by using a filmmaker's greatest art supplies—actual human beings (rather than the abstract figures depicted in such an effective, yet limited, fashion in the paintings).

Lee also uses, with mixed results, a film buff's mental catalogue. In interviews and publicity Lee has cited two films as direct inspiration for *Bamboozled*: director Sidney Lumet's 1976 satire *Network* and Mel Brooks's 1968 farce *The Producers*. Though he certainly drew many of his film's strengths from these sources, it's possible that *Bamboozled*'s cool critical and commercial reception can also be partially blamed on these homages. In addition to some overt textual references to *Network* (most notably Manray recalling William Holden's iconic speech by declaring onstage, "Cousins, I want you to go to your windows, yell out, scream with all the life you can muster up inside your bruised and battered assaulted bodies, 'I'm sick and tired of niggers and I'm not going to take it anymore!'"), Lee was excited to borrow that film's drastic shifts between comedy and drama. "We wanted the laughs to stop and get serious," Lee explained. "I love films where you mix it up, where a film doesn't keep the same rhythm, the same tone all the way through."

This tonal shift is jarring, as the last third of the film becomes an anxiety-driven, violent bloodbath. Though this nihilistic finale was certainly foreshadowed by the tense, dangerous material in the film's first seventy minutes, it may have been disturbing to filmgoers in ways that discouraged the word-of-mouth buzz necessary for it to find a wider audience. The last act also featured the introduction of an out-of-left-field sexual backstory for Sloan, reviving past accusations of Lee's mishandling of female characters.

But it was Lee's nod to *The Producers* that both shaped the film's plot and took Lee's trademark ambiguity to a confusing extreme. Like Brooks's comedy about a play designed intentionally to flop, Delacroix decides to combat his boss's racist requests and expectations by creating a show bound to fail spectacularly. "Dunwitty wants a coon show; that's what I intend to give him," Delacroix plots. "The show will be so negative, so offensive and racist, hence I will prove my point [that] the network does not want to see Negroes on television unless they are buffoons." In the same scene he explains that he expects this experiment will get him fired, his ultimate goal. Already this is a bit confusing, as those two goals (proving his point, getting fired), while not mutually exclusive, seem to have some contradicting dynamics (the former requires the show to be good enough to get into production to demonstrate his theory, but the latter needs the show to be bad enough to fail).

Though *Bamboozled* certainly intends to show Delacroix

being seduced by the show's eventual success, shifting his goals as he sells his soul, the idea of creating an intentionally bad program is undermined even before it begins. By building the show around Savion Glover, a spellbinding tap dancer whose brilliance can make audiences ignore even the shock of blackface makeup, Delacroix seems to be setting the show up to transcend the limitations necessary to fail. This continues during *Bamboozled*'s remarkable auditions sequence, in which Delacroix and Sloan defy the tactics used by Bloom and Bialystock in *The Producers*, consistently dismissing the absurd, awful, and ridiculous in favor of genuine genius. For the house band, they choose a group played by the masterfully dexterous, musically brilliant Philadelphia act the Roots instead of the Mau Maus. The latter is a clownish rap group whose vacuous, pseudo-revolutionary lyrics clash with *Mantan: The New Millennium Minstrel Show*'s themes, but whose desire to audition for a "coon show," and to ultimately have a mainstream TV show built around them ("Fucking Monkees had a show . . . the Partridge Family . . . if those motherfuckers had a show . . . ?"), implies they would willingly adjust their values for Delacroix's intended shipwreck.

Most notably, Delacroix and Sloan dismiss an R&B singer played by Tuffy Questell, who performs the repugnant song "I Be Smackin' Them Hoes," despite the fact that he perfectly fits the Def Comedy Jam/*Showtime at the Apollo* emcee model. Instead, they hire Honeycutt, portrayed by Thomas Jefferson Byrd, whose stunning audition demonstrates a brilliant distillation of African American oratorical traditions. Channeling everyone from Rudy Ray Moore to James Brown to the Last Poets, Honeycutt references actual minstrel-show history (a dialect Shakespeare routine: "To be or not to be, you know . . . that is the motherfucking question . . .") and dissects the nature of the black minstrel tradition ("Do blackface and a monkey shine, cut a jig at the same time. 'Cause niggers is a beautiful thing . . ."). Had Delacroix wanted to prove that white TV execs embraced the worst stereotypes and create a show bound to fail, certainly the hoe smacker would be a better choice than this riveting genius whose deep understanding of the nature of minstrelsy is likely to elevate the quality of their production. But *Bamboozled* isn't *The Producers*. Even though the ambiguity of Delacroix's motivations may have made this film more confusing for some viewers, it seems that both Delacroix and Lee had an idea that they were creating something special here. Filling screen time with anything less than brilliance would be a waste.

Not to imply that Lee wanted to make his show-within-a-film seem attractive to viewers of *Bamboozled*. The director does all he can to make the scenes from *Mantan: The New Millennium Minstrel Show* stand out as repugnant. Though *Bamboozled* was mostly shot on grainy digital video stock, the footage of the show is shot on rich Super 16mm film and presented with oversaturated colors to make these sequences grotesquely seductive (filmmaker Zeinabu irene Davis has written that these scenes demonstrate the African American cultural concept of "beautiful-ugly"). The shiny, greasy-looking, pitch-black makeup, glistening blood-red lips, and beads of sweat breaking through the sinister masks make the ominous nature of this minstrel show viscerally obvious. These scenes, in fact, look nothing like television: they are awkward, stagey, staccato routines, which are profanity-laced and not-ready-for-prime-time. In doing this, Lee increases the depth of discomfort, causing most of the comedy routines on *Mantan* to lose any comic punch.

The *Mantan* segment that maintains the most comedic impact is *Bamboozled*'s adaptation of a well-known routine called "indefinite talk." This classic black minstrel bit is perhaps the easiest one to study because of its inclusion in 1943's *Stormy Weather*, one of mainstream Hollywood's few black-cast films prior to the 1970s black action movie boom. In that backstage musical black comedians Flournoy Miller and Johnny Lee (both in blackface) perform what scholar Arthur Knight calls "the most remarkable" black blackface routine in cinema history. The routine (which Redd Foxx credits Miller with developing) involves a lively conversation between two characters who, with deft comic accuracy, keep interrupting each other, prematurely responding to the unspoken information they just cut off. It is an exercise in precise timing, a glorious subversion of the call-and-response tradition, and a sly commentary on the ambiguity caused by minstrelsy's malapropisms and mangled pronouns. It is also a surrealist romp, undermining the familiar dynamic of the knowing audience laughing at clueless Sambos by having the duo impossibly know exactly what they're talking about, while the amused audience is left in the dark.

What follows is an excerpt from Miller and Lee's *Stormy Weather* routine:

FM: He's gonna marry that widow whose husband used to . . .

JL: She's a fine lady! But listen, I heard that one time she . . .

FM: That was her daughter! You see, I'm keeping time with her.

JL: You is?

FM: Yeah, I've been engaged to her ever since the . . .

JL: I didn't know you knowed her that long. I worked with her brother and one day on the job the first thing I know . . .

FM: That was your fault! Now what you shoulda done was . . .

JL: I did!

FM: Now that's why I like talking to you, because we usually seem to agree with each other!

Miller had made this routine a part of his act by the 1920s, originally with his minstrel-stage, vaudeville, and Broadway costar Aubrey Lyles. He later did this signature piece with Lee, Mantan Moreland, and, in the 1951 low-budget minstrel-show nostalgia exploitation film *Yes Sir, Mr. Bones*, Scatman Crothers. Moreland went on to perform the routine in the 1940s in two Charlie Chan movies and in the 1950s with partner Nipsey Russell. As heard on a series of party records released on the Laff label in the early 1970s, Moreland was still performing the routine until shortly before his death in 1973. By the estimation of black comedy historian Mel Watkins, it was as familiar to black audiences as Abbott and Costello's "Who's on First?" was to white audiences.

Which makes it puzzling that Lee has his characters perform the routine incorrectly. Though the sequence in which they perform it features Davidson and Glover employing fine contemporary comic skills, the essence of the renowned routine is lost. The duo finish several sentences, and frequently pantomime specific answers, filling in comically crucial blanks with unambiguous hand gestures, leaving little of the indefinite talking indefinite.

Two excerpts from their routine follow:

SG: Lookee here, you know my lady Lucindy?

TD: Oh, you mean the one with the big *(indicates large breasts with hand gestures)*

SG: Oh no, not her, the one with the little, uh . . . *(mimes squeezing a behind)*

TD: Oh her!

SG: Yes, you see, uh, tomorrow's her birthday, and I want to get her something really nice, like one of those . . .

TD: No don't get her one of those. What you need to do is get her one of them . . .

SG: Oh no, no, now she hates them.

TD: That's too bad. Why don't you get her a dress?

TD: Ah boy, you getting fancy now! Why don't I just come on over and we get a double date?

SG: Oh no, man, I heard your lady is wild!

TD: No, no, that was her second cousin, the one that's married to Lil' Bit.

SG: Oh well, uh, because you know, uh, on our first date she let me . . . *(makes lewd, thrusting hand gestures)*

TD: That bitch didn't!

With respect to Watkins's "Who's on First?" comparison, certainly the routine is less familiar to contemporary black audiences than it was last century (Miller and Lee's scene is one of the few performances from *Stormy Weather* not enshrined on YouTube, though that likely has more to do with the burnt cork than the comedic content). And clearly Spike Lee gave Tommy Davidson room to improvise inside of skits (Davidson consistently inserts contemporary hip-hop asides into classic minstrelsy). It's also not surprising that a physical performer like Glover would have a predilection for gestures and body language. But in a film that is the most focused address of the black minstrel tradition in cinematic history, for Lee to allow the essence of the best-preserved black minstrel routine to be undermined seems to suggest either intentional sabotage or a deep misunderstanding of African American minstrel comedy.

Or maybe it's something in between those two: a calculated agenda of denial of the black minstrel tradition's place in African American comic culture. As demonstrated in his accusations of minstrelsy directed at gangsta rappers, Lee seems to associate minstrelsy with the perpetuation of any negative stereotypes of blacks, as well as the presentation of those in a space where whites can see them. Also implied are his concerns about the damage that past and present perpetuations of racist stereotypes have on contemporary African Americans. *Bamboozled* is not reviving historical theatrical practices to study them for their nuances and artistic influence, but instead to comment on contemporary mores. While white racism is eviscerated in the film, black behavior is also thoroughly critiqued, as Lee's satiric eye focuses on the contemporary antics of unself-aware rappers, over-the-top actors like Cuba Gooding Jr., thoughtless black consumers, absurdly histrionic melisma singers, and many other familiar contemporary African American characters. The worst of today's myriad crimes against black dignity, the film seems to say, are perfectly represented by the most odious of performance traditions: blackface minstrelsy. Lee may be undercutting the potency of indefinite talk because a demonstration that stereotype-burdened minstrelsy spawned innovative black brilliance does not fit his agenda.

Which isn't to imply that Lee is some kind of conservative, positivity-first, church values–spouting do-gooder. *Bamboozled*'s depiction of black comedy at its purest ignores uplift and bourgeois values: it's an all-black stand-up club where well-dressed patrons hear Paul Mooney (playing Delacroix's father) do dick jokes and drop the N-word dozens of times ("keeps my teeth white"). Lee loves low comedy, and he's surely pleased that a great deal of African American low comedy comes from sources other than minstrelsy. He likely prefers the oral traditions, toasts, street/pimp culture, storytelling, and other forms of humorous discourse that have allowed Richard Pryor to be vulnerably human, Bill Cosby to be a jazzy raconteur, Rudy Ray Moore to be a potty-mouthed poet, and Snoop Dogg to be a human cartoon, all without relying on the minstrel techniques practiced by Billy Kersands, Stepin Fetchit, Mantan Moreland, and their cohorts.

Lee himself was able to reject minstrelsy despite his early comic self-representation. The Mars Blackmon character he plays in *She's Gotta Have It* (and subsequent Nike commercials) is a fast-talking comic figure whom other characters sometimes view as a buffoon. In much of Lee's onscreen work he plays childlike, stereotypically slick characters whose manhood is often diminished to a degree by his juxtaposition with tall, handsome *über*-men like Denzel Washington and Michael Jordan. But one important difference between Lee's own comic characters and the stars of the black minstrel stages is that the tropes, cadences, and clownishness Lee is evoking do not recreate, reference, or undermine something previously performed by whites, or for that matter, expected by white audiences. When the trailer for *She's Got to Have It* hit screens, with Blackmon rattling off a slick hustler's rap trying to sell a black-and-white art film using the same tools an urban street vendor uses to sell tube socks and bootlegs, it was jarring. This was a character related to familiar black neighborhood figures, yet he had never been seen on-screen. Lee's characters may have been clowns, may have explored sloth, may have toyed with stereotypes, may have messed around with greed, lust, and irresponsibility, but these were demonstrations of genuine vices and foibles, not echoes of contrived black screen representations that had come before. This put Lee in the lofty position of the Man Who Cried Coon, allowing him to call out gangsta rappers ("the twenty-first-century version of a minstrel show") and producers and casts of contemporary black TV shows ("I would rather see *Amos 'n' Andy*; at least they were just straight-up about Uncle Tommin'") for crimes against black dignity.

Lee played that card in a TV interview with Ed Gordon on BET in 2009 in which he invoked the names he revived in *Bamboozled* a decade prior. "A lot of stuff that's out today is coonery and buffoonery . . . we could do better. We got a black president. Are we going back to Mantan Moreland and Sleep'n' Eat?" This reaction was inspired by seeing advertisements for TNT's black-cast sitcoms *House of Payne* and *Meet the Browns* (Lee said he did not watch the shows, but had the ads forced upon him during the network's NBA telecasts). This criticism was directed at the programs' producer, a man who had usurped Lee's position as America's best-known, most prolific black filmmaker, Tyler Perry.

Tyler Perry (born in New Orleans in 1969) produced his first play, an inspirational musical, in 1992. While the history of African American theater goes at least as far back as the African Company's works in the 1820s, the contemporary explosion of commercially successful independent black plays for black audiences began in the 1980s when playwright Shelly Garrett perfected his formula of directing material and advertising (most prominently on black radio) toward an all-black, predominantly female audience, resulting in years of sold-out performances for his touring comedy *Beauty Shop*. Subsequent creators like Perry, David E. Talbert, and Je'Caryous Johnson tweaked the formula by judiciously adding more church-oriented content. The network of venues where these plays thrive is often called the "chitlin' circuit," after the theaters and clubs that earned that name in prior eras, but the world of gospel stage plays differs from its predecessors in that tickets are often pricey, and despite the low comedy and raucous laughs in most plays, audiences consider it a respectable, cultural night out. The traditional line between the church and the juke joint is erased.

Though there had been a few attempts to cross these works over to the mainstream (*Beauty Shop* was adapted as an ABC sitcom that lasted six weeks in 1990), none succeeded until Perry's 2005 film adaptation of his play *Diary of a Mad Black Woman*. The feature opened as the number-one film in the U.S., grossed $50 million despite near-universal critical panning, and forced a recognition of the influence of the gospel stage play circuit, both by the mainstream entertainment industry and by a number of cultural critics quick to compare Tyler Perry to Lincoln Perry and his predecessors. Russell Scott Smith's 2006 *Salon* article on Perry titled "The New Amos 'n' Andy?" wondered if he was "a new stereotype-spouting minstrel," and quoted Gary Anderson, artistic director of Detroit's Plowshares Theatre, calling Perry's characters minstrel revivals ("He has the lazy coon, the pickaninny and the loose woman who wants everyone's man"). In his 2009 book *Brain-*

washed: Challenging the Myth of Black Inferiority, Tom Burrell (a pioneer in black-audience advertising) lamented that "nothing that occurred during Amos 'n' Andy's radio and television reign could match the words and actions of black comedies like [Tyler Perry's] Madea and The Browns." USC professor Todd Boyd was puzzled by Perry's success, saying that "minstrel shows are probably more progressive" than his films.

Though loud women, brutish men, cackling fools, and sassy, eye-rolling archetypes had always populated his plays (and the videos of the plays, which sold briskly in African American communities and played frequently in communal spaces like hair salons), these stereotypes seemed less odious without the white gaze brought on them by mainstream success. Perry's first offense was that his tremendous success allowed the white establishment to see that black audiences enjoyed black stereotypes on their own time. (Notably, audiences for these successful films remained predominantly black; a 2011 study published in the *Journal of Communication* found white audiences have little interest in seeing movies with black casts.) His revival of material indelibly associated with minstrelsy was another. The TV ads that Lee likely saw featured Mr. Brown (a clownish character portrayed on stage, TV, and cinema screen by Perry discovery David Mann) spouting absurd malapropisms in a cartoonish voice. Though Perry's sitcoms demonstrate some innovation by injecting dire urban situations and melodrama into the standard three-camera-laugh-track sitcom format (*House of Payne* is about a young father forced to move his family into his uncle's home after his drug-addict wife burns down their house), Perry never seems worried about drawing upon caricatures that embarrass the black bourgeoisie.

To many Perry's worst crime against black dignity is Madea,

his female alter ego at the heart of his empire. Perry contends that the brash, gun-toting, truth-telling matriarch resonates with audiences because she is an honest, if exaggerated, representation of familiar and necessary figures in the black community. Black drag has roots in black minstrel shows, which featured clownlike burly men in dresses and convincing female impersonators (Little Richard broke into showbiz as "Princess Lavonne" in the Sugarfoot Sam from Alabam minstrel show). Many consider the practice a crime against black manhood. "I hate to see black men in drag, symbolically castrated," film critic Sergio Mims wrote on the African American film Web site Shadow and Act, and syndicated columnist Daryl James declared, "the Black man in drag is one of the new coons." While performers like Flip Wilson, Martin Lawrence, and Eddie Murphy have enjoyed commercial triumphs portraying female characters, other black actors agree with Mims and James. During his interview with Oprah Winfrey, Dave Chappelle recalled producers begging him to wear drag. "I don't need a dress to be funny," he bitterly reflected. Conversely, Murphy has scoffed at his Oscar nomination for playing a James Brown–like character in *Dreamgirls*, insisting that his transformations into overweight females in his *Nutty Professor* films and *Norbit* are better examples of true acting. Perry also dismisses these critiques. "Why are black people complaining about what other comedians are doing?" he questioned. "It's a comedic moment, people just need to chill, let that shit go, man."

That uncharacteristically PG-13 statement was made during Perry's tireless press tour for his 2011 film *Madea's Big Happy Family*. Suffering a modest career setback (his 2010 adaptation of Ntozake Shange's play *For Colored Girls Who Have Considered Suicide When the Rainbow is Enuf* was a critical and commercial disappointment, only the second of his then ten films to not rank number one or number two in its opening weekend's box office), Perry appears to have calculated that courting controversy might boost ticket sales (*Madea's Big Happy Family* eventually opened at number two). Though Spike Lee had challenged Perry's work in 2009, and has remained publicly quiet on the matter since (other than writing on his Web site, "I'm not feuding with Tyler Perry"), Perry had harsh words for Lee that he repeated in several press junkets (often with no instigation): "Spike can go straight to hell! You can print that. I am sick of him talking about me, I am sick of him saying, 'This is a coon; this is a buffoon.' I am sick of him talking about black people going to see movies. This is what he said: 'You vote by what you see,' as if black people don't know what they want to see."

More interesting was this diatribe, which he repeated with some variation several times: "Langston Hughes said that Zora Neale Hurston was the new version of the 'darkie.' This woman wrote *Their Eyes Were Watching God*, she spoke from a southern point of view. Here Langston is in New York with his Harlem slickness and he couldn't understand it. I speak from the South, people love it. Why in the hell would I sit here worried about Spike Lee?" Putting aside that Richard Wright might be a better example (Hughes, who loved low comedy and may have dug Madea plays, once called Hurston "a perfect 'darkie' " in her dealings with white friends, but didn't attack her work like Wright), it's fascinating that Perry sees himself as Zora Neale Hurston in this formula. Like the southern rappers who have no shame in their "country" ways, Georgia-based Perry sees accusations of minstrelsy as an attack on his region by northerners whose "slickness" has removed them from their essence. Like Hurston, perhaps, Perry isn't shamed by white folks' laughter, and is proud of "common" black folks' ways.

Also note that he doesn't refute charges of coonery and buffoonery, he just lets the market decide.

Certainly, Perry was calling out Lee to get publicity (he later told *Ebony* that he would not do so again, citing sensitivity to Lee's children), although he was sincere in defending not only his work but also the black fans who love it. Lee never responded to Perry's attack. He also ignored a request by Oscar-winning comedienne Mo'Nique to mediate the nonfeud on her talk show. The director had made his case quite succinctly in *Bamboozled*.

The most amazing sequence in *Bamboozled* is the powerful montage that appears before, during, and after Delacroix's murder. This coda combines scores of images from cinema history now considered offensive, and features some of America's earliest films (including American Mutoscope's 1901 short *Laughing Ben*); some of Hollywood's most iconic movies (*The Birth of a Nation, Gone With the Wind*); white superstars in blackface (Mickey Rooney, Judy Garland, Eddie Cantor); a number of iconic black stars in stereotypical roles (Butterfly McQueen, Farina Hoskins, Stepin Fetchit); and animated images of cannibals at the cooking pot, Little Black Sambo facing tigers, Uncle Tom tomming, and mammies vigorously washing black babies. This new millennial montage may be the greatest survey of racially insensitive images ever assembled.

If Lee is commenting on how the entire body of ugly, stereotypical media images contributes to the racism that damages the psyches of white and black Americans, then there is no reason he should differentiate between black, white, and animated performers; between comic minstrel shows, plantation melodramas, and the grimly serious propaganda of *Birth of a*

Nation; between nineteenth, twentieth, and twenty-first century productions ("New Millennium? It's the same bullshit, just done over!" Womack declares in the film). As Lee demonstrates gracefully with brisk editing in a scene of a room of white writers trying to craft a black television script, a legitimate argument can be made that Pigmeat Markham's minstrel revival on *Laugh-In*, the clownish sitcoms of the seventies, and the media exploitation of the racial tensions surrounding O. J. Simpson's murder trial have all tattooed dehumanizing stereotypes onto the minds of white Americans. Thus, Lee is doing the right thing by lumping together seventy-plus diverse, shocking images.

But if *Bamboozled* wants to get into the heads of the black performers and creators at the heart of his film's narrative, then perhaps some nuances could have been explored. Maybe distinctions could have been drawn between Garland blacking up in a backstage musical, a cartoon jungle savage bouncing on a drum, and Mantan Moreland performing original, acrobatic, physical comedy. Lee's script does pay some lip service to the talent, worthiness, and tragedy of past generations' African American practitioners of the black minstrel tradition. But he always does so with qualified, faint, or sarcastic praise, never assuming that any of these comics could have had pride or agency in the work they did; that despite the painfully limited options available for black performers in mainstream film and stage, these particular artists may have found their calling, expressed their genius, and found a twisted form of freedom in the seemingly dumb antics of low comedy. That *Bamboozled*'s black practitioners/perpetrators of minstrelsy are shot to death for their crimes, seemingly deservedly so, makes the script's nods to the forefathers of black film comedy hardly seem sincere.

Certainly the comic who gets the worst of it in *Bamboozled* is the one whose name gets the most mileage, Mantan Moreland. "How does he make his eyes do that?" Manray asks in response to a video of a bug-eyed dice routine. "He was gifted," Delacroix answers, his phrase resonating in audiences' ears as an absurd joke. But Moreland *was* gifted. Though dismissed in the Bill Cosby–hosted 1968 TV documentary "Black History: Lost, Stolen, or Strayed" as a Stepin Fetchit impersonator, Moreland (born in 1902 in Louisiana) was nothing of the sort. The man Mel Watkins described as a "jittery, chubby, moonfaced [comic who] even when motionless projected boundless energy and excitement" was worlds away from the slothlike comedy of Lincoln Perry's Fetchit. He was an amazing physical comedian, occasionally demonstrating the dexterity of the Three Stooges' Curly Howard, and frequently contorting his elastic face into expressive, cartoonish masks. He also combined his resonant voice and Redd Foxx–esque comic timing to deliver killer punch lines. Though he specialized in the bulging eyes and fear of ghosts that came to be benchmarks of stereotypical black representation, in his hundred-plus screen appearances he not only provided comic relief for white casts (most famously as Birmingham Brown, chauffeur to Chinese detective Charlie Chan, portrayed by Caucasian actor Sidney Toler in "yellowface"), but also appeared in black-cast movies for black audiences, as well as on countless chitlin'-circuit stages during his sixty-year career. Some of the Moreland clips Lee uses are in fact from the 1942 black-cast film *Lucky Ghost,* the picture Cosby uses to illustrate the most heinous black stereotypes in "Lost, Stolen, or Strayed." This is the same footage that was lengthily excerpted in *That's Black Entertainment*, where in proper context we see Moreland's ridiculous character as a sympathetic figure among African American villains, heroes, clowns, and beauties. *Bamboozled* has some complicated commentary on black spectatorship. We are shown clearly that black laughter gives white viewers permission to laugh at the coon show. But it is unclear if the blacks in the audience of *Mantan's New Millennium Minstrel Show* are responding to the absurdity, the satire, the low comedy, or the applause signs. Presenting black laughter so ambiguously obscures Moreland's great triumph: for over half a century his clowning not only amused white theatergoers, but also endeared him to many thoughtful black audiences. "We liked Mantan Moreland," actor Ossie Davis observed. "His stereotypical presentation didn't make us look too bad."

In a later *Bamboozled* scene, Sloan tells Manray, "African Americans had to perform in blackface. You know that entertainer Bert Williams? He was brilliant. . . . Bert Williams and the rest they had to blacken up because they had no choice." To demonstrate, *Bamboozled* features several sequences of Davidson and Glover blacking up, shot in disconcerting close-ups, presenting the act as brutal torture. In Marlon Riggs' documentary on black stereotypes, *Ethnic Notions*, we see a similar scene, where actor Leni Sloan, portraying Bert Williams, blackens up in front of a backstage mirror, at first casually, then with the activity growing increasingly painful as he recounts tales of discrimination he faced despite his fame. Playwright Ralph Allen, fresh off the success of his Broadway burlesque revival *Sugar Babies*, also dramatized Williams's life in his flop 1986 musical *Honky Tonk Nights*. The playwright blames that play's failure in part on his decision to make his Williams-inspired character angry, despite Allen's extensive research actually convincing him that Williams "was a quiet man . . . essentially kind and happy." Spike Lee and Leni Sloan are artistically victorious in portraying the application of blackface as agony. But it is a jump in logic to conclude that because his stage persona was maudlin and because blackface seems inherently odious to contemporary sensibilities, Williams felt bitter about wearing blackface and was forced to do so. The soul-wrenching dressing room scenes in *Bamboozled* are amazing, and convey brilliantly Lee's thoughts about the suffering of artists forced to compromise or sell out, but it may not tell us much about Bert Williams and his contemporaries.

That *Bamboozled*'s imagining of the inherent agony of blacking up may be historically revisionist doesn't diminish the film's power: Lee isn't a historian; he's an artist with an agenda and a masterful presenter of a passionate position. Likewise, there doesn't have to be a contradiction in appreciating Tyler Perry's embrace of the low, the loud, and Ladies' Wear, and in appreciating the positions of his critics. Louis Armstrong's genius can't be written off because of the pleasure he took in romanticizing plantations, or wearing a cannibal king's crown. Zora Neale Hurston could make the white folks laugh and Richard Wright could take issue with her without either figure losing stature. One isn't inherently wrong for feeling pride or shame in craving Flav's Fried Chicken, humming "Ain't Nobody Here but Us Chickens," chuckling at an Amos 'n' Andy dialect routine, or catching a Zulu coconut or a *Good Times* rerun.

The glory and the frustration of opening up this burnt-cork-sullied can of worms is that it is not a journey that uncovers answers or solves puzzles. It's an exercise in problematization, as the more you learn, the more it muddies both historical and contemporary perceptions of black minstrelsy. However, doing dozens of interviews on the subject, reading scores of books, studying hundreds of articles, listening to hundreds of songs, and watching thousands of hours of footage reveal some themes that undeniably recur, even if we are hesitant to characterize them as conclusions.

It seems reasonable to deduce that regardless of one's opinion of white minstrel performers in blackface, African American minstrels were operating on a different plane. They transmogrified white imitations of blackness, they brought in their own cultural traditions, and they used the forum and form to practice entertainment innovations that still powerfully resonate. It demonstrated no contradiction or character flaw for Hurston to hate white minstrelsy while loving the work of the black artists who built upon that tradition.

It also feels safe to say that since the dawn of black minstrelsy African American artists have demonstrated that masking and foolishness can provide freedom as well as bondage. Though it may be painful to see such images in *Bamboozled*'s montage, many artists acted a fool and "blacked up" not just to get paid, and not just because of limited choices. They did so because the harsh realities of American racism could be temporarily eased by acting crazy, by becoming someone else. Many black audience members felt a similar release watching such antics.

Those audiences also demonstrated another of this subject's fascinating facets: the alchemy of spectatorship. The weight of the burden of stereotypes shifts dramatically when the white gaze is removed from black audience productions. This was true when the Rabbit Foot's Minstrels played to rural black crowds while en route to grand, segregated white-audience theaters in the North, and it's true when a Tyler Perry stageplay bootleg screens on a TV in a Detroit nail salon.

Some may feel the black minstrel tradition's muscles flexed most powerfully in 1895 when it birthed the glorious, amusement-park-scaled, 500-performer, epic theatrical behemoth *Black America*. But others may think it happened in 2005 when a three-inch-tall blackface pixie tore up a $55 million check. To champion the artistry and importance of early black minstrels isn't to diminish the shame, pain, or queasiness felt by those confronted with this practice. The heirs of the black minstrel tradition aren't just today's performers drawing from the uncouth comedy of blacks in blackface, but also the black intellectuals, activists, essayists, and artists building upon generations of dissent, disapproval, and demonstration.

Bamboozled, with its powerful dramatic distillations of pain and shame, joins lofty company in the antiminstrelsy Hall of Fame. Ralph Ellison's 1958 essay "Change the Joke and Slip the Yoke," perhaps the most powerful rebuke of minstrelsy ever written, argued that the damage of this white creation on black Americans was comparable to physical violence. Marlon Riggs's 1987 documentary *Ethnic Notions* examined the brutal legacy of stereotypes, using visual poetry to illustrate the damaging impact of Sambo, Mammy, and their cartoonish cousins. Caryl Phillips's 2005 fictionalization of Bert Williams's story, *Dancing in the Dark*, despite mischaracterizing the legendary entertainer, brought to life the confusion ethnic caricature can bring to racial identity. These are just a few of many milestones in black antiminstrelsy discourse, an art form almost as old as blackface comedy.

Black minstrelsy briefly burned brightly as America's top entertainment. Its artistic innovations subsequently made it easy for mainstream Hollywood to limit black screen representation to stereotypes honed on its stages. And it has succeeded in continuously reviving its signature techniques, jokes, characters, and themes, creating in every era new stars that rely on old tropes, some with sly subversion and some with one-dimensional straightforwardness. Throughout this long history an army of Spike Lees, Richard Wrights, Bill Cosbys, *Chicago Defenders*, and NAACPs has demonstrated equal inspiration and creativity to keep the lazy Sambos, malapropian mumble-mouths, and shameless fools in check. This timeless facet of American cultural history has spawned impressive works of both hilarious, shameless abandon and poignant, deliberate condemnation.

The black minstrel tradition is funny that way.

SOURCES

EPIGRAPH

Wilmore, Larry. "Is Blackface Ever OK?" *The Daily Show*, Comedy Central. November 11, 2009. Television.

CHAPTER 1: **RACIAL PIXIES**

Author interviews and correspondence: Daphne Brooks, Arnold "Gatemouth" Moore, Ira Padnos, Sascha Penn, Mel Watkins.

Abbott, Lynn, and Doug Seroff. *Out of Sight: The Rise of African American Popular Music, 1889–1895*. Jackson: University Press of Mississippi, 2002.

———. *Ragged but Right: Black Traveling Shows, "Coon Songs," and the Dark Pathway to Blues and Jazz.* Jackson: University Press of Mississippi, 2007.

"Antoine Dodson Warns a PERP on LIVE TV! (Original)." YouTube.com, July 29, 2010. Web.

Bogle, Donald. *Toms, Coons, Mulattoes, Mammies, and Bucks*, 4th ed. New York: Continuum, 2001.

Brown, Sterling A. "Negro Character as Seen by White Authors." *Journal of Negro Education* 3, no. 2 (April 1933): 179–203.

Chappelle, Dave. Interview by Anderson Cooper. *Anderson Cooper 360*, CNN. July 7, 2006. Television.

———. Interview by James Lipton. *Inside the Actor's Studio*, Bravo. September 10, 2006. Television.

———. Interview by Oprah Winfrey. *The Oprah Winfrey Show*, ABC. February 3, 2006. Television.

Chappelle's Show. Comedy Central. July 16, 2006. Television.

Chilton, John. *Let the Good Times Roll: The Story of Louis Jordan and His Music*. Ann Arbor: University of Michigan Press, 1994.

"The Christmas Story." *Amos 'n' Andy*, CBS. December 25, 1953. Television.

Crawford, Byron. "Minstrel Show Rap: Southern Hip-Hop Reaches Its Logical Conclusion." XXLmag.com. September 22, 2006. Web.

Cripps, Thomas. *Slow Fade to Black*. New York: Oxford University Press, 1977.

Crouch, Stanley. "Tupac Shows Risk of Being Rapped Up in Stage Life." *New York Daily News*, September 11, 1996.

Dramatic Mirror. Review of *Bandanna Land*. November 20, 1908. Quoted in Smith, *Bert Williams*, 108.

Du Bois, W. E. B. *The Souls of Black Folk*. Chicago: A. C. McClurg & Co., 1903.

Ellison, Ralph. *The Collected Essays of Ralph Ellison*. Edited by John Callahan. New York: Random House, 1995.

Farley, Christopher John. "Dave Speaks." *Time*, May 23, 2005, 68–73.

Indianapolis Freeman. "Williams and Walker in Vaudeville at Koster and Bilal's, New York City." February 29, 1897. Quoted in Sampson, *Ghost Walks*, 125.

Jones, LeRoi. *Blues People: Negro Music in White America*. New York: William Morrow, 1963.

Kendall, Mark. "A Time to Sing," *Pomona College Magazine* 45, no. 2 (2009).

Lott, Eric, *Love & Theft: Blackface Minstrelsy and the American Working Class*. New York: Oxford University Press, 1993.

Mamenta, Joanne. "Diamond Teeth Mary, 97, Dies." *Bradenton (FL) Herald*, April 9, 2000.

Miller, Monica. *Slaves to Fashion: Black Dandyism and the Styling of Black Diasporic Identity*. Durham, NC: Duke University Press, 2009.

New York Daily News. Review of *Simply Heavenly*, August 8, 1957. Quoted in Woll, *Black Musical Theater*, 236.

New York Herald Tribune. Review of *My Magnolia*. July 13, 1926. Quoted in Woll, *Black Musical Theater*, 114.

"Not Gone—Not Forgotten." *Chicago Defender*, May 27, 1957, p. 18.

Oliver, Paul. *The Story of the Blues*. Boston, MA: Northeastern University Press, 1998.

Pope, Kyle. "How Dave Spent His Summer (and Fall, Winter, and Spring) Vacation." *Blender*, April 2006, 70–78.

Powell, Kevin. "Heaven Hell Dave Chappelle." *Esquire*, May 2006, 92–99, 147–148.
"The Rare Coin." *Amos 'n' Andy*, CBS. March 20, 1952. Television.
Riggs, Marlon, dir. *Ethnic Notions*. KQED, 1977. Film.
Robinson, Simon. "On the Beach with Dave Chappelle," Time.com, May 15, 2005. Web.
Sampson, Henry T. *Blacks in Blackface: A Source Book on Early Black Musical Shows.* Metuchen, NJ: Scarecrow Press, 1980.
———. *The Ghost Walks: A Chronological History of Blacks in Show Business, 1865–1910.* Metuchen, NJ: Scarecrow Press, 1988.
Smith, Eric Lidell. *Bert Williams: A Biography of a Pioneer Black Comedian.* Jefferson, NC: McFarland, 1992.
Watkins, Mel. *On the Real Side: Laughing, Lying, and Signifying—the Underground Tradition of African-American Humor That Transformed American Culture, from Slavery to Richard Pryor.* New York: Simon & Schuster, 1994.
———, ed. *African American Humor: The Best Black Comedy from Slavery to Today.* Chicago: Lawrence Hill Books, 2002.
White, Shane, and Graham J. White. *Stylin': African American Expressive Culture from Its Beginnings to the Zoot Suit.* Ithaca, NY: Cornell University Press, 1999.
Wittke, Carl. *Tambo and Bones: A History of the American Minstrel Stage.* Durham, NC: Duke University Press, 1930.
Woll, Allen. *Black Musical Theatre: From* Coontown *to* Dreamgirls. Baton Rouge: Louisiana State University Press, 1989.
Wright, Richard. "Between Laughter and Tears." *New Masses*, October 5, 1937, 22–23.

CHAPTER 2: **DARKEST AMERICA**

Author interviews and correspondence: Nick Tosches, Mel Watkins.

Abbott, Lynn, and Doug Seroff. *Out of Sight: The Rise of African American Popular Music, 1889–1895.* Jackson: University Press of Mississippi, 2002.
———. *Ragged but Right: Black Traveling Shows, "Coon Songs," and the Dark Pathway to Blues and Jazz.* Jackson: University Press of Mississippi, 2007.

Allen, William Francis, Charles Pickard Ware, and Lucy McKim Garrison, eds. *Slave Songs of the United States.* New York: A. Simpson & Co., 1867.

Bean, Annemarie, James V. Hatch, and Brooks McNamara, eds. *Inside the Minstrel Mask: Readings in Nineteenth-Century Blackface Minstrelsy*. Middletown, CT: Wesleyan University Press, 1996.

Bernard, John. *Retrospections of America, 1797–1811.* New York: Harper & Bros., 1887. Quoted in Boskin, *Sambo*, 61.

Black America, advertisement of. In Abbott and Seroff, *Out of Sight*, 392.

Black America, reviews of. Quoted in Sotiropoulos, *Staging Race*, 23.

Boskin, Joseph. *Sambo: The Rise and Fall of an American Jester.* New York: Oxford University Press, 1986.

Boston Herald. Review of Georgia Minstrels. Quoted in Trotter, *Music:* 280.

Centennial Exhibition, Philadelphia, 1876, guidebook description of. Quoted in Rydell, *All the World's a Fair*, 28.

Charters, Ann. *Nobody: The Story of Bert Williams.* New York: Macmillan, 1970.

Clemens, Samuel. *The Autobiography of Mark Twain.* New York: Harper & Bros., 1959.

Cobb, Thomas R. R. *An Inquiry into the Law of Negro Slavery in the United States of America.* Philadelphia: T. & J. W. Johnson & Co., 1858. Quoted in Boskin, *Sambo*, 54.

Cockrell, Dale. *Demons of Disorder: Early Blackface Minstrels and Their World.* New York: Cambridge University Press, 1997.

Colored American, The. Review of *Darkest America*, November 11, 1896. Quoted in Sampson, *Blacks in Blackface*, 5.

Cook, James W. "Dancing Across the Color Line." *Common-Place* 4, no. 1 (October 2003). Web.

Crèvecoeur, J. Hector St. John de. *Sketches of Eighteenth Century America.* New Haven: Yale University Press, 1925. Quoted in Boskin, *Sambo*, 60.

Dickens, Charles. *American Notes for General Circulation.* London: Chapman & Hall, 1842.

Douglass, Frederick. "Gavitt's Original Ethiopian Serenaders." *North Star*, June 29, 1849, 1.

Du Bois, W. E. B. "The Negro in Literature and Art." In *Writings*, New York: Library of America, 1986: 862–67.

Ellison, Ralph. "Change the Joke and Slip the Yoke." In *Shadow and Act.* New York: Random House, 1964: 45–59.

Emerson, Ken. *Doo-Dah! Stephen Foster and the Rise of American Popular Culture.* New York: Simon & Schuster, 1997.

Entr'acte. Review of Haverly's Colored Minstrels, August 6, 1880. In Sampson, *Ghost Walks*, 43–45.

Fletcher, Tom. *100 Years of the Negro in Show Business!* New York: Burdge & Co., 1954.

Handy, W. C. *Father of the Blues: An Autobiography.* New York: Macmillan, 1941.

Haverly's Colored Minstrels, 1879 and 1880 descriptions of. Quoted in Toll, *Blacking Up*, 205.

Henderson's Colored Minstrels, review of. Quoted in Wittke, *Tambo and Bones*: 92.

Hill, Errol G., and James V. Hatch. *A History of African American Theatre.* New York: Cambridge University Press, 2003.

Huggins, Nathan Irvin. *Harlem Renaissance.* New York: Oxford University Press, 1971.

Indianapolis Freeman. Review of Richards & Pringle's Georgia Minstrels, October 24, 1896. Quoted in Abbott & Seroff, *Out of Sight*, 106.

Inter-Ocean, The (Chicago). Review of the Hyers Sisters Company, March 21, 1889. In Sampson, *Ghost Walks*, 58.

"Jim Crow" (lyrics). Quoted in Emerson, *Doo-Dah*, 65.

Johnson, J. Rosamond, ed. *Rolling Along in Song: A Chronological Survey of American Negro Music.* New York: Viking, 1937.

Johnson, James Weldon. *Black Manhattan.* New York: Knopf, 1930.

Kemble, Frances Anne. *Journal of a Residence on a Georgia Plantation in 1838–1839.* New York: Harper & Bros., 1863. Quoted in Boskin, *Sambo*, 46.

Lhamon, W. T. *Raising Cain: Blackface Performance from Jim Crow to Hip Hop.* Cambridge, MA: Harvard University Press, 1998.

Lott, Eric. "Blackface and Blackness: The Minstrel Show in American Culture." In Bean et al., *Inside the Minstrel Mask*, 3–32.

———. *Love & Theft: Blackface Minstrelsy and the American Working Class.* New York: Oxford University Press, 1993.

Mahar, William J. *Behind the Burnt Cork Mask: Early Blackface Minstrelsy and Antebellum American Popular Culture.* Urbana, IL: University of Illinois Press, 1999.

———. "Ethiopian Skits and Sketches: Contents and Contexts of Blackface Minstrelsy, 1840–1890." In Bean, Hatch, and McNamara, eds., *Inside the Minstrel Mask*, 179–220.

Marshall, Arthur, description of the Essence of Old Virginia. Quoted in Stearns, *Jazz Dance*, 50.

McCabe & Young's Minstrels. Reply to St. Augustine authorities, 1889. Quoted in Abbott and Seroff, *Out of Sight*, 66, and in Sampson, *Ghost Walks*, 58.

Miner's Journal. Review of *Darkest America*, 1897. In Abbott and Seroff, *Out of Sight*: 334–35.

Nathan, Hans. *Dan Emmett and the Rise of Early Negro Minstrelsy.* Norman: University of Oklahoma Press, 1962.

New York Clipper. Review of *Black America*, June 8, 1895. Quoted in Abbott and Seroff, *Out of Sight*, 392.

———. Review of Cleveland's Colored Minstrels, March 7, 1891. Quoted in Abbott and Seroff, *Out of Sight*, 113.

———. Review of *Darkest America*, July 13, 1895. Quoted in Abbott and Seroff, *Out of Sight*, 334.

New York Herald. Advertisement for the Virginia Minstrels, February 6, 1843. Quoted in Cockrell, *Demons of Disorder:* 151.

Nichols, Thomas L. *Forty Years of American Life*. London: John Maxwell, 1864.

Old Plantation concession, descriptions of. Quoted in Rydell, *All the World's a Fair*, 87, 147.

Oliver, Paul. *Songsters and Saints: Vocal Traditions on Race Records.* New York: Cambridge University Press, 1984.

Reynolds, Harry. *Minstrel Memories: The Story of Burnt Cork Minstrelsy in Great Britain from 1836 to 1927.* London: A. Rivers, 1928. Quoted in Sampson, *Ghost Walks*, 42.

Russell, Sylvester. "Smart Set in 'Enchantment': The Smartest Colored Comedy Ever Produced in America." *Indianapolis Freeman*, November 1, 1902. In Abbott & Seroff, *Ragged but Right*, 83.

Rydell, Robert W. *All the World's a Fair: Visions of Empire at American International Expositions, 1876–1916.* Chicago: University of Chicago Press, 1984.

Sampson, Henry T. *Blacks in Blackface: A Source Book on Early Black Musical Shows.* Metuchen, NJ: Scarecrow Press, 1980.

———. *The Ghost Walks: A Chronological History of Blacks in Show Business, 1865–1910.* Metuchen, NJ: Scarecrow Press, 1988.

Saturday Advertiser (Dunedin, New Zealand). Review of Hicks's Georgia Minstrels, July 7, 1877. In Sampson, *Ghost Walks*, 28.

Smith, J. F. D. *A Tour in the United States of America.* London: G. Robinson, 1784. Quoted in Boskin, *Sambo*, 60.

Sotiropoulos, Karen. *Staging Race: Black Performers in Turn of the Century America.* Cambridge, MA: Harvard University Press, 2006.

Southern, Eileen. "Blackface Musicians and Early Ethiopian Minstrelsy." In Bean, Hatch, and McNamara, *Inside the Minstrel Mask*, 43–63.

———. "The Georgia Minstrels: The Early Years." In Bean et al., *Inside the Minstrel Mask*: 163–175.

———. *The Music of Black Americans: A History*. 3rd ed., New York: W. W. Norton, 1997.

Stearns, Marshall, and Jean Stearns. *Jazz Dance: The Story of American Vernacular Dance*. New York: Macmillan, 1968.

St. Louis Dispatch. Review of *Darkest America*, May 1897. Quoted in Sampson, *Blacks in Blackface*, 6.

Toll, Robert C. *Blacking Up: The Minstrel Show in Nineteenth-Century America*. New York: Oxford University Press, 1974.

Tosches, Nick. *Where Dead Voices Gather*. Boston: Little, Brown, 2001.

Trotter, James M. *Music and Some Highly Musical People*. Boston: Lee & Shepard, 1880.

Virginia Minstrels, English review of, 1846. Quoted in Nathan, *Dan Emmett*, 125.

Watkins, Mel. *On the Real Side: Laughing, Lying, and Signifying—the Underground Tradition of African-American Humor that Transformed American Culture, from Slavery to Richard Pryor*. New York: Simon & Schuster, 1994.

———, ed. *African American Humor: The Best Black Comedy from Slavery to Today*. Chicago: Lawrence Hill Books, 2002.

Weatherford, Willis D., and Charles S. Johnson. *Race Relations: Adjustment of Whites and Negroes in the United States*. New York: D. C. Heath & Co., 1934. Quoted in Watkins, *African American Humor*, 1.

White, Newman I. *American Negro Folk-Songs*. Cambridge, MA.: Harvard University Press, 1928.

Winans, Robert B. "Early Minstrel Show Music, 1843–1852." In *Musical Theatre in America: Papers and Proceedings of the Conference of Musical Theatre in America*, ed. Glenn Loney. Westport, CT: Greenwood, 1984, 71–97.

Wittke, Carl. *Tambo and Bones: A History of the American Minstrel Stage*. Durham, NC: Duke University Press, 1930.

Woll, Allen. *Black Musical Theatre: From* Coontown *to* Dreamgirls. Baton Rouge: Louisiana State University Press, 1989.

CHAPTER 3: OF CANNIBALS AND KINGS

Author interviews and correspondence: Charles Chamberlain, Antoinette K-Doe, Lefty Parker, Quintron, Ned Sublette, Panacea Theriac

Abbott, Lynn, and Doug Seroff. *Ragged but Right: Black Traveling Shows, "Coon Songs," and the Dark Pathway to Blues and Jazz.* Jackson: University Press of Mississippi, 2007.

Armstrong, Louis. *Satchmo: My Life in New Orleans.* New York: Prentice-Hall, 1954.

Brothers, Thomas. *Louis Armstrong's New Orleans.* New York: W. W. Norton, 2006.

From Tramps to Kings: 100 Years of Zulu. Exhibition, Louisiana State Museum, New Orleans, 2009. (Much of the information in the exhibit is included in an untitled document from the Louisiana State Museum in New Orleans, which can be found here: http://lsm.crt.state.la.us/education/Zulu_curriculum.pdf.)

Gill, James. *Lords of Misrule: Mardi Gras and the Politics of Race in New Orleans.* Jackson: University Press of Mississippi, 1997.

Hearsey, Henry James. "The Negro Problem and the Final Solution." *Daily States,* August 7, 1900. Quoted in Gill, *Lords of Misrule,* 163.

Hill, Errol G., and James V. Hatch. *A History of African American Theatre.* New York: Cambridge University Press, 2003.

Keitz, Gustave. Article on "race war." *Times-Democrat,* 1900. Quoted in Gill, *Lords of Misrule,* 163.

Kinser, Samuel. *Carnival, American Style: Mardi Gras at New Orleans and Mobile.* Chicago: University of Chicago Press, 1990.

Louisiana Weekly. Petition resenting Zulu parade (advertisement). Quoted in Trillin, "The Zulus," 42.

Louisiana Weekly. Editorial about Zulu Krewe, March 12, 1938. Quoted in Mitchell, *Mardi Gras Day,* 183.

Mitchell, Reid. *All on a Mardi Gras Day: Episodes in the History of New Orleans Carnival.* Cambridge, MA: Harvard University Press, 1995.

Murray, Albert. *Stomping the Blues.* New York: McGraw-Hill, 1976.

Saxon, Lyle. *Fabulous New Orleans.* New York: Century Co., 1928.

Sublette, Ned. *The Year Before the Flood: A Story of New Orleans.* Chicago: Chicago Review Press, 2009.

Spera, Keith. "Singer's Widow Revived Career." *Times-Picayune,* February 25, 2009, B1, B4.

Times-Picayune. Article on boycott of Zulus, February 5, 1961. Quoted in Michell, *Mardi Gras Day*, 184.
Trillin, Calvin. "The Zulus." *New Yorker,* June 20, 1964, 41–119.
Wilson, Manuel. 1954 remark on Zulus being "modern." Quoted in Trillin, "The Zulus," 76.

CHAPTER 4: NOBODY

Belasco, David. "Rosemary: A Preface to the Life of Bert Williams." In Rowland, *Bert Williams*, ix–xiii.
Brawley, Benjamin. *The Negro in Literature and Art in the United States.* New York: Duffield & Co., 1918.
Brooks, Tim. *Lost Sounds: Blacks and the Birth of the Recording Industry, 1890–1919.* Urbana: University of Illinois Press, 2004.
Charters, Ann. *Nobody: The Story of Bert Williams.* New York: Macmillan, 1970.
Chude-Sokei, Louis. *The Last "Darky": Bert Williams, Black-on-Black Minstrelsy, and the African Diaspora.* Durham, NC: Duke University Press, 2006.
Debus, Allen G. "Bert Williams on Stage: Ziegfeld and Beyond." Liner notes to Bert Williams, *The Middle Years, 1910–1918*. St. Joseph, IL: Archeophone Records, 2002.
———, and Richard Martin. "The Incomparable Bert Williams: The Williams and Walker Years." Liner notes to Bert Williams, *The Early Years, 1901–1909*. St. Joseph, IL: Archeophone Records, 2004.
Douglas, Ann. *Terrible Honesty: Mongrel Manhattan in the 1920s.* New York: Farrar, Straus & Giroux, 1995.
Du Bois, W. E. B. "The Negro in Literature and Art." In *Writings.* New York: Library of America, 1986, 862–867.
Forbes, Camille F. *Introducing Bert Williams: Burnt Cork, Broadway, and the Story of America's First Black Star.* New York: Basic Civitas, 2008.
Hennessey, Meagan, and Richard Martin. Liner notes to Bert Williams, *His Final Releases, 1919–1922*. St. Joseph, IL: Archeophone Records, 2001.
Hughes, Langston. *The Big Sea: An Autobiography.* New York: Knopf, 1940.
Hurston, Zora Neale. "Characteristics of Negro Expression." In *Folklore, Memoirs, and Other Writings.* New York: Library of America, 1995, 830–845.
In Dahomey, review of. Quoted in Forbes, *Introducing Bert Williams*, 112.

"J.B.," interview with Bert Williams, *The Soil*, 1916. Quoted in Rowland, *Bert Williams*, 93–95; and Smith, *Bert Williams*, 181–182.

Johnson, James Weldon. *Black Manhattan*. New York: Knopf, 1930.

Johnson, Robert E. "Ben Vereen Still Under Fire for Blackface Act at Gala; He's Shocked." *Jet*, February 12, 1981, 13–18, 60.

Lhamon, W. T., Jr. "Whittling on Dynamite: The Difference Bert Williams Makes." In Eric Weisbard, ed., *Listen Again: A Momentary History of Pop Music*. Durham, NC: Duke University Press, 2007.

New York Age. "The Secret of Williams and Walker's Success." February 27, 1908. Quoted in Smith, *Bert Williams*, 102.

New York Age. Article on Bert Williams funeral rites, 1922. Quoted in Charters, *Nobody*, 147.

Phillips, Caryl. *Dancing in the Dark*. New York: Knopf, 2005.

Pierpont, Claudia Roth. "Behind the Mask." *New Yorker*, December 12, 2005.

Rowland, Mabel, ed. *Bert Williams, Son of Laughter: A Symposium of Tribute to the Man and His Work, by His Friends and Associates with a Preface by David Belasco*. New York: English Crafters, 1923.

Smith, Eric Ledell. *Bert Williams: A Biography of the Pioneer Black Comedian*. Jefferson, NC: McFarland & Co., 1992.

Walker, George. "The Real 'Coon' on the American Stage." *Theatre Magazine*, August 1906, 224.

Walrond, Eric. "Bert Williams Foundation Organized to Perpetuate Ideals of Celebrated Actor." *Negro World*, April 21, 1923. In *Winds Can Wake Up the Dead: An Eric Walrond Reader*. Louis J. Parascandola, ed., Detroit: Wayne State University Press, 1998, 64–65.

Washington, Booker T. "The Greatest Comedian the Negro Race Has." *American Magazine* 70 (September 1910): 601. Quoted in Smith, *Bert Williams*, 145.

Williams, Bert. "The Comic Side of Trouble." *American Magazine*, January 1918, 33–35, 58, 60–61.

———. "The Negro on the Stage." *Green Book Album*, December 4, 1910, 1341–1344. Quoted in Smith, *Bert Williams*: 146.

CHAPTER 5: I'SE REGUSTED

Author interviews and correspondence: Zeinabu irene Davis, Allyson Field, Ross Lipman, Jack Mulqueen, Jacqueline Stewart, Mel Watkins, Ian Whitcomb.

Abbott, Lynn, and Doug Seroff. *Out of Sight: The Rise of African American Popular Music, 1889–1895.* Jackson: University Press of Mississippi, 2002.

———. *Ragged but Right: Black Traveling Shows, "Coon Songs," and the Dark Pathway to Blues and Jazz.* Jackson: University Press of Mississippi, 2007.

Andrews, Bart. *Holy Mackerel! The Amos and Andy Story.* New York: Dutton, 1986.

Baraka, Amiri. "The Academic Cowards of Reaction." TheBlacklisted Journalist.com, March 1, 2002. Web.

Barron, James. "Andy Rooney Returns to '60 Minutes,'" *New York Times,* March 5, 1990, C14.

"Black History: Lost, Stolen, or Strayed." *Of Black America.* CBS. July 2, 1968. Television.

"Blaxploitation." *Black Panther,* October 7, 1972, 2, 9, 11.

Bogle, Donald. *Heat Wave: The Life and Career of Ethel Waters.* New York: HarperCollins, 2011.

———. *Prime Time Blues: African Americans on Network Television.* New York: Farrar, Straus & Giroux, 2002.

———. *Toms, Coons, Mulattoes, Mammies, and Bucks,* 4th ed. New York: Continuum, 2001.

Callaway, Earl. "Stepin Fetchit Stages Comeback on TV and Hit Record." *Chicago Defender,* November 20, 1968, 15.

Clayton, T. "Amos 'n' Andy Threw Shadow Across the Lives of Top Negro Actors." *Ebony,* October 1961, 67–73.

Cosby, Bill. Interview by Dick Cavett. *The Dick Cavett Show.* ABC, November 10, 1971. Television.

Cripps, Thomas. *Making Movies Black: The Hollywood Message Movie from World War II to the Civil Rights Era.* New York: Oxford University Press, 1993.

Crowell, James R. "Amos 'n' Andy." *Psychology,* August 1930. Quoted in McLeod, *The Original Amos 'n' Andy,* 43.

Danny Thomas Presents the Wonderful World of Burlesque. NBC. December 11, 1966. Television.

Dunning, John. *On the Air: The Encyclopedia of Old-Time Radio.* New York: Oxford University Press, 1998.

Ely, Melvin Patrick. *The Adventures of Amos 'n' Andy: A Social History of an American Phenomenon.* New York: Free Press, 1992.

Ford, John, dir. *Judge Priest.* Fox Film Corporation, 1934. Film.

Foxx, Redd, and Norma Miller. *The Redd Foxx Encyclopedia of Black Humor*. Los Angeles: W. Ritchie Press, 1977

Ganz, Cheryl. *The 1933 Chicago World's Fair: A Century of Progress*. Urbana: University of Illinois Press, 2008.

Gates, Henry Louis. "An Amos 'n' Andy Christmas." *New York Times*, December 23, 1994, 35.

———. "TV's Black World Turns—But Stays Unreal." *New York Times*, November 12, 1989, A1.

Gray, Herman. *Watching Race—Television and the Struggle for Blackness*. Minneapolis: University of Minnesota Press, 2004.

Inge, M. Thomas. *Truman Capote: Conversations*. Jackson: University Press of Mississippi, 1987.

Ingram, Billy. "Amos 'n' Andy: Standard and Stain." TVParty.com, 2004. Web.

Jones, William G. *Black Cinema Treasures: Lost and Found*. Denton: University of North Texas Press, 1991.

Khaldi, Walid, dir. *Spencer Williams: Remembrances of an Early Black Film Pioneer*. Golden Moon, 1996. Film.

———. *That's Black Entertainment*. Revis Media, 2002. Film.

Knight, Arthur. *Disintegrating the Musical: Black Performance in American Musical Film*. Durham, NC: Duke University Press, 2002.

Liebenson, Donald L. "Folk Art or Racial Stereotypes? Vintage Films Remain Problematic." *Chicago Tribune*, September 18, 1997, 5, 6.

MacDonald, J. Fred. *Blacks and White TV: African Americans in Television Since 1948*. Chicago: Nelson-Hall Publishers, 1983.

MacMinn, Aleene. "Stepin Fetchit, 76, Stages Comeback." *Los Angeles Times*, October 25, 1968, G21.

McLeod, Elizabeth. *The Original Amos 'n' Andy: Freeman Gosden, Charles Correll, and the 1928–1943 Radio Serial*. Jefferson, NC: McFarland & Co., 2005.

Osborne, Brad, dir. *In The Shadow of Hollywood—Race Movies and the Birth of Black Cinema*. AMS Production Group, 2007. Film.

Page, Clarence. "Amos, Andy, and Tony Soprano." *Chicago Tribune*, June 10, 2001, sec. 1, p. 21.

Riggs, Marlon, dir. *Color Adjustment*. California Newsreel, 1992. Film.

Robinson, Edward A. "The Pekin: The Genesis of American Black Theater." *Black American Literature Forum* 16, no. 4 (Winter 1982): 136–138.

Sampson, Henry T. *Blacks in Blackface: A Source Book on Early Black Musical Shows*. Metuchen, NJ: Scarecrow Press, 1980.

———. *The Ghost Walks: A Chronological History of Blacks in Show Business, 1865–1910.* Metuchen, NJ: Scarecrow Press, 1988.

———. *Swingin' on the Ether Waves: A Chronological History of African Americans in Radio and Television.* Metuchen, NJ: Scarecrow Press, 2005.

Smith, Eric Lidell. *Bert Williams: A Biography of a Pioneer Black Comedian.* Jefferson, NC: McFarland, 1992.

Stewart, Jacqueline. *Migrating to the Movies.* Berkeley: University of California Press, 2005.

Thurman, Tom, dir. *Movies of Color—Black Southern Cinema.* FBN Motion Pictures, 2002. Film.

Watkins, Mel. *On the Real Side: Laughing, Lying, and Signifying—the Underground Tradition of African-American Humor that Transformed American Culture, from Slavery to Richard Pryor.* New York: Simon & Schuster, 1994.

———. *Stepin Fetchit: The Life and Times of Lincoln Perry.* New York: Pantheon, 2005.

———. "What Was It About Amos 'n' Andy." *New York Times,* July 7, 1991, 71.

Woll, Allen. *Black Musical Theatre: From* Coontown *to* Dreamgirls. Baton Rouge: Louisiana State University Press, 1989.

CHAPTER 6: **DYN-O-MITE**

Author interviews and correspondence: Daphne Brooks, Oscar Brown Jr., Chuck D, Clinton Ghent, Jacqueline Stewart, Milt Trenier, Don Waller.

Aaron, Charles and Mike Rubin. "Hot-Tub Orgies and Kung Fu Beatdowns: A Short History of the Hip Hop Skit." *Spin,* March 1999, 94–98.

Achman, Christine. *Revolution Televised: Prime Time and the Struggle for Black Power.* Minneapolis: University of Minnesota Press, 2004.

Arceneaux, Michael. "Black Folks We'd Like to Remove from Black History." TheRoot.com. February 21, 2010. Web.

Austen, Jake. *TV-a-Go-Go.* Chicago: Chicago Review Press, 2005.

"Black History: Lost, Stolen, or Strayed." *Of Black America.* CBS. July 2, 1968. Television.

Bogle, Donald. *Primetime Blues: African Americans on Network Television.* New York: Farrar, Straus & Giroux, 2002.

Bossip staff. "T.O. Joins Minstrel Monstrosity." Bossip.com, April 13, 2008. Web.

Brown, Jamie Foster. "Flavor Flav Exchanges Reality TV for Real Acting." *Sister 2 Sister*, May 2008, 36–44.

———. "Flavor Flav Introduces His True Love." *Sister 2 Sister*, August 2008, 92–99.

Calhoun, Claudia. "The Def Jam Generation." PaleyCenter.org, 2009. Web.

Carter, Bill. "In the Huxtable World, Parents Knew Best." *New York Times*, April 26, 1992, 21.

Chris Rock: Kill the Messenger. HBO. September 27, 2008. Television.

Coates, Ta-Nehisi. "Mushmouth Reconsidered: You Can't Say That on TV—but Bill Cosby Can." *Village Voice*, July 14, 2004, 34, 36.

Cole, Nat "King," as told to Lerone Bennett. "Why I Quit My TV Show." *Ebony*, February 1958, 29–35.

Collier, Eugenia. "'Sanford and Son' is White to the Core." *New York Times*, June 17, 1973, 1, 3.

The Comedy Central Roast of Flavor Flav. Comedy Central, August 12, 2007. Television.

Cosby, Bill. Interview. *The Bill Cosby Show Season One*. Shout Factory, 2006. DVD.

Cosby, Bill, and Tom Mossman, dirs. *Bill Cosby on Prejudice*. Pyramid Film & Video, 1971. Film.

Cosby, Bill, and Alvin S. Poussaint. *Come On, People: On the Path from Victims to Victors*. Nashville: Thomas Nelson, 2007.

Danny Thomas Presents the Wonderful World of Burlesque. NBC. December 11, 1966. Television.

Davis Jr., Sammy. Interview by Alex Haley. *Playboy*. December 1966, 99–124.

Denhart, Andy. "Flavor of Love 2 Finale Watched by 7.5 Million, and More Viewers 18–49 Than Any Other Cable Show in History." Reality Blurred.com, October 18, 2006. Web.

Dyson, Michael Eric. *Is Bill Cosby Right?: Or Has the Black Middle Class Lost Its Mind*. New York: Basic Civitas Books, 2005.

Flav, Flavor. *The Icon The Memoir*. Las Vegas, NV: Farrah Gray Publishing, 2011.

Foxx, Redd, and Norma Miller. *The Redd Foxx Encyclopedia of Black Humor*. Los Angeles: W. Ritchie Press, 1977.

Gates, Henry Louis. "TV's Black World Turns—But Stays Unreal." *New York Times*, November 12, 1989, A1.

Gay, Jason. "Blackout, Prime Time Apartheid: How Television Has Divided the Races." *Boston Phoenix*, February 26, 1998.

Gray, Herman. *Watching Race—Television and the Struggle for Blackness*. Minneapolis: University of Minnesota Press, 2004.

Haliluc, Alina, and Valerie Palmer-Mehta. "Flavor of Love and the Rise of Neo-Minstrelsy on Reality Television." In Elwood Watson, ed. *Pimps, Wimps, Studs, Thugs, and Gentlemen: Essays on Media Images of Masculinity*. Jefferson, NC: McFarland, 2009, 85–105.

Hicks, L. Wayne. "Hey! Hey! Hey! Fat Albert and the Cosby Kids." TVParty.com, 2005. Web.

Hurston, Zora Neale. *Collected Plays*, edited by Jean Lee Cole and Charles Mitchell. New Brunswick, NJ: Rutgers University Press, 2008.

Khaldi, Walid, dir. *That's Black Entertainment*. Revis Media, 2002. Film.

Leonard, John. "Funny, Funky, and, Ah, Flip." *Life*, January 22, 1971, 12.

———. "Leave It to Cosby." *New York*, October 22, 1984, 154.

Littleton, Darryl. *Black Comedians on Black Comedy: How African Americans Taught Us to Laugh*. Montclair, NJ: Applause Books, 2006.

MacDonald, J. Fred. *Blacks and White TV: African Americans in Television Since 1948*. Chicago: Nelson-Hall, 1983.

Miller, Troy, dir. *Katt Williams: It's Pimpin' Pimpin'*. Salient Media, 2008. Film.

Mooney, Paul. *Black Is the New White*. New York: Gallery Books, 2009.

native. "New Minstrel Show Winner." NativeNotes.net, May 20, 2008. Web.

Price, Joe X. *Redd Foxx, B.S.* Chicago: Contemporary, 1979.

Reeves, Marcus. *Somebody Scream! Rap Music's Rise to Prominence in the Aftershock of Black Power*. New York: Faber & Faber, 2008.

Riggs, Marlon, dir. *Color Adjustment*. California Newsreel, 1992. Film.

Sanneh, Kelefa. "Last Laugh: The Prickly Comedy of Katt Williams." *New Yorker*, April 13, 2009, 26–31.

Sampson, Henry T. *Blacks in Blackface: A Source Book on Early Black Musical Shows*. Metuchen, NJ: Scarecrow Press, 1980.

———. *The Ghost Walks: A Chronological History of Blacks in Show Business, 1865–1910*. Metuchen, NJ: Scarecrow Press, 1988.

———. *Swingin' on the Ether Waves: A Chronological History of African Americans in Radio and Television*. Metuchen, NJ: Scarecrow Press, 2005.

Smith, Ronald L. *Cosby*, rev. ed. Amherst, NY: Prometheus Books, 1997.

"So Long, Patrick Henry." *I Spy*. NBC. September 15, 1965. Television.

Torres, Sasha, ed. *Living Color: Race and Television in the United States.* Durham, NC: Duke University Press, 1998.

Travis, Dempsey J. *The Life and Times of Redd Foxx*. Chicago: Urban Research Press. 1999.

Troy, Gil. *Morning in America: How Ronald Reagan Invented the 1980s.* Princeton, NJ: Princeton University Press, 2007.

Watkins, Mel. *On the Real Side: Laughing, Lying, and Signifying—the Underground Tradition of African-American Humor that Transformed American Culture, from Slavery to Richard Pryor.* New York: Simon & Schuster, 1994.

"When John Comes Marching Home." *Sanford and Son*. NBC. February 14, 1977. Television.

Williams, Todd. "Flavor Flav—Bum Rush the Show." *Rolling Out*, April 10, 2008, 22–23.

Wilson, Flip. Interview by Gary Owens. *Laugh-In Magazine*, January 1969, 48–49.

Wiltz, Teresa. "Love Him, or Leave Him?" *Washington Post*, November 2, 2006, C1.

Zook, Kristal Brent. *Color by Fox: The Fox Network and the Revolution in Black Television*. New York: Oxford University Press, 1999.

———. *I See Black People: The Rise and Fall of African American–Owned Television and Radio.* New York: Nation Books, 2008.

CHAPTER 7: THAT'S WHY DARKIES WERE BORN

Author correspondence: Will Friedwald, Elijah Wald.

Bergreen, Laurence. *Louis Armstrong: An Extravagant Life.* New York: Broadway Books, 1997.

Bogle, Donald. *Heat Wave: The Life and Career of Ethel Waters.* New York: HarperCollins, 2011.

Chilton, John. *Let the Good Times Roll: The Story of Louis Jordan and His Music.* Ann Arbor: University of Michigan Press, 1994.

Dennison, Sam. *Scandalize My Name: Black Imagery in American Popular Music.* New York: Garland Publishing, 1982.

Dormon, James H. "Shaping the Popular Image of Post-Reconstruction American Blacks: The 'Coon Song' Phenomenon of the Gilded Age." *American Quarterly* 40, no. 4 (December 1988): 450–471.

Gillespie, Dizzy, with Al Fraser. *To Be, or Not . . . to Bop.* Garden City, NY: Doubleday, 1979.

Holiday, Billie, with William Duffy. *Lady Sings the Blues.* Garden City, NY: Doubleday, 1956.

Friedwald, Will. *A Biographical Guide to the Great Jazz and Pop Singers.* New York: Pantheon, 2010.

———. *Sinatra! The Song Is You: A Singer's Art.* New York: Scribner, 1995.

———. *Stardust Melodies: A Biography of Twelve of America's Most Popular Songs.* New York: Pantheon, 2002.

Grimes, Bruce. "Randy Newman: 12 Songs." *Rolling Stone,* April 16, 1970.

Marcus, Greil. *Mystery Train: Images of America in Rock 'n' Roll Music.* New York: Dutton, 1975.

Meckna, Michael. *Satchmo: The Louis Armstrong Encyclopedia.* Westport, CT: Greenwood, 2004.

Ratliff, Ben. *The New York Times Essential Library: Jazz; A Critic's Guide to the 100 Most Important Recordings.* New York: Times Books, 2002.

Riggs, Marlon. *Ethnic Notions.* California Newsreel, 1987. DVD.

Robeson, Paul, Jr. *The Undiscovered Paul Robeson: An Artist's Journey, 1898–1939.* New York: Wiley, 2001.

Teachout, Terry. *Pops: A Life of Louis Armstrong.* New York: Houghton Mifflin Harcourt, 2009.

CHAPTER 8: **EAZY DUZ IT**

Author interviews and correspondence: Bob Abrahamian, Bril Barrett, Chuck D, Jamaa Fanaka, Rudy Ray Moore, J. P. Schauer, Rick Wojcik.

Asim, Jabari. "Peaches Over Peachez." WashingtonPost.com, October 9, 2006. Web.

Beron, Justin. "Cosby—Hold the Racial Jive, Please." *San Francisco Chronicle,* February 5, 2009, 1.

Cepeda, Raquel, ed. *And It Don't Stop.* New York: Faber & Faber, 2004.

Christian, Margena A. "Parental Advisory: The History of N.W.A." *Ebony,* June 2011, 94–99.

Cizmar, Martin. "Whatever Happened to N.W.A.'s Posse?" *L.A. Weekly,* May 6, 2010, 75–76, 80.

Coleman, Brian. *Check the Technique: Liner Notes for Hip-Hop Junkies.* New York: Villard, 2007.

Cosby, Bill. Interview by Tim Russert. *Meet the Press,* NBC. October 14, 2007.

———, and Alvin S. Poussaint. *Come On, People: On the Path from Victims to Victors*. Nashville: Thomas Nelson, 2007.

Crawford, Byron. "Minstrel Show Rap: Southern Hip-Hop Reaches its Logical Conclusion." XXLmag.com. September 22, 2006. Web.

Crouch, Stanley. "A Fireside Chat with Stanley Crouch." Interview by Fred Jung. All About Jazz, February 22, 2005. Web.

———. "The Electric Company—How Technology Revived Ellington's Career." *Harper's*, June 2009, 73–77.

———. "Mr. Parks, You'll Be Missed." *New York Daily News*, March 9, 2006, 39.

Du Bois, W. E. B. *The Souls of Black Folk*. Chicago: A. C. McClurg & Co., 1903.

Dyson, Michael Eric. *Is Bill Cosby Right?: Or Has the Black Middle Class Lost Its Mind*. New York: Basic Civitas Books, 2005.

Fassler, Joe. "Flavor Flav vs. KFC: A Dispatch from Flav's Fried Chicken." TheAtlantic.com, January 27, 2011. Web.

Flav, Flavor. *The Icon The Memoir*. Las Vegas, NV: Farrah Gray Publishing, 2011.

George, Nelson. *Hip Hop America*. New York: Penguin, 1999.

Gonzales, Michael, and Havelock Nelson. *Bring the Noise: A Guide to Rap Music*. New York: Three Rivers Press, 1991.

Hardy, Ernest. "How Shit Be: Freestyle Riffs and Ruminations on Black Music and Pop Culture at the Dawn of 2007." *L.A. Weekly*, January 11, 2007.

Hiatt, Brian. "For the Children." EW.com, November 16, 2004. Web.

House Committee on Energy and Commerce, "Stereotypes and Degrading Images," 110th Cong., 1st sess., September 25, 2007.

James, Darius. "Gangstaphobia." *Spin*, May 1994, 64–66.

Lee, Spike. Interview by Paul Fisher. CrankyCritic.com, 2000. Web.

Lhamon, W. T. *Raising Cain: Blackface Performance from Jim Crow to Hip Hop*. Cambridge, MA: Harvard University Press, 1998.

Lil Wayne. Interview by Jimmy Kimmel. *Jimmy Kimmel Live*. ABC, March 3, 2009. Television.

Long, Richard A. *The Black Tradition in American Dance*. New York: Smithmark Publishers, 1995.

Lott, Eric. *Love and Theft: Blackface Minstrelsy and the American Working Class*. New York: Oxford University Press, 1993.

Olorunda, Tolu. "Lil' Wayne, 'Whip It Like a Slave,' and the Crisis of Coonery." AllHipHop.com, August 3, 2009. Web.

Owen, Frank. "Public Service." *Spin*, March 1990, 57–61, 86.

Perpatua, Matthew. "Flavor Flav Closes Fried Chicken Restaurant in Iowa." Rollingstone.com, April 25, 2011. Web.

Reid, Shaheem. "RZA Addresses Comments About the South That Offended Jay Electronica." MTV.com, June 2, 2010. Web.

Rose, Tricia. *The Hip Hop Wars*. New York: Basic Civitas Press, 2008.

Sarig, Roni. *Third Coast: OutKast, Timbaland, and How How Hip-Hop Became a Southern Thing*. New York: Da Capo Press, 2007.

Sharpton, Al. Interview by Elvis Mitchell. *The Blacklist: Volume One*. Perfect Day Films, 2008. Film.

Shocked, Michelle, and Bart Bull. "Gangster Rappers Preserve White Myths." *Billboard*, June 20, 1992, 6.

Walker, Jimmie. "Nardwuar versus Jimmie 'Dyn-O-Mite' Walker." Interview by Nardwuar. Nardwuar.com, August 14, 2001. Web.

Watkins, Mel. *On the Real Side: Laughing, Lying, and Signifying—the Underground Tradition of African-American Humor That Transformed American Culture, from Slavery to Richard Pryor.* New York: Simon & Schuster, 1994.

Westhoff, Ben. *Dirty South: Outkast, Lil Wayne, Soulja Boy, and the Southern Rappers Who Reinvented Hip-Hop*. Chicago: Chicago Review Press, 2011.

Whalen, Faraji. "The Disgruntled Fan." In Kenji Jasper and Ytasha Womack, eds. *Beats, Rhymes, and Life: What We Love and Hate About Hip-Hop*. New York: Random House, 2007, 35–54.

Wiltz, Teresa. "Love Him, or Leave Him?" *Washington Post*, November 2, 2006, C1.

Woldu, Gail Hilson. *The Words and Music of Ice Cube*. Westport, CT: Praeger, 2008.

CHAPTER 9: **WE JUST LOVE TO DRAMATIZE**

Atkinson, Brooks. "Harlem Fandango." *New York Times*, September 16, 1931, 15. Quoted in Hurston, *Collected Plays*, xxiii.

———. "The Play: Musical Comedy in Sepia." *New York Times*, October 8, 1930, 29.

Boyd, Valerie. *Wrapped in Rainbows: The Life of Zora Neale Hurston*. New York: Scribner, 2003.

Brickell, Herschel. "Zora Neale Hurston's Second Novel Fine Story of Woman Who Loved and Enjoyed Life." *New York Post*, September 14, 1937, 11. Quoted in West, *Zora Neale Hurston*, 112.

Brown, Sterling. "Luck Is a Fortune." *The Nation*, October 16, 1937. In Gates and Appiah, *Zora Neale Hurston*, 20–21.

———. "Old Time Tales." *New Masses,* February 25, 1936. Quoted in Boyd, *Wrapped in Rainbows,* 281.

Ferguson, Otis. "You Can't Hear Their Voices." *New Republic,* October 13, 1937. In Gates and Appiah, *Zora Neale Hurston,* 22–23.

Gates, Henry Louis, Jr. "*Their Eyes Were Watching God:* Hurston and the Speakerly Text." In Gates and Appiah, *Zora Neale Hurston,* 154–203.

———, and K. A. Appiah, eds. *Zora Neale Hurston: Critical Perspectives Past and Present.* New York: Amistad, 1993.

Hemenway, Robert E. *Zora Neale Hurston: A Literary Biography.* Urbana: University of Illinois Press, 1977.

Hibben, Sheila. "Vibrant Book Full of Nature and Salt." *New York Herald Tribune Weekly Book Review,* September 26, 1937. In Gates and Appiah, eds., *Zora Neale Hurston,* 21–22.

Hurston, Zora Neale. *Collected Plays.* Edited by Jean Lee Cole and Charles Mitchell. New Brunswick, NJ: Rutgers University Press, 2008.

———. *Folklore, Memoirs, and Other Writings.* New York: Library of America, 1995.

———. *Novels and Stories.* New York: Library of America, 1995.

———. "You Don't Know Us Negroes." Quoted in Kaplan, "Zora Neale Hurston," 219; and Boyd, *Wrapped in Rainbows,* 268.

Kaplan, Carla. "Zora Neale Hurston, Folk Performance, and the 'Margarine Negro.'" In George Hutchinson, ed., *The Cambridge Companion to the Harlem Renaissance.* New York: Cambridge University Press, 2007.

Kennedy, Randall. "Looking for Zora." *New York Times Book Review,* December 30, 1979, 8. Quoted in West, *Zora Neale Hurston,* 244.

Locke, Alain. Review of *Their Eyes Were Watching God. Opportunity,* June 1, 1938. In Gates and Appiah, *Zora Neale Hurston*: 18.

Moon, Henry Lee. "Big Old Lies." *New Republic,* December 11, 1935. In Gates & Appiah, *Zora Neale Hurston,* 10.

Preece, Harold. "The Negro Folk Cult." *The Crisis* 43 (December 1936). Quoted in Boyd, *Wrapped in Rainbows,* 282–283.

Schuyler, George. "Views and Reviews." *Pittsburgh Courier,* December 25, 1937. Quoted in West, *Zora Neale Hurston,* 109.

Stearns, Marshall, and Jean Stearns. *Jazz Dance: The Story of American Vernacular Dance.* New York: Macmillan, 1968.

Washington, Mary Helen. Foreword to Hurston, *Their Eyes Were Watching God.* New York: HarperCollins, 1990, vii–xiv. Quoted in West, *Zora Neale Hurston,* 237.

West, M. Genevieve. *Zora Neale Hurston and American Literary Culture.* Gainesville: University Press of Florida, 2005.

Wright, Richard. "Between Laughter and Tears." *New Masses,* October 5, 1937. In Gates and Appiah, *Zora Neale Hurston,* 16–17.

CHAPTER 10: NEW MILLENNIUM MINSTREL SHOW

Author interviews and correspondence: Zeinabu irene Davis, Jim Dawson, Allyson Field, Sergio Mims, Rudy Ray Moore.

Abbott, Lynn, and Doug Seroff. *Out of Sight: The Rise of African American Popular Music, 1889–1895.* Jackson: University Press of Mississippi, 2002.

———. *Ragged but Right: Black Traveling Shows, "Coon Songs," and the Dark Pathway to Blues and Jazz.* Jackson: University Press of Mississippi, 2007.

Allen, Ralph. "Same As You." *American Heritage,* Winter 2005, 20–31.

Arnold, Darren. *The Pocket Essential Spike Lee.* Harpenden, UK: Pocket Essentials, 2003.

BET staff. "Mo'Nique Invites Spike Lee and Tyler Perry to Resolve Their Differences Face to Face." BET.com, April 29, 2011. Web.

"Black History: Lost, Stolen, or Strayed." *Of Black America,* CBS, July 2, 1968. Television.

Braxton, Greg. "Ex-Actor Gets Laughs—as Playwright: Shelly Garrett's Play Has Become a Word-of-Mouth Smash; Soon Companies Will be Taking It on the Road." *Los Angeles Times,* August 20, 1989, C46.

Tom Burrell. *Brainwashed: Challenging the Myth of Black Inferiority.* New York: Smiley Books, 2010.

Chappelle, Dave. Interview by Oprah Winfrey. *The Oprah Winfrey Show.* ABC, February 3, 2006. Television.

Christian, Margena A. "Becoming Tyler." *Ebony,* October 2008, 72–83.

———. "Black Theater Evolves from 'Chitlin' Circuit to Mainstream Stage." *Jet,* May 21, 2007, 60–64.

Davis, Zeinabu irene. "'Beautiful-Ugly' Blackface: An Esthetic Appreciation of *Bamboozled.*" *Cineaste* 26, no. 2 (2001): 16.

Dyson, Michael Eric. *Debating Race.* New York: Basic Civitas Press, 2007.

Ellison, Ralph. "Change the Joke and Slip the Yoke." In *Shadow and Act.* New York: Random House, 1964.

Foxx, Redd, and Norma Miller. *The Redd Foxx Encyclopedia of Black Humor*. Los Angeles: W. Ritchie Press, 1977.

Fuchs, Cynthia, ed. *Spike Lee Interviews*. Jackson: University Press of Mississippi, 2002.

Hill, Errol. *Shakespeare in Sable: A History of Black Shakespearean Actors*. Amherst: University of Massachusetts Press, 1984.

James, Darryl. "The Bridge: Diary of a Mad Black Man." *Los Angeles Sentinel*, March 16, 2006.

Johnson, Roy S. "His Own Man," *Ebony*, August 2011, 80–85.

Khaldi, Walid, dir. *That's Black Entertainment*. Revis Media, 2002. Film.

Knight, Arthur. *Disintegrating the Musical: Black Performance in American Musical Film*. Durham, NC: Duke University Press, 2002.

Kurtz, Eliza, dir. *Biography: Eddie Murphy*. A&E. 2008. Television.

Lauterbach, Preston. *The Chitlin' Circuit: And the Road to Rock 'n' Roll*. New York: W. W. Norton, 2011.

Lee, Spike, dir. *Bamboozled*. New Line Cinema, 2000. Film.

———. Interview by Ed Gordon. *Our World with Black Enterprise*. BET, May 30, 2009. Television.

———. Foreword to *Michael Ray Charles*. New York: Tony Shafrazi Gallery, 1998.

———. "No Feud with Tyler Perry." 40acres.com, March 17, 2010.

———. *Spike Lee's Gotta Have It: Inside Guerrilla Filmmaking*. New York: Fireside Books, 1987.

Lee, Spike, and Kaleen Aftab. *That's My Story and I'm Sticking to It*, 2nd ed. New York: W. W. Norton, 2006.

Lee, Spike, and Samuel D. Pollard, dirs. *The Making of Bamboozled*. New Line Home Video, 2001. Film.

Massood, Paula J., ed. *The Spike Lee Reader*. Philadelphia: Temple University Press, 2008.

Mims, Sergio. "Just Have to Get This Off My Chest . . ." ShadowandAct.com, May 13, 2009. Web.

Murray, Sonia. "The Talented Mr. Perry." *Essence*, February 2009, 113–117.

Murphy, Keith. "The Takeover." *Vibe*, March 2008, 17.

Newman, Patricia. "Leni Sloan Revives a Raucous (and Racist) U.S. Institution—The Minstrel Show." *People*, September 24, 1979, 89–90.

O'Hehir, Andrew. Review of *Bamboozled*, Spike Lee (2000). Salon.com, October 6, 2000. Web.

Ormond, Ron, dir. *Yes Sir, Mr. Bones*. Spartan Productions, 1951.

Perry, Tyler. *Don't Make a Black Woman Take Off Her Earrings*. New York: Riverhead Books, 2006.

Phillips, Caryl. *Dancing in the Dark*. New York: Knopf, 2005.

Riggs, Marlon, dir. *Ethnic Notions*. KQED, 1987. Film.

Roberts, Richard, Randy Skretvedt, and Brent Walker. "Commentary." *Showtime USA*, vol. 2. DVD. VCI Entertainment, Tulsa, 2007.

Sampson, Henry T. *Blacks in Blackface: A Source Book on Early Black Musical Shows*. Metuchen, NJ: Scarecrow Press, 1980.

Smith, Russell Scott. "The New Amos 'n' Andy?" Salon.com. February 23, 2006. Web.

Stewart, Jacqueline. "Review of *Bamboozled*, Spike Lee, (2000)." *The Moving Image*, Fall 2002, 166–170.

Stone, Andrew L., dir. *Stormy Weather*. Twentieth Century–Fox, 1943. Film.

THR staff. "Tyler Perry: 'Spike Lee Can go Straight to Hell.'" Hollywood reporter.com, April 19, 2011. Web.

Tosches, Nick. *Where Dead Voices Gather*. Boston: Little, Brown, 2001.

"Tyler Perry Talks Black Men in Drag (part 3 of 4—Episode 106 of NoMoreDownLow.TV)." YouTube.com, March 11, 2011. Web.

Watkins, Mel. *On the Real Side: Laughing, Lying, and Signifying—the Underground Tradition of African-American Humor that Transformed American Culture, from Slavery to Richard Pryor.* New York: Simon & Schuster, 1994.

Weaver, Andrew J. "The Role of Actors' Race in White Audiences' Selective Exposure to Movies." *Journal of Communication* 61, no. 2 (April 2011): 369–385.

ACKNOWLEDGMENTS

The authors gratefully acknowledge the kindness and help of Bob Abrahamian, damali ayo, Bril Barrett, Daphne Brooks, the Carolina Chocolate Drops, Charles Chamberlain, Amy Cherry, William Clark, Chuck D, Zeinabu irene Davis, Jim Dawson, Kathryn A. Duys, Ken Emerson, Jamaa Fanaka, Joe Fassler, Allyson Field, Devon Freeny, Will Friedwald, Clinton Ghent, Ross Lipman, Sergio Mims, Jack Mulqueen, Jim Newberry, Ira Padnos, Lefty Parker, Sascha Penn, Miss Pussycat, Mr. Quintron, J. P. Schauer, Jeff Shreve, Jacqueline Stewart, Ned Sublette, Nick Tosches, Milt Trenier, Elijah Wald, Don Waller, Mel Watkins, Eric Weisbard, Ian Whitcomb, Rick Wojcik, and David Wondrich.

INDEX

Note: Page numbers in *italics* indicate a photograph or illustration.